EGYPT-
OMANIA

EGYPT-OMANIA

Our Three Thousand Year Obsession

with the Land of the Pharaohs

BOB BRIER

palgrave
macmillan

First published in 2013 by PALGRAVE MACMILLAN® in the United States—a
division of St. Martin's Press LLC, 175 Fifth Avenue, New York, NY 10010.

Where this book is distributed in the UK, Europe and the rest of the world, this
is by Palgrave Macmillan, a division of Macmillan Publishers Limited, registered
in England, company number 785998, of Houndmills, Basingstoke, Hampshire
RG21 6XS.

Palgrave Macmillan is the global academic imprint of the above companies and
has companies and representatives throughout the world.

Palgrave® and Macmillan® are registered trademarks in the United States, the
United Kingdom, Europe and other countries.

ISBN 978-1-137-27860-9

Library of Congress Cataloging-in-Publication Data

Brier, Bob.
    Egyptomania / Bob Brier.
        pages   cm
    Includes bibliographical references.
    1. Egyptology—History. 2. Egypt—Antiquities. 3. Egypt—Civilization—To
332 B.C. 4. Archaeology and history—Egypt. I. Title.
DT60.B749   2013
932.0072—dc23

                                                                    2013016347

A catalogue record of the book is available from the British Library.

Design by Letra Libre, Inc.

First edition: November 2013

10 9 8 7 6 5 4 3 2 1

Printed in the United States of America.

For Rus

CONTENTS

ACKNOWLEDGMENTS

There are so many people who helped at various stages of this book that it is best to thank them chronologically. Rus Gant haunted the flea markets of London with me, found objects I never knew existed, and then photographed them for me! Pat Remler was of course in on the early formation of the collection, was there for all the adventures, and, as ever, was fearless in acquiring the goodies, even when we didn't have the money. Her "cruel-but-fair" editing helped immensely. Then, when the book was in its earliest stages, my favorite nit-picker, Judith Turner, caught the errors and helped keep the book on track.

My agent, Liza Dawson, helped tremendously to transform *Egyptomania* from my fantasy to a real book. Her associate, Anna Olswanger, was right there to help close the deal. Once we had a contract for the book, things really got hectic. Mary Chipman, techie extraordinaire, formatted, styled, edited, photographed, and did almost anything needed to ready the manuscript for the publisher, all the while improving the book. As our deadline approached and some really difficult photographs had to be taken, Brandon Remler stepped in on short notice and did the job. Also, a special thanks to Zahi Hawass for his wonderful introduction.

At Palgrave Macmillan, my first editor, Luba Ostashevsky, wasn't able to see the book through publication but was helpful in the early discussions. Later the manuscript was handed over to Karen Wolny, who was invaluable in determining the final content and form of the book. At the very end, I was delighted to have Elisabeth Dyssegaard as the final editor.

Thank you all. I couldn't have done it without you. I know that sometimes it was frantic, but I think we all had fun, which is what Egyptomania is all about.

INTRODUCTION

Ancient Egypt was a unique culture whose magic reaches down the millennia to us through words such as mummies, pyramids, the Sphinx, Tutankhamun, pharaohs, and curses. Few Egyptologists are able to use adventures and secrets from the realm of the pharaohs to capture people's hearts. Bob Brier is one of them. The wonderful book you are about to read will explain to us the history of Egyptomania since the Greek and Roman period. Bob has done magnificent research and gathered together important information that will be both useful to scholars and interesting to the general public.

Napoleon Bonaparte's expedition to Egypt in 1798 initiated the modern era of Egyptomania: We can say that Bonaparte, Vivant Denon (the head of his scientific team), and others discovered ancient Egypt for everyone. The publication of the *Description de l'Égypte* and the discovery of the Rosetta Stone can be thought of as the keys that opened the door for the world to understand the land of the pharaohs.

I myself began to witness many aspects of Egyptomania during my travels to give lectures all over the world. I will never forget my first lecture tour to the United States in 1977. During this tour, I gave a public talk in a hotel in Connecticut. To my amazement, the people who sat in the first row were wearing paper pyramids on their heads!

This was very strange to me, something I had never seen before. At the end of my lecture, the people with the pyramid hats began to ask me about pyramid power. I told them that I had never heard about this before. They began to explain to me that if you put meat under a pyramid, it will never rot, and razors under a pyramid will stay sharp forever. I could see that some of the audience members were holding books about pyramid power, including a book about the experience of someone who had spent a night inside the Great Pyramid, and many other books that had nothing to do with science.

My second stop was in Santa Barbara, and I will never forget what I saw there. Some people said they slept under pyramid shapes, others talked about reincarnation (all the ladies had been Cleopatra or Nefertiti), and most of them believed that slaves had built the pyramids. I did not have the chance to correct all of these beliefs, but it was good just to laugh and enjoy all of this Egyptomania.

Part of my lecture was about Egyptomania. I talked about early explorers such as Howard Vyse, who used to use dynamite to open pyramids—he even opened a hole in the Great Sphinx with explosives; Waynman Dixon, who found the so-called air shafts in the Great Pyramid; Giovanni Belzoni and his discovery of the tomb of Seti I, and the mysterious tunnel in that tomb. But the discovery of the tomb of Tutankhamun was the key that opened the floodgates to Egyptomania. November 4, 1922, is a day that will never be forgotten.

The water boy who found the tomb of Tutankhamun for Carter is still remembered in the village of Qurna on the west bank of Luxor. It was very dramatic for this child, who brought his water jars to the Valley of the Kings. It was as he dug a hole in the sand to set up his jars that he found the first step of the tomb. Carter put a beautiful necklace from the tomb around the boy's neck and took a photo of him. This photo still hangs in the home of his family, the Abdel Rassouls, and his grandchildren show it with pride to all the journalists and tourists who visit their house.

When I came back from my lecture tour in the States, the words "pyramid power" had captured my mind. I could imagine the scene of these people putting pyramids on their heads or sleeping under pyramid shapes. My office as Chief Inspector of the Pyramids at Giza was right next to the Great Pyramid. This office is like a monument now, and the inspectors of this area look at it and remember our great days in this place. But here I will mention two stories connected with this office. The first is when I wanted to test pyramid power. I bought a pound of meat and put half of it inside the Great Pyramid and the other half inside my office. I brought a few reporters to see this experiment. The results were just as you would expect, and I told the reporters that the pyramids in the States must have more power than the real pyramid!

The second story connected with my office at Giza concerns a media battle between me and those who believed that the Great Pyramid had been built by some other civilization, not the ancient Egyptians. This debate became hot news in the international press. There were lots of rumors that I was finding evidence of lost civilizations and hiding it. Then one day a young man from California who was spreading all this nonsense on the Internet came to my office. When he came to Giza, he asked to see my bathroom. I asked why, and he told me that people were saying that at 12 noon I went to my bathroom and opened a tunnel and went through to the Great Pyramid to hide evidence of lost civilizations and then came back. I told him to come with me to the bathroom and look for the tunnel, and I even gave him an ax to dig with—I wanted to finish this craziness for once and for all.

The positive side of all of this publicity was that people were absolutely fascinated by Egypt. The term "Egyptomania" began to morph into other manias, such as pyramidmania, Tutmania, and mummymania.

Pyramidmania was the term I could say the most about because I have been connected with pyramids most of my life. My office next to the Great Pyramid saw the visits of many famous people, such as Mickey Rooney, Roger Moore, Princess Diana, Dr. Ruth, and others. People came to see me to get permission to enter the pyramid alone, sleep for one night inside, or climb the pyramid; I had to refuse most of these requests. Groups such as the Rosicrucians or the Shriners, another group called 11/11, and others came to ask for permission to enter the Great Pyramid for two hours at dawn. I would see them weeping and praying, saying words that no one could understand. At sunrise they would go to the Sphinx and be so happy because they thought all their sins had been forgiven.

Other groups collected money from people and claimed that they would excavate under the Labyrinth at Lahun (a Middle Kingdom pyramid complex) and under the Giza Pyramids to discover records that would save the world from destruction. Another man from California believed that the Great Pyramid contained the scroll of David and wanted to excavate there. Others claimed that the pyramids were built according to the constellation Orion. Many theories were discussed about the construction of the pyramids. Pyramids were built everywhere: in Copenhagen; at the Louvre; and in Waukegan, Illinois, where Jim Onan built a house for himself in the shape of a pyramid, fronted by a huge statue of Ramesses II, with queens' pyramids for garages. Memphis, Tennessee, had a mayor who was in love with Egypt and built a pyramid in the center of the city. He even brought an exhibition from Egypt on Ramesses the Great to the city.

Pyramids were the main attraction for the first part of my life as an Egyptologist. But when I left my job as director of the pyramids and took the position of secretary general of the Supreme Council of Antiquities (SCA), I began to become aware of other aspects of Egyptomania and saw the enormous interest that people have in topics such as the Valley of the Kings, Tutankhamun, mummies, and Cleopatra.

My personal experience with the Valley of the Kings began in 1974, when I was working on the West Bank of Luxor. One night I went with the chief of the guards to climb the Qurn, the pyramidal peak that guards the valley. We arrived at the top at midnight, which was a perfect time to enjoy the magic of this desert landscape. Another high point of my early time in Luxor was meeting Sheikh Ali Abdel-Rassoul, the last living member of the family that discovered the First Royal Cache of mummies in 1871 (and the family of Carter's water boy). This discovery, and what happened when the government found out about the cache, is beautifully explained by Bob in Chapter 6. If you have a chance, try to see a film called *The Mummy*, also called *The Night of Counting the Years*, directed by Shadi Abdel Salam. One scene in this movie shows men and women standing on the West Bank of the Nile to mourn their ancestors and say farewell as the royal mummies sail down the river toward Cairo. When the mummies arrived at the customs area in Boulaq, the officer on duty could not find an appropriate category in which to put them, so he had the ancient kings and queens of Egypt enter the city as salted fish.

Sheikh Ali Abdel-Rassoul owned the El-Marsam Hotel on the West Bank, where we young archaeologists used to gather in the evenings. He and I loved to talk, and he told me many interesting stories about his family, including the water boy who had discovered the tomb of Tutankhamun, and about many of the archaeologists who had excavated in the Valley of the Kings. One day he took me to the tomb of Seti I and told me how he had excavated here in 1960, in a mysterious tunnel that leads from the king's burial chamber back into

the mountain. He had cleared about 100 meters, but then the antiquities department stopped his work because the tunnel had become too
dangerous and his workers were finding it hard to breathe. Sheikh Ali
believed that I would become an important archaeologist and asked
me if someday I would continue his work in the tunnel. He believed
that I would discover the real tomb of Seti I. But he said, "If you discover the treasure of the tomb, the only thing I need from you is to tell
the world that I am the one who told you this secret." In 2005, I did
begin to excavate this tunnel, with a well-trained team of Egyptian archaeologists. We had to find a method to make the tunnel safe, and we
ended up supporting the ceiling with a series of iron frames. We found
that the tunnel began to curve after 120 meters, then continued until
it reached a total depth of 174.5 meters into the mountain. We found
stairs and also a grid on some of the walls, showing that they were being prepared for decoration. But we came to a dead end. I believe that
Seti I's architects intended to build a tomb within a tomb, a new style
for the Nineteenth Dynasty, but had to abandon the project because
Seti I's reign was cut short.

In this magical book, you will read some wonderful stories about
Tutmania. I am happy that I was able to contribute to people's fascination with the golden boy king and to our scholarly understanding
of his reign. In 2005, I took a portable computed tomography (CT)
scanning machine that had been given to us as a gift by the National
Geographic (NG) Society and Siemens to scan Tut's mummy for the
first time. Terry Garcia, from the NG, helped to bring this machine to
the SCA and to open a new era for technology in archaeology. I was
amazed how much the media talked about the curse, especially after
the machine stopped before we could scan the mummy. It turned out
that it had just overheated, and we were able to start it again after an
hour by cooling it with inexpensive plastic fans. Our scan showed that

Tutankhamun had suffered an accident and fractured his left thigh shortly before he died. Several years later, we did DNA tests, which revealed that he had malaria and circulation problems. Through our DNA studies, we were also able to identify the mummies of many members of his immediate family. As a side benefit of these tests, we noticed that the mummy itself was in danger of deterioration because of dust and the breath of the many tourists who visited his tomb, so we had a new showcase designed in Germany and moved the mummy from his sarcophagus into this case.

Tutankhamun's treasures began their first tour in November 1961 at the Washington Gallery of Art and then traveled to many cities in the United States, Japan, France, England, and the Soviet Union. The National Gallery was the first stop on Tut's next tour, when 45 objects went to the United States in November 1976. Many stories connected to Tutmania come out of these tours. One that I like is about a woman who was looking at the golden mask when she saw she was not alone—the actor Cary Grant was looking at the mask too. She was so overwhelmed that she fainted.

I was able to choose 50 small objects from Tutankhamun's treasure to be included in a tour that began in Basel, Switzerland, went to Bonn, then traveled to the United States and on to Australia and Japan. Through this tour, which captured the hearts of many people around the world, we were able to bring more than $120 million to Egypt. I was able to attend the opening of the exhibition in each city in the States, and there were Tutmania stories connected with all of these events. My best story comes from Atlanta, Georgia, where I gave a lecture to 4,500 people in the Fox Theater. Before I came to the States, I had received letters through my children's fan club from three eight-year-old young ladies who wanted to meet me after the lecture. I wrote back to them to tell them that we would call out their names after the

lecture. After I had finished answering questions, I called the names of
the girls, and they came up to the front. The one in the middle walked
toward me, and I bent down to her. She looked at me and said, "Hug
me." I did, and she said, "More!" The audience loved it and gave her
a standing ovation.

You will read in this book about the discovery of the First Royal
Mummy Cache in 1871 and about the discovery of the Second Royal
Mummy Cache in the tomb of Amenhotep II (KV 35) by Victor Loret
in 1898. One of my favorite archaeological adventures was the discovery of the Valley of the Golden Mummies at Bahariya Oasis. We
excavated about 250 of the estimated 10,000 mummies from the valley, mostly covered with gold, and were able to explore the history of
this area during the Greco-Roman period. This discovery captured the
imagination of the whole world.

In addition to the scans and DNA studies of Tutankhamun, we
used CT technology and DNA to reveal the secrets of the royal mummies of the New Kingdom, the kings and queens discovered in the
royal caches. We made a number of important discoveries through this
new technology: Among other things, we identified what is most likely
the mummy of Queen Hatshepsut and discovered that Ramesses III
was murdered in a harem conspiracy.

My main experience with Cleopatra-mania came from my search
with Kathleen Martinez for the tomb of Cleopatra and Mark Antony.
The world was thrilled by Martinez's theory, which led us to excavate
inside a temple near Alexandria called Taposiris Magna.

In this book, Bob Brier begins his search for the birth of Egyptomania with the Greco-Roman period. Then he introduces the topic of
Napoleon Bonaparte and his scholarly expedition in Egypt. He tells
us how one of the obelisks from Luxor Temple was taken to France
to be erected in the Place de la Concorde and how Cleopatra's Needle

traveled to London. Bob tells us how this obelisk attracted Londoners and introduced Egyptomania to England. The London obelisk weighed about 187 tons, and the trip to England was a great adventure. Then there is what Bob calls Egyptomania American style. The story of the New York obelisk, which weighs about 193 tons, is another great tale. The state of this obelisk was brought to my attention several years ago, so I wrote to the mayor of New York to ask that arrangements be made to restore it. Two friends of mine, Richard Paschael and Dorothy McCarthy, continued to ask the city for help with this, and conservation of the obelisk is scheduled to go forward this year. Obelisks are wonderful ambassadors for Egypt. I am personally amazed when I see that there are 13 obelisks in Rome—the city is decorated with these Egyptian monuments.

I think this book is one of the most important books on Egyptomania since scientific research on this topic began in the United States. It is fascinating to see how Egyptomania has spread to small towns in countries all over the world. I believe that these small cities and even villages have become fascinated by ancient Egypt because of the great documentaries (many of them featuring Bob!) made by organizations such as the Discovery Channel, National Geographic, the History Channel, Nova, the BBC, FOX, and others.

Until recently, the big surprise was that Egyptomania never reached modern Egypt. But when we sent a robot inside the Great Pyramid to reveal the secret chambers, we did a live film. All of Egypt stayed up until 5 A.M. to see this program, and I could see the love and Egyptomania inside the hearts of many Egyptians.

Zahi Hawass
Cairo, March 2013

EGYPT-OMANIA

ONE

Birth of a Collection

When I was a kid growing up in the East Bronx, I collected acorns. I'd gather them in the fall, sort them by size and color, and organize them in small compartments I made in a shoebox for the purpose. The collection stayed intact for a week or so until the worms came out and my mother threw away the box. Later it was baseball cards. I wasn't really interested in baseball or the players on the cards. It was order that interested me—a numbered set waiting to be completed. Then there were postage stamps. In the 1950s, every kid collected postage stamps. You got your relatives who received letters from foreign countries to save the stamps. If someone worked for a company that got regular shipments from abroad, you had duplicates to trade. You soaked the stamps off the envelopes, then—and here's the fun part—you organized them and put them in an album. This is how we learned about exotic countries like Turks and Caicos Islands. I vividly remember the triangular stamps for Tana Tuva and the very small stamps issued by San Marino. Stamps were wonderful things to collect.

When I became an Egyptologist, the obvious thing to collect was Egyptian antiquities, but there are problems. First, antiquities are expensive. More important, collecting antiquities is off-limits to Egyptologists. We all work on excavation sites where artifacts are unearthed, and it would look suspicious if I had an apartment full of antiquities. So, no antiquities for me.

But there is a solution for those of us with the collecting gene—books! They satisfy the need to acquire, possess, and organize, and there is a rationalization for the collection—Egyptology books help my career. I *need* books to do research, publish, get tenure, and receive promotions.

I remember first seeing Thomas Pettigrew's 1834 *Egyptian Mummies*[1] 40 years ago in a dusty secondhand bookshop on New York's Fourth Avenue. The illustrations by George Cruikshank (Charles Dickens's illustrator) were highlighted with real gold to indicate gilt on the mummies' faces. It cost me a full week's salary at the time, but eating peanut butter and jelly sandwiches was a small price to pay for such a treasure. I didn't stop with Egyptology books. There were travel books; art books; books on Egypt from the seventeenth, eighteenth, and nineteenth centuries with fabulous engravings. What about fiction set in Egypt? There are hundreds of novels out there, good and bad, that deal with mummies and pharaohs. They too could be hunted down, acquired, and cataloged. And this is where the real decision had to be made, one that separates the collectors from the merely interested. Do I collect the bad along with the good? Thomas Mann's *Joseph in Egypt* series is great literature, so I would definitely pick that up, but do I really need S. S. Van Dine's 1930 thriller *The Scarab Murder Case?* Of course I do. It sits on the shelf next to Ellery Queen's dreadful 1932 *The Egyptian Cross Mystery.*

From books it was only a small step to prints, engravings, comics, watercolors, posters, and everything else that now fills my apartment. From two-dimensional prints it was easy to move to objects. And what objects there are! In 1808 the famous English Wedgwood porcelain factory produced an extraordinary Egyptian tea service to commemorate Admiral Nelson defeating Napoleon Bonaparte at the Battle of the Nile. The teapot lids sport crocodiles, and ersatz hieroglyphs wind around the plates and cups. It's fabulous, but Josiah Wedgwood's Egyptian set (Color Plate 2) is no more wonderful than my cheap World War II–era made-in-Japan tea service with hand-painted pyramids, palm trees, and camels. Both sets are displayed in close proximity to Barbie of the Nile and the King Tut Cologne bottle with a stopper vaguely resembling the boy king's gold mask (Color Plate 46). We all know that something can be so bad that it's good. The true collector has no shame.

Almost every aspect of my life has been touched by the lure of Egypt. There is the Kamut Flakes cereal (Fig. 1.1) that claims its origins in Egypt. At Halloween we give out Yummy Mummies (Fig. 1.2) and the like, and Cleopatra soap, complete with a beautiful portrait of Cleo, is sold in most convenience stores in Greece. Old magazines are a wonderful source of additions to my collections. There are loads of magazine ads with Egyptian themes, some done by the best artists of the time. Remember "I dreamt I was Cleopatra sailing down the Nile in my Maidenform bra"? Magazines of the 1920s are packed with beautiful art deco and art nouveau Egyptian-themed ads for perfumes, soaps, and even car tires.

To compound the danger of unbridled enthusiasm, my wife, Pat, also an Egyptologist, is as bad as I am when it comes to Egyptomania. There are no checks and balances in our house. When we are on the hunt, there is no one to say, "I don't think so, better to pay the rent this month."

Once we heard that a small auction house in Devon, England, was selling the letters and papers of Waynman Dixon, a young British engineer sent to Egypt in 1872 to build bridges over the Nile.

Fig. 1.1   *Kamut Flakes are supposedly grown from 36 original kernels of wheat found in an Egyptian tomb at Dahshur.*

The Egyptian red tape and slow pace of doing business were driving him mad, so he decided to explore the ancient monuments. Inside the Great Pyramid he saw a crack in the wall of the Queen's Chamber and took a sledgehammer to it to see what was behind. These were the Wild West days of Egyptology, when one didn't automatically think of asking for permission. Dixon discovered two mysterious passages called "the Air Shafts." Recently one was explored by robotic cameras, which were not able to reach the end of the passage. The air shafts' purpose remains a mystery. Dixon also visited Alexandria, where he

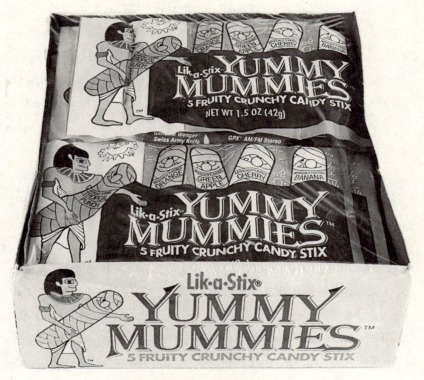

Fig. 1.2 *Yummy Mummies candy made no claims of any connection to ancient Egypt but they were shaped like mummies.*

saw the obelisk known as Cleopatra's Needle that had been previously offered to England languishing in the sand because money hadn't been provided to transport it. He vowed to bring it back to London.

After his brother raised the funds, Dixon designed an iron caisson, very much like a cigar tube, into which the obelisk would be slid, sealed, and then towed to England by steamer. The voyage was dramatic. The ship hit a gale in the Bay of Biscay, six brave seamen lost their lives, and the obelisk was temporarily lost at sea but remained afloat and subsequently was recovered by another ship. The obelisk coming to London was a major Egyptological event. For the first time in more than a century, a monumental Egyptian antiquity left

Egyptian soil. The story was chronicled in the *Illustrated London News* of the day. A few years ago when Dixon's papers came on the auction block, Pat and I had a chance to own a unique piece of the history of Egyptology. Perhaps we would discover some unknown aspects of the obelisk's journey to the Thames Embankment. But could we afford it?

The archive was divided into eighteen individual lots. Some were letters, some were photographs, and some were Dixon's watercolors of Egypt. *Lot 476 A Collection of Twenty-Two Watercolors* was estimated to sell for £1,000 to £2,000. Less than $100 each for rather nice paintings by Waynman Dixon seemed quite reasonable. *Lot 477 Collection of Twenty-Seven Detailed Manuscript Letters from Waynman Dixon while in Egypt* was expected to sell for £1,500 to £2,000. This was a bargain considering that they dealt with important events like the discovery of the Air Shafts in the Queen's Chamber and the loss of the obelisk at sea. We were hoping that the material would go for the low end of the estimates. After all, this was a minor auction house selling possessions of a relatively obscure figure. We calculated that we should be able to get it all for about $15,000, just about all we had in the bank.

We couldn't go to England to bid on the lots so I called the auction house to make sure we could do it over the phone—not nearly as much fun as being there, but still we were in the game. The auction house gave me a time to be by the phone, and someone would call me when the lots came up. Pat and I recalculated and confirmed that it would take everything we had in the bank to get it all, but we were game. The call came.

The first lot was *A Large Collection of Loose Photographs Mainly Related to Waynman Dixon's Travels in Egypt*. Estimate: £400 to £800. We bid £400, then £500, and kept on going. When the lot reached the high estimate, we were still in and wondering who was bidding against us. At £1,000 we dropped out. It was just too high; we had to save our cash for the other lots. The next few lots were also photographs and we went high, even higher than we planned, but we were still outbid. Was it the same buyer? When the letters came up we were ready to go very high, well above the high estimate. We started at £1,500, quickly passed the high estimate, and then it kept on going right up to £3,000. I told the young lady on the other end of the phone that we were out, but Pat urged me to "Go for it." I put in one more bid, but again we were outbid. Someone out there was a Waynman Dixon fan. The bidding for the other lots went pretty much the same. I bid beyond the high estimate, and the unidentified villain outbid me. In the end we were able to buy only one lot of the watercolors and an architectural drawing of the obelisk. Who could have wanted Waynman Dixon's papers so much? Was it someone we knew?

A year later we found out. I was looking through a current Sotheby's auction catalog of books and prints, and there was the Waynman Dixon material, back up for auction! Well, not exactly. The photographs were not there. It seemed as if a dealer of antique photographs had outbid us, decided he didn't want the rest of the material after all, and now it was one big lot in a Sotheby's auction. The finances were still the same—we could just barely afford it, if—big if—we could get it for the low estimate. The photography dealer had probably been the only one who outbid us in the first place, so we had high hopes. We were right. We got it.

My favorite letter is the one in which Dixon tells his family that his name will be "immortalized" because of his discovery of the air shafts (the mysterious small tunnels) in the pyramid. (He was right, but only among Egyptologists.) He even tells how Auguste Mariette, the Director of the Service des Antiquities, called him on the carpet for not asking permission to take a sledgehammer to the pyramid. The lost-and-found saga of the Dixon Papers was a high point of building our Egyptomania collection. We were broke but happy. Within a few months the hunt was on again.

At some point, I realized I wasn't the only one who thought this was neat stuff. When friends came over to the house, they were fascinated by our Egyptomania. They weren't just being polite. They asked questions, wanted to know the history of each piece, where I found the Victorian thermometer in the shape of an obelisk or the Singer Sewing Machine with Egyptian decorations. The musically inclined were drawn to the hundreds of 1920s sheet music pieces with their art deco covers and titles such as "Old King Tut Was a Wise Old Nut" or "Cleopatra Had a Jazz Band." I loved the sheet music because of the wonderful factual errors they contained. "Old King Tut" was written when Tutankhamen's tomb was first discovered in 1922. The excavators hadn't gotten to the burial chamber yet to discover that Tut was a boy king, so he appears on the sheet music as an old man with a cigar! Writers frequently confused mummies with fossils: "Now that you've turned to stone. . . ." Or sometimes the lyrics got the era wrong: "A million years ago. . . ." I have spent hundreds of hours at flea markets, searching through stacks of sheet music for Egyptian titles. Now it was all worth it. I have a collection.

When our art-loving friends visit, they gravitate toward the art on the walls, the engraving of Napoleon at the Sphinx, or the detailed epic scene of the Holy Family in Egypt. Military buffs love the documents from Napoleon's Egyptian campaign along with the medals, letters, and swords embellished with pharaohs' heads.

Egypt excites people in ways no other country can. Ask any museum curator what the two biggest attractions are—Egypt and dinosaurs. Why the fascination with ancient Egypt? I have been trying to answer that question for 30 years. Part of it is escapism. Egypt is a land far, far away and long, long ago. It's exotic; the hieroglyphs seem indecipherable, the pyramids appear unbuildable, the art is unsurpass-able, it's thousands of years old, and it's still here.

For decades I taught a Wednesday night course on Egyptian hi-eroglyphs at the New School for Social Research in New York. Some-times there were more than 100 people in the class. Why? It certainly wasn't going to help them get a job or earn more money. For the most part, the students already had careers, and most were professionals—physicians, lawyers, opera singers, artists, and computer nerds. The course lasted four terms—two years—and many of the students re-peated the sequence several times! Something drew them in. What was it? For some, drawing the hieroglyphic birds, plants, and feet was a therapeutic release from present-day concerns. For others, the hiero-glyphs were the door to ancient Egypt, an entry into a mysterious dis-tant civilization. Part of it is escapism, but that's not the whole story of why people are drawn to ancient Egypt.

What about all those little kids begging to be taken to the Egyp-tian section of the museum? They never want to see the Greek vases. What is it that Egypt has that Greece doesn't? One thing is mummies. Mummies give us a chance to confront death in a nonthreatening way. Where else can a child—or adult—stare at a dead body? Usually a dead body is a sign that someone has been lost—been hit by a car, died of cancer, or simply aged. With a mummy, we are not looking at a loser; we have a winner, someone who is 3,000 years old and isn't just dust or a pile of bones in a coffin. We are looking at a recognizable human being who was walking and talking just like us, but 30 centuries ago. Perhaps when we look at a mummy there is a bit of envy. It's almost like the person succeeded in beating the Grim Reaper. In a way, they are immortal, and we all would like a piece of that. So we're hooked; for whatever reason, we buy into ancient Egypt, learn the hieroglyphs, read the books, visit the museum collections, and look at the art. The next step is going to mummy movies, buying sheets and pillowcases with pharaohs and lotus flowers on them, watching the same *How They Built the Pyramids* documentary on the History Channel four times. Before you know it, you are buying obelisk salt and pepper shakers and searching for Egyptian-themed tchotchkes wherever you go.

In 1990, Long Island University asked me to mount an exhibition of Egyptomania at their Hillwood Art Museum. The museum is quite large, so there was plenty of room to show my treasures. There were engravings from the Napoleonic *Description de l'Égypte* beside *The Living Mummy* comic book and Palmolive soap ads evoking Cleopatra's beauty secrets.

Dave Jason, the Music Department's resident expert on ragtime and jazz, played and sang from vintage sheet music. Children at the opening were given Yummy Mummy candies as souvenirs. By museum standards, the opening was an incredible success. We expected a few hundred people; 1,500 came. Student interns made frantic trips to the grocery store for more food and drink. The *New York Times* praised it.

Writing the exhibition catalog forced me to think about Egyptomania in new ways. I began to realize that interest in ancient Egypt peaked after certain events. When Napoleon invaded Egypt in 1798, he brought artists and scientists ("savants") to study Egypt. When they returned to France, their publication, *Description de l'Égypte,* sparked a giant wave of Egyptomania. Other peaks occurred when massive obelisks were brought from Egypt to Paris, London, and New York in the nineteenth century, igniting the mass production of Egyptomania-related objects. I have spent many pleasant days in search of the silver obelisk-shaped mechanical lead pencils that Victorian ladies wore around their necks. Once at a postcard fair, I was looking through a dealer's Egypt box and spotted an ordinary view of the New York

Obelisk. When I turned it over to see the message, there was a printed invitation from the Secretary of the Navy to the installation of the obelisk in Central Park in 1881.

Perhaps the biggest explosion of interest in ancient Egypt came with the discovery of Tutankhamen's tomb in 1922. The world went wild for all things Egyptian. Ladies wore Egyptian-styled dresses and Egyptian perfume. One of my favorite Tut items is a bronze cigarette box imitating a wood chest found in the tomb. The antique dealer selling it insisted it was Victorian, even after he was told that it couldn't be since the chest wasn't discovered until 1922! Half a century after the tomb's discovery, there was a second revival of the Tut frenzy when the Tutankhamen exhibition toured the United States and Europe. Since then Tutankhamen items have been ubiquitous.

The Egyptomania exhibition led to meeting another Egyptomania collector who would become a close friend. Soon after the exhibition opened, I received a call from Rus Gant, a photographer for the Boston Museum of Fine Arts's expeditions to Egypt. He collected Egyptomania and wanted permission to photograph the collection. A week later, Rus was in the gallery clicking away. He still retained a 1960s hippie allure. He was tall and thin, wore his hair long, and had the refined eye of an art connoisseur. He had managed a Japanese art gallery; excavated in Egypt; was a computer expert and interior designer; but above all, he was a collector of Egyptomania. Years before my Egyptomania exhibition, the Boston Museum of Fine Arts had mounted an exhibition of ancient Egyptian antiquities of the New Kingdom. It built an Egyptian-style palace room, complete with pillars, windows, and beautifully decorated walls. When the exhibition was over, the wood panels comprising the room were chucked unceremoniously into a dumpster where Rus discovered them. He quickly hired a truck, loaded it with the panels, and drove to the nearest self-storage facility where he rented a room, saving a wonderful bit of Egyptomania. Years later our paths crossed in London, and, as they say at the end of *Casablanca,* it was the beginning of a beautiful friendship.

In the 1990s, Pat and I began making documentary films about my research on mummies and pyramids for the Learning Channel. Pat did much of the research, and I appeared in front of the camera. For ten years we traveled the world, and every country we visited was a chance to search for new objects. Sometimes we found treasures, sometimes we didn't.

Paris is very good for paper Egyptomania. There are dealers who sell old magazines of all kinds. I went on the hunt for issues of the *Illustration* magazine from the 1920s that contained weekly accounts of Howard Carter's excavation of Tutankhamen's tomb. One dealer had long tunnels beneath his store that served as his warehouse. For two days, Pat and I pored through thousands of magazines in search of Tut articles. We found loads with beautiful sepia photographs of the treasures being excavated but also things we never knew existed. Who knew that the 1900 Christmas issue of *Illustration* was Egyptian-themed with lovely color drawings of pyramids and temples?

Of all the cities we searched for Egyptomania, none compares to London. Fortunately for me, the production company that I worked with on the documentaries was based in London so I spent many months there editing the shows. On each trip to London I left behind a significant portion of my salary and returned to New York with suitcases stuffed with mummy pencils, Egyptian sewing machines, even Howard Carter's letters written from the Valley of the Kings before he discovered Tutankhamen's tomb.

When I was in London editing my TV series *Unwrapped: The Mysterious World of Mummies,* Rus was also living there, helping the British Museum put its Egyptian collection online. Fortunately, we bumped into each other on the street not far from the British Museum. Rus invited Pat and me to his place. If Sherlock Holmes had collected Egyptomania, this is what it would have looked like, only better! Walls of floor-to-ceiling bookcases filled with Egyptomania books, but with a different slant from mine. Rus was not an Egyptologist, so there were no technical excavation reports, no hieroglyphic dictionaries. Rus had amassed a dazzling collection of nineteenth-century books about Egypt with beautifully decorated spines and covers. Gold palm trees stretched up the spines; pyramids, Arabs, camels, and temples were embossed on covers. Lined up on yards and yards of red bookshelves, they were a work of art. Victorian glass and wood display cases held Rus's remarkable collection of antique cigarette tins, all with Egyptian scenes (Color Plates 7–10). There were Egyptian Deities, Camels, Cleopatra, Helmar, and loads of other Oriental cigarette brands. Other antique museum cases held jewelry from the 1880s, when ladies wore winged-scarab broaches, hat pins with pharaohs' heads, and necklaces with silver mummies (Color Plates 27 and 28). The walls that didn't have bookcases were hung with Orientalist paintings, the perfect backdrop for a remarkable collection. Rus slept in a huge antique Chinese bed decorated with intricate carvings. The entire apartment was one big cabinet of curiosities, heavy on the Egyptomania. Rus had been in London for quite a while scouting all the places where one might find Egyptomania, and he offered to show me his haunts. Our first stop was Portobello Road.

Portobello Road is famous for its Saturday array of antique dealers' stalls offering practically everything old. One dealer sells nothing but antique pens and pocketknives and started keeping mummy pens and knives for me. The dealer specializing in cigarette cases had 1920s black art deco cases, inlaid in gold with scenes from the *Egyptian Book of the Dead* (Color Plate 18). Several dealers sold pages from the *Illustrated London News*. The *ILN,* as it is called, was the *Life* magazine of England from the 1860s right into the twentieth century. The early issues were printed before photography could be reproduced in newspapers so armies of skilled artists created beautiful woodblock prints as illustrations. *ILN* was a wonderful source of inexpensive high-quality Egyptomania. For a few pounds I was buying illustrated contemporary accounts of the great archaeological discoveries of the nineteenth century. There was the 1881 discovery of the cache of royal mummies at Deir el-Bahri, complete with four full-page illustrations. I could follow discoveries of the great British Egyptologist Sir Flinders Petrie over several decades, illustrated by beautiful drawings of the objects he discovered. H. Rider Haggard, the author of *King Solomon's Mines,* serialized his novel *Cleopatra* in the *ILN.* For six months, each issue had beautiful full-page Egyptian woodblock prints of Cleopatra's adventures.

Rus, Pat, and I trolled the stalls looking for wonderful things, but not only at Portobello. Every Tuesday a flea market at Camden Passage magically appeared, and we were there by 6:00 A.M. to get the best. Monday it was Covent Garden.

I bought hundreds of *Illustrated London News* pages from Mo Hudson's stall on Portobello Road. Dealers in vintage newspapers don't make much money (no page is more than $20) so they are not used to high-priced items. As Pat and I were leaving London, I told Mo that if he ever found anything important he should call Rus, in London, and Rus would contact me. Six months later my phone in New York rang. It was Rus.

"Mo has found Howard Carter's letters. They're for sale." Howard Carter material is the holy grail of Egyptomania. Carter was a reclusive bachelor, and very little of his personal material ever appears for sale. This was an entire steamer trunk full of papers. Rus explained that Mo had called him and described the material as best he could. Mo didn't really understand what it was, but the person who owned it did, and the price was thousands of pounds. Rus had examined it and concluded that the trunk originally belonged to Lady Amherst, Howard Carter's patron. It was Lady Amherst who had launched his career in Egyptology. Carter never intended to be an archaeologist. He came from a family of artists, and his father made his living by doing portraits of the pets of the English aristocracy. One of his father's clients was Lady Amherst, who collected Egyptian antiquities and supported excavations. In the 1880s, she received a letter from Egyptologist Percy Newberry asking if she could send him an artist for his excavation— "preferably not a gentleman as he won't make too many demands."[2] Lady Amherst dispatched 17-year-old Howard Carter to Egypt, and a great archaeological career was launched.

While he copied tomb paintings and inscriptions, Carter was also learning the techniques of excavating and within a few years was supervising workmen on his own. Years later he was appointed chief inspector of Luxor, and in 1922, he made his famous discovery of Tutankhamen's tomb. Throughout his career Carter wrote to Lady Amherst, telling of his discoveries and describing the antiquities he was trying to obtain for her collection at Didlington Hall. The story of Lady Amherst does not have a happy ending. Sometime in the 1920s, the Amherst's family lawyer ran off with all their money. The Amhersts were ruined. Didlington Hall was sold and along with it the collection of antiquities and most of the Amhersts' possessions. Among the items auctioned off was a trunk containing Lady Amherst's papers. This is what Mo Hudson had found.

Rus had examined the contents of the chest only briefly, but even from his sketchy description over the phone, it sounded wonderful. Carter's early letters to Lady Amherst described his discovery of Queen Hatshepsut's Tomb in the Valley of the Kings as well as excavations of other tombs. Some had little drawings by Carter in the margins to give her ladyship an idea of the beauty of the objects discovered. The collection contained far more than just Carter's letters. Virtually every prominent Egyptologist of the early part of the twentieth century had written to Lady Amherst, and the letters were all in the trunk. There was even the deed to Didlington Hall. This wasn't just a cool bit of Egyptomania, it was an important slice of the history of Egyptology, and we didn't want it to get away.

Pat and I were on the next plane to Heathrow and went straight to Rus Gant's place. The director of our documentaries had our cash waiting for us there. Mo Hudson joined us, and we all jumped into a cab for the big adventure. The cab took us to a neighborhood so far from central London that there wasn't even a tube station near it. When we arrived at the very modest house, there were no lights on, and all the blinds were drawn. Mo rang the bell, and a man in his 50s dressed in khaki fatigues opened the door. The place looked like it hadn't seen daylight or been dusted in years. There was a single bare bulb hanging from the ceiling and not much furniture. In the center of the room was the chest. I asked our host, Terry, how he came by the chest, and he replied that his father had bought it at auction many years ago. Terry collected military medals and uniforms and wanted the money to buy more medals. I understood such things.

The chest itself was wonderful, not your ordinary steamer trunk. It was round-topped with Lady Amherst's name and address written inside. We all looked at the contents as best we could in the dim light; it seemed marvelous. Lady Amherst had written and published a book on Egypt, and there was her manuscript, corrected by Gaston Maspero, Director of the Egyptian Museum in Cairo. There were several hundred letters from various Egyptologists. Best of all were Carter's, still in their envelopes addressed to Lady Amherst, written on stationary of the Service des Antiquities. We were all very excited but tried to keep our cool. "Yes, this is very good, but the price is a bit too high." Internally we were jumping up and down, doing a happy dance. After very brief negotiations we arrived at a price and the deal was done, but getting it home proved more difficult than anticipated. We asked if we could call a cab, but there was no phone in the house! (Cell phones were still a few years off.) Mo and I walked down a few blocks to a local pub and called a cab from the pay phone. Soon we were all in the cab with one of the best Egyptomania finds of all time.

Rus, Pat, and I continued to comb London in search of Egyptomania. Jewelry, books, prints, cigarette tins, all came our way until Rus's job at the British Museum finally ended and he moved back to Boston. Not long afterward, he called us. He was downsizing, moving into a smaller apartment, and was looking for a home for some of his collection. Did we want to buy any of his things? Every few months, Pat and I would drive up to Boston and buy part of Rus's collection.

Eventually the three of us began an inventory of our joint collection, spending many happy weekends photographing, cataloging, and seeing what we had. The cataloging took on the form of an archaeological excavation. We had all these artifacts, and now we had to reconstruct their past. We quickly discovered that Egyptomania had its own stratigraphy, its own chronology. As the project went forward, we had long discussions about why certain kinds of objects appear at certain times. We began to see the bigger picture and realized that the history of Egyptomania was a story worth telling. Arthur Weigall, perhaps the best of all the Egyptology writers, once said, "It should be the goal of the writer on archaeology to make the dead come alive, not to put the living to sleep." That's my hope for *Egyptomania: Our Three Thousand Year Obsession with the Land of the Pharaohs.*

TWO

Rome and the Birth of Egyptomania

Egypto • mania *n. The extreme fascination with all aspects of ancient Egypt.*

When Herodotus, a Greek traveler, visited Egypt around 450 BC, he couldn't believe his eyes. The pyramids and temples, the strange gods, the Nile overflowing its banks all overwhelmed him, but what amazed him most was Egypt's antiquity: "The priests read to me from a written record the names of three hundred and thirty kings, in the same number of generations."[1] Even in 450 BC Egypt was ancient, a land of wonder. Compared to the Egyptians, the Greeks were newcomers. Greek writing went back only a few centuries; Egypt's was thousands of years old. When Herodotus visited Egypt, the pyramids were already 2,000 years old, about the same span of time that divides Herodotus and us.

WHAT FASCINATED THE GREEKS

Herodotus exclaimed that Egypt contained more remarkable things than any country in the world. He was captivated by the same things that fascinate us today—Egypt's antiquity, its hieroglyphs, art, and most of all mummies. Herodotus's interest in mummies is a boon to modern Egyptologists. The ancient Egyptian embalmers never wrote down how they mummified; it was a trade secret. Herodotus's account of mummification is the earliest we have.

Herodotus revered Egypt and was delighted to trace almost all aspects of Greek civilization back to the Egyptians. He said Greeks learned to build in stone from the Egyptians, was proud to proclaim that Greek gods were derived from the Egyptian pantheon, and even credited Egypt for the Greek legal code. A hundred years after Herodotus, the philosopher Plato attributed the invention of writing to Egypt.[2] The Greeks were just wild about their much older neighbor.

When Alexander the Great conquered Egypt in 330 BC, he had himself crowned pharaoh and built shrines and temples to Egyptian gods. Greek kings were mortal; Alexander wanted to be a pharaoh, a god on earth. After Alexander died, Egypt was ruled for three centuries by Greeks, all named Ptolemy, all depicting themselves on temple walls as Egyptian pharaohs. Later the Romans under Julius Caesar continued this fascination with Egypt.

CLEOPATRA CONQUERS CAESAR

Julius Caesar visited Egypt late in the Ptolemaic Dynasty (305 BC to 30 BC), when Egypt was on the decline. He came to settle a civil war that threatened Rome's supply of Egyptian grain. At that time the Roman army was the greatest military force on earth, but Caesar was about to be conquered by both Egypt and Cleopatra. Cleopatra was in her early 20s, and ruling Egypt, when she was deposed by her younger brother, Ptolemy. Caesar eventually straightened things out (Ptolemy conveniently drowned), and Cleopatra was restored to the throne. Cleopatra then took Caesar on a tour of Egypt on her royal barge. Although Caesar was well educated and well traveled, he had never seen anything like Egypt's pyramids and temples. Rome was still quite provincial, built mostly of mud bricks, so Egypt's gigantic stone structures thousands of years old amazed him. Most visitors to Egypt never ventured south of Alexandria. Cleopatra gave Caesar the full tour, sailing as far south as Luxor. Not only was Egypt unlike anything Caesar had ever seen, so was Cleopatra. Most Roman women were uneducated and relegated to the kitchen. Cleopatra had an extensive education, spoke several languages, and was ruling over one of the greatest civilizations in the world. By the time Caesar departed for Rome, he was hooked, and Cleopatra was pregnant with his son, Caesarion (Little Caesar).

Caesarion was born in Alexandria, and we have an ancient depiction of the birth, for Cleopatra erected a "birth house," a small temple commemorating the boy's divine birth (Fig. 2.1). On the walls she is shown giving birth sitting on a specially constructed birthing stool—the normal birthing position for women in ancient Egypt. This is a sensible position since gravity assists the delivery. When two young engineers on Napoleon's Egyptian campaign, Jean-Baptiste Prosper Jollois and Édouard de Villiers, recorded this scene in 1799, the wall where the newborn was shown was damaged, but we can make out Caesarion's feet emerging from Cleopatra. A goddess assists the squatting Cleopatra at the birth.

Fig. 2.1   Napoleon's artists copied a scene on an Egyptian temple wall showing Cleopatra, third from the left, giving birth to Caesarion. Egyptian women traditionally gave birth sitting on a birthing stool.

In 46 BC, when Caesarion was about two years old, Caesar brought Cleopatra and his young son to Rome. They stayed for two years, and Rome's aristocracy was introduced to the Queen of Egypt. For the first time Romans experienced refinement Egyptian style. When Rome's calendar needed adjusting, Cleopatra sent her astronomer Sosigenes to Rome to straighten things out. Here was an educated young woman who ruled a vast empire as a goddess. No one like Cleopatra had ever been seen in Rome. Enthralled by their visiting royalty, many Roman women converted to the cult of Isis, but the Roman Senate was uneasy. Caesar was getting a taste of what it was to be viewed as a god, and he liked it. He went so far as placing a statue of Cleopatra in the Temple of Venus Genetrix, suggesting the divinity of his young guest. A cabal of senators, concerned that Caesar might want to rule Rome as a demigod, assassinated him on the steps of the Senate on the Ides of March.

Like the goddess Isis, Cleopatra was now a widow with an infant son to protect. She fled Rome, returned to Egypt, and aligned herself with another Roman general, Mark Antony. After the pair were defeated by Octavian's navy at the Battle of Actium in the Ionian Sea, both Antony and Cleopatra committed suicide. Octavian then killed Caesarion and seized control of Egypt, making it a Roman province. Octavian, who changed his name to Augustus, had always viewed Cleopatra as the enemy and did not take kindly to devotees of Isis or to any other Egyptian fads. However, that did not stop him from bringing two obelisks to Rome, rededicating them to the sun. Obelisks were almost always erected in pairs at the entrances to Egyptian temples. The pharaohs inscribed their names on all four sides, ensuring that the gods would know which pharaoh had created such great monuments. Augustus was eager to emphasize the continuity between the pharaohs and himself, but without the trappings of the various cults prevalent at the time. The imperial taste for obelisks was not an expression of Egyptomania but rather a political statement to emphasize the dominance of Rome over its new province. In the following decades, however, later Roman emperors were infatuated with Egypt, and that is when true Egyptomania begins.

ISIS FOR ALL

The Egyptian goddess Isis became a patron saint for sailors who brought grain from Egypt to Rome. At various ports, sailors erected shrines to Isis Pelagia—Isis of the sea—hoping her magic would protect them. According to Egyptian mythology, Isis's husband, Osiris, was sealed in a wooden chest and thrown into the Nile by his evil brother, Seth. Eventually the chest washed ashore on Byblos (Lebanon). Isis set out on a voyage to recover the body and bring it back to Egypt. She succeeded and, through her powerful magic, resurrected Osiris, who becomes the god of the dead. It's not surprising that sailors adopted Isis as their protector.

Roman women took to worshiping Isis as a mother goddess. After Isis resurrected Osiris, she became pregnant and had a son, Horus, whom she successfully protected from various dangers. Isis was a goddess Roman women could identify with; they could understand her grief at the loss of her husband and her fear for her son's safety. In their homes, Roman women kept small bronze statues of Isis suckling the infant Horus—a precursor to Christianity's Madonna and child. Isis frequently wore a crown with a solar disk that would later morph into the Madonna's halo. Roman devotees of Isis frequently wore small vials of Nile water around their necks for protection, a precursor of holy water. Egyptian-themed mosaics and frescoes graced the floors and walls of private villas of the wealthy. Usually they were scenes of the Nile showing exotic crocodiles and hippopotami, but sometimes there were religious scenes of initiates worshiping Isis.

HADRIAN'S GRAND TOUR

Sailors and women were not the only Romans swept up in Egyptomania; even Roman emperors were bitten by the bug. Hadrian is probably the emperor most closely tied to Egypt. His imperial tour of Egypt during the years 130–131 AD took more than eight months. Starting in Alexandria, he visited Memphis and Saqqâra, where he dedicated a sanctuary to the sacred Apis bull, then traveled south on the Nile. When the imperial party reached Middle Egypt, a tragedy stuck that would forever link Hadrian with Egyptian archaeology. Hadrian was traveling with his wife, Empress Sabina, and Antinous, his lover. (Sabina was not happy about this.) When Antinous drowned in the Nile, the grief-stricken Hadrian decreed that a city be built in honor of the now-deified Antinous. The city, Antinopolis, had a triumphal arch, a circus, and a carefully planned grid of streets. Much of the city was still standing when Napoleon's savants visited and recorded it in 1799 (Fig. 2.2). It is a good thing they did; in the 1830s, Mohamed Ali, Egypt's ruling pasha, ever eager to westernize Egypt, ordered the city torn down and its blocks burned in kilns to produce quicklime, a key ingredient in the mortar he needed to build sugar refineries. The Napoleonic engravings are the only accurate records we have of Antinopolis.

After the Egyptian priests had performed the rituals deifying Antinous, the imperial party continued south, to Luxor, their southernmost destination. Hadrian's party left a vivid record of their visit to the Colossi of Memnon, which are actually statues of the pharaoh Amenhotep III. The statues once stood at the entrance to his mortuary temple, where he was worshiped after his death. The temple disappeared over the

Fig. 2.2 Emperor Hadrian built a city in Egypt to commemorate the death of his young lover, Antinous. Napoleon's savants recorded the ruins of the city for the Description de l'Égypte. *The city was destroyed soon after.*

centuries because its blocks were reused in later building projects. Today the colossi stand isolated on an open plain. The Greeks believed one colossus was a statue of Memnon, son of a legendary king of Egypt, and the other a statue of Eos, the Dawn. The statue on the north side (the one on the right) was famous in antiquity because it emitted a sound at dawn. Hadrian proudly recorded that the statue spoke to the royal party.

Hadrian's fascination with Egypt was not a passing fancy. When he returned to Rome, he added an Egyptian wing to his Villa Hadriana outside the city. The Egyptian wall murals are now gone, but not the statues of the youthful, well-muscled Antinous as a pharaoh. They are beautiful but were carved in Rome by non-Egyptian sculptors and don't look quite Egyptian. These Antinous statues are very early Egyptomania.

ROMANS IN THE AFTERLIFE

As a Roman province, Egypt supplied most of Rome's grain ("Egypt is the breadbasket of Rome" was the saying). Many retired Roman soldiers were granted plots of land in Egypt's fertile Fayoum, an area in the north. The Fayoum was just right for Romans. It was temperate in climate with a large lake and soil suitable for growing wine grapes. Soon Roman settlements were springing up on Egyptian soil. These settlers kept many of their customs but soon adopted the Egyptian belief in immortality. They wanted to live forever, and the Egyptian way of death seemed like their best bet. The ancient Egyptians were resurrectionists: They believed that the body would literally get up and go again in the next world. Therefore, the body had to be preserved—that's why they practiced mummification. After a body was mummified, it was placed inside an anthropoid (human-shaped) coffin. At

Fig. 2.3   Mummy masks on coffins were stylized and were not intended to look like the deceased.

the top of the coffin, by the head, was a stylized mummy mask—the face of the deceased (Fig. 2.3). These mummy masks were not realistic likenesses but were merely intended to stand in for the deceased if something happened to the body, a Plan B, as it were.

Romans living in Egypt embraced mummification but improved on the stylized mummy mask, replacing it with a realistic portrait of the deceased that was painted on a wooden board and bound into the mummy wrappings where the mask used to be (Fig. 2.4). These

Fig. 2.4   Roman mummy portraits were the first realistic portraits in the world.

realistic portraits created a sensation when they were discovered by British Egyptologist Flinders Petrie excavating at Hawara in the Fayoum. There, staring back at Petrie, were dozens of the Roman inhabitants, dead for 2,000 years but looking straight at him. Today there is still something unnerving about these portraits when one encounters them in museums. The leading authority on these portraits, Euphrosyne Doxiadis, agrees. "An experience I had in Berlin convinced me of the power inherent in the best of the Fayoum faces: I was left in a storage room on my own with about twenty portraits, and when the door closed behind me I felt a strange sensation—that I was not alone. None of these portraits were still on the mummy, and yet they transmitted the energy of human beings."[3]

Antinous statues were excavated in Hadrian's villa, so we know who produced them. And the Fayoum portraits were discovered in a Roman city, so we know when they were painted. But when something is discovered out of context, it can be difficult to figure out what is going on. This is just what happened during the seventeenth century, when the Isis Tablet first appeared on the scene.

THE ISIS TABLET

The Isis Tablet is my favorite bit of Egyptomania, but when it was found, no one knew its origins. It first appeared in Rome around 1628 and was bought by Charles Emmanuel I, King of Savoy.[4] It is a large metal rectangular plaque, about 50 by 30 inches, made of bronze with hieroglyphs and figures of Egyptian gods inlaid in silver and gold. When seventeenth-century antiquarians looked at the tablet, they could recognize the goddess Isis by her distinctive headdress, the solar disk surrounded by horns, and called it the Mensa Isiaca, the Isis table. Everyone was convinced that it was an ancient Egyptian artifact, perhaps a temple altar some long-deceased Roman had brought back from Egypt. A century later, the Jesuit scholar Athanasius Kircher published his massive four-volume work on ancient languages, *Oedipus Aegyptiacus* (1652–1654). Volume III was devoted to Kircher's claim that he had deciphered the ancient Egyptian hieroglyphic language. As primary texts for his thesis, Kircher used inscriptions on obelisks that the Roman emperors had brought back to Rome and the hieroglyphs on the Isis Tablet (Fig. 2.5). Kircher's translations were pure fantasy but were widely accepted during the Renaissance. Kircher and his followers didn't realize that the hieroglyphs on the tablet really don't say anything; the tablet wasn't from Egypt.

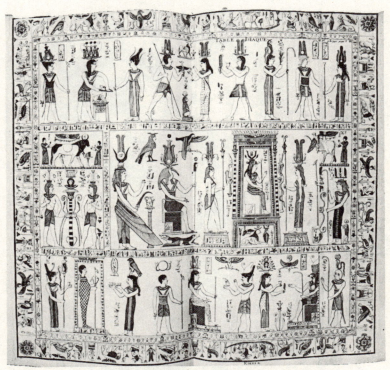

Fig. 2.5   The Isis Tablet fooled seventeenth-century antiquarians who thought it was made in Egypt. It is really an early piece of Egyptomania created by a Roman.

Fig. 2.6   The Roman magistrate Gaius Cestius was so taken with Egypt that he was buried in a pyramid.

Evidence suggests that the Isis Tablet was probably manufactured in Rome around the first century AD. We don't know the exact circumstances of its production, but I can imagine a likely scenario. Some wealthy Roman returning from Egypt wanted to set up an Isis shrine at home. He had seen Egyptian temple inscriptions, copied them as best he could, and, in his fervor to become a devotee of Isis, commissioned a metal smith to produce the tablet. He wasn't trying to fool anyone, he was creating an early bit of Egyptomania. By the seventeenth century, when the tablet was discovered, knowledge of hieroglyphs had been lost. Very few travelers were going to Egypt, so it was easily mistaken for an ancient Egyptian artifact.

Ancient Rome's infatuation with Egypt lasted for centuries; Roman villas sported Egyptian-themed murals, mosaics, and statues. A decade after Cleopatra's suicide, the Roman magistrate Gaius Cestius built his pyramid tomb outside Rome's city wall. Over the centuries the city has grown, and today this imposing 100-foot-tall structure is at a busy intersection, a reminder of Rome's fascination with Egypt (Fig. 2.6). Roman noblemen had pyramid-shaped tombs, but obelisks were the favored Egyptian souvenir of emperors. In fact, Rome has more upright obelisks today than any other city in the world.

THE DECLINE OF THE OLD GODS

With the conversion of Emperor Constantine to Christianity in AD 319, the ancient Egyptian religion declined along with the Roman Empire. Emperors no longer supported the temples of Egypt, so the priests, custodians of the sacred writings, dwindled in number, and eventually only a few old priests could read hieroglyphs. In 391 Emperor Theodosius I decreed that all Egyptian temples be closed. Some isolated temples in upper Egypt continued the old religion, but not for long. On August 24, 394, a priest of Isis named Esmet-Akhom carved the last dated hieroglyphic inscription on a wall at Philae temple. It was a drawing of the god Mandulis along with a prayer. Soon after there was no one alive who could read his prayer.

The rise of Christianity was the death blow to the ancient Egyptian religion. Not only was it no longer fashionable to worship Isis, it could cost you your life, and mummification was forbidden. Mummification suggested a pagan physical resurrection of the body, not a spiritual one as in Christianity. Soon Christian zealots in Rome were pulling down pagan obelisks that Rome's emperors had so proudly erected. Only one obelisk was permitted to remain standing, the one Caligula brought to Rome in the first century AD and erected at his circus, where St. Peter was later martyred. Because this obelisk witnessed the death of St. Peter, patriarch of the church, it alone was not toppled. As the centuries passed and Europe entered the Dark Ages, knowledge of Egypt was lost and Rome's obelisks disappeared under centuries of debris.

In Greece and Rome, Egyptomania evolved from a reverence for ancient Egypt's antiquity, hieroglyphs, and mummies. Greeks and Romans wanted to be like Egyptians and live forever. By the Middle Ages, the fascination with all things Egyptian had vanished, as had most knowledge of Egypt. The only source of information about the land of the pharaohs was the Bible. It would not be until the Renaissance that Egyptomania would rise again, but in a very different form. During the seventeenth century, an interest in Egypt arose, but it was more a curiosity than a religious quest. The event that jump-started Egyptomania during the Renaissance was the moving of an obelisk, something that had not been attempted in more than 1,000 years.

After the emperor Constantine legalized Christianity, he made Rome the capital of this new religion. In an attempt to make Rome worthy, Constantine began building. The circus where St. Peter had been martyred 300 years earlier was torn down, and upon its foundation a basilica was constructed in the shadow of the obelisk Caligula had brought from Egypt. Throughout the Middle Ages, as Christianity took hold, the obelisk remained upright. At the time of the Renaissance, St. Peter's Basilica was more than 1,000 years old and beginning to show its age. A spectacular new basilica was begun less than a quarter of a mile from the old one, which, along with the obelisk, had been neglected. Visited by only the most informed and persistent pilgrims, the obelisk's pedestal disappeared beneath accumulated rubbish. The suggestion was constantly put forward that the obelisk should be moved to the site of the new St. Peter's Basilica, where it would be appreciated, but no one was willing to attempt such an undertaking. When Michelangelo was asked to try, he replied, "And what if it breaks?"

FONTANA MOVES THE OBELISK

When Pope Sixtus V took office in 1585, he formed a committee of four cardinals, a bishop, and city council members to select an architect to move the obelisk. Applicants for the job were to submit their plans. In September 1585, more than 150 architects and engineers came to Rome from as far away as Greece with plans ranging from brilliant to ridiculous. Many did not want to lower the obelisk, fearing it would break when pivoted to the horizontal, and suggested it be levered straight up off its pedestal and moved while upright. The committee selected seven finalists, among them Domenico Fontana. Fontana came from a family of architects and had worked with his older architect brother, Giovanni, before he moved to Rome. Early in the pope's career, when he was a cardinal, Fontana assisted him with architectural matters. Fontana undoubtedly had the inside track, but he also came prepared. He presented an exquisite miniature model of the scaffold he intended to build complete with a lead obelisk he had cast to scale. His was an extremely detailed plan including calculations to determine the weight of the obelisk, something that had never been done before. It impressed the committee, and Fontana was given the job.

Today Fontana's moving of the Vatican obelisk is considered one of the great engineering feats of the Renaissance, and rightly so. Details of how the ancient Romans transported and erected the obelisks—the boats, the mechanics, how many men, how much time it took—have not survived. There was no manual, no eyewitness accounts, nothing to go on save the simple fact that somehow the ancients had done it, more than once. It took a considerable number of skills to move an obelisk, and the risk was high. In addition to his engineering skills, Fontana also needed organizational skills to oversee the required army of workers.

Once Fontana determined the weight of the obelisk, he calculated that he would need 40 windlasses to lift it. Windlasses traditionally were used on ships to raise sails and anchors. The basic element is a gear box within a horizontal wheel around which rope is wound or unwound. Levers radiating from the wheel give the men turning the wheel a mechanical advantage, greatly increasing the weight that can be lifted. Although a windlass is horizontal, the pull can be converted vertically by running rope through a pulley suspended above the object to be lifted.

Windlasses were Fontana's main source of power to lift the obelisk off its base, but as a backup, he also intended to insert five huge levers under the obelisk for extra lifting power if the windlasses were not adequate. It was a brilliant plan, but not everyone was convinced it would work. Could 40 windlasses be used in tandem?

The scaffold that supported this work was actually two halves of a framework on either side of the obelisk that were joined at the top for stability. Fontana called it his *castello,* or castle. Think of a giant ladder with the obelisk standing right in the middle (Fig. 2.7). The structure was supported by four "masts" on each side composed of four huge tree trunks that had been hand hewn into gigantic timbers. The timbers were held together by iron hoops with massive bolts going through them. For additional strength, wood wedges were hammered between the hoops and the timbers to maintain tightness. If anything shifted during the work, the wedges could be adjusted.

The surface of the obelisk was protected by a double layer of wood planks held together by a cage composed of iron strips four and a half

Fig. 2.7   The Vatican obelisk being lowered in front of the original St. Peter's Basilica in 1586.

inches wide that bolted together and ran the full length of the obelisk. The ropes going through the blocks and tackles at the top of the scaffold were attached to this iron cage. When the windlasses turned, the ropes were reeled in, pulling straight up on the cage, and the obelisk would rise off its pedestal straight up in the air. At least that was Fontana's plan.

When the Romans set the obelisk on its pedestal in Rome, they lowered it onto four massive bronze nodules that Fontana called "dumplings" (*gnocchi*), but which are traditionally called *astragals* because they resemble bones of the foot. Thus, the obelisk didn't rest directly on its stone base; there was daylight between the pedestal and the bottom of the obelisk, and Fontana capitalized on this feature. He threaded his iron cage under the obelisk and up its sides so that when the windlasses turned and the pulleys transferred the forces to the obelisk, it would be pulled from the bottom as well as from the sides. The space between the obelisk and pedestal also enabled Fontana to insert the immense levers supplementing the lifting force generated by the windlasses. The iron strapping alone weighed 4,000 pounds. It was a grand plan, well thought out, but would it work? The truth is, no one was sure.

Fontana was clearly worried about the windlasses. He numbered each one so his foremen on top of the scaffold could shout down orders to master builders stationed by each one. "Ease up on windlass 32" would thus be guaranteed a quick response. For weeks before the obelisk was to be lowered, Fontana trained his teams. Three or four horses turned each windlass, and one by one they were fine-tuned until all had the same tension. Throughout the fall and winter, preparations had gone forward: The iron straps were forged, pulleys carved, timber cut, foundations poured, horses procured, windlasses shaped and tested. Finally, on April 30, 1586, Fontana was ready to lower his obelisk.

Two hours before dawn, two masses were said, and all workers involved in the project took communion. Even before first light, crowds had been growing. For six months endless cartloads of iron and wood had streamed into Rome; this was the biggest show in town, and no one wanted to miss it. A barricade was set up around the work area, and the entire police force of Rome was called in to keep order. It was explained that any nonworker crossing the barricade was subject to penalty of death. Strict silence was to be maintained by all spectators so Fontana's orders could be heard. To make absolutely certain there could be no confusion of orders, a 20-foot-high platform was constructed for a trumpeter. When the workers heard the blast of the trumpet, they were to begin turning the windlasses. High on top of the scaffold was a great bell. When it was rung, work was to stop instantly. With a trumpet to signal "begin" and a bell for "stop," there wasn't going to be any confusion on this project.

At one end of the square, 20 carters waited with 20 strong replacement horses in case any of the windlass horses tired. At the base of the obelisk, Fontana had 12 carpenters with sledgehammers ready to pound in wedges when the obelisk began to rise so that it would never be supported by ropes alone. These dozen carpenters were supplied with iron helmets to protect them from bolts that might fall from the top of the scaffold. Fontana had invented the hard hat! Thirty men climbed high on the scaffold to monitor it for movement or signs of weakness. Below, 35 men were positioned to work three levers inserted under the south side of the obelisk and another 18 to work two levers at the north end.

When dawn finally came, all of Rome had gathered to watch "God's work," as Fontana called it. There were dukes and princes, cardinals and foreigners who had traveled great distances to see the obelisk move. Every window of every house that faced the square was filled with heads, stretching to see something of the work. The crowds were so great that Swiss Guards, the Vatican security force, and light cavalry were spread along the barricade to ensure order and silence.

Fontana asked all assembled, workers and spectators, to kneel and pray for a successful outcome. When everyone rose, Fontana signaled the trumpeter, and almost immediately 907 men, 75 horses, and 40 windlasses moved as one. The ground shook as with an earthquake, and then a loud *crack,* like a lightning bolt, was heard across the square. Immediately the bell was rung and work halted. One of the iron hoops at the top of the scaffolding had snapped. It was repaired, and everything was inspected carefully again. Months earlier, when Fontana had dropped a plumb line to measure the height of the obelisk, he discovered it was leaning slightly. Now as he examined the scaffold, he saw that the obelisk was perfectly upright. The first turns of the windlasses had moved it; his plan was working.

With the hoop repaired and the scaffold inspected, the trumpeter was told to give the signal to commence work. Once again horses and men went into motion. Slowly the obelisk rose into the air, but as it inched upward, more and more iron bands snapped. Fontana later said they looked as if they had been made of the softest material that had been cut by a knife. No longer confident that the bands could support the obelisk, Fontana brought in more than a quarter of a mile of cord that Roman rope makers had fashioned from hemp and wrapped it around the obelisk and its iron basket. Now, with the obelisk securely encased in its giant net, Fontana was confident it could once again move safely upward.

Throughout the day the trumpet sounded, the windlasses turned, and the obelisk moved up. Rope had trumped iron and supported the Vatican obelisk. At dinnertime, baskets of food were brought to the square so the workers would not have to leave their stations. Fontana was not going to worry about rounding up 907 men to continue work after dinner. By 10 P.M., after 14 rotations of the windlasses, the obelisk had risen more than two feet above its pedestal. Iron and wood wedges had been hammered into the space between the bottom of the obelisk and the pedestal, and with the obelisk resting securely on wedges, everyone returned home. The first day, not without its drama, ended in a resounding success.

The next day, Fontana began removing the massive 600-pound dumplings, a task that took more than a week. On May 7, Fontana was ready to lower the obelisk onto the huge sledge on which it was to be pulled to the new site.

With the obelisk safely lowered, Fontana built a causeway from the old site to the new site 260 yards away (Fig. 2.8). Huge beams were

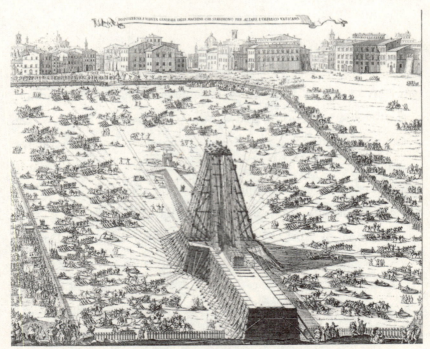

Fig. 2.8   Erecting the obelisk at St. Peter's on September 10, 1556.

inserted through the width of the causeway and bolted together so the earth wouldn't slide under the great weight it would support. When the obelisk moved on top of it, pulled by several windlasses, it looked something like a railroad trestle. The plan was to raise the obelisk with the sledge still attached, providing an extra layer of protection for the needle.

In the predawn of September 10, two masses were celebrated, everyone prayed for a successful outcome, and Fontana's highly trained team took up their stations. Once again, the trumpet blew, windlasses turned, and the tip of the obelisk began its slow skyward journey. When the obelisk reached 45 degrees, the bell was sounded, work stopped, and food was delivered to the site for the workers. After dinner, the process continued—three turns of the windlasses, inspection of the scaffold and ropes, and then three more turns. After 52 turns of the windlasses, the obelisk was upright, and cannons were fired to notify the city of the successful operation.

HOW TO EXORCISE AN OBELISK

Fontana's accomplishment was one of the great engineering triumphs of the Renaissance, but the goal was not just physical. The obelisk was a symbol of Christianity's triumph over paganism. Rome's needle was seen as a lofty and graceful pedestal for the Holy Cross that would be attached to its top, but the show was not yet over. The pope ordered that a ritual of exorcism be performed on the obelisk.

The ritual of exorcism is intended to cast out Satan and his demons and is not to be taken lightly. Today, only a specially trained priest can perform an exorcism, and that is usually done in consultation with psychologists to be certain that the person is truly possessed. While normally performed on a person, objects too can be exorcised. Clearly the obelisk was viewed as a pagan monument that might house malevolent forces. In a sense, there was a double whammy, both Egyptian and Roman. Because the Egyptians had quarried the obelisk, the church had Egyptian gods to contend with. Then there were the early Romans who moved the obelisk to Rome; they too were pagans. The church still believed that Egyptian gods were a force to be reckoned with. This sense of ancient Egypt as a source of occult power continued for centuries. With no one capable of reading the hieroglyphs, it was easy to believe they had mysterious powers. This all changed at the end of the eighteenth century, when a young military officer from Corsica became obsessed with Egypt.

THREE

Napoleon on the Nile

In the spring of 1798, Napoleon Bonaparte, a 29-year-old general fresh from a victorious Italian campaign, was the toast of Paris. However, unemployed heroes are dangerous to have around, so the Directory, the ruling body of Revolutionary France, decided to put him in charge of the "Army of England," which was then preparing to invade Britain. Napoleon inspected the ships and troops for the invasion, concluded that they had no chance of success, and declared he wanted no part of it. Instead, he suggested it would be better to strike a fatal blow to the British economy by invading Egypt and cutting off England's land route to India. Although Bonaparte gave the Directory solid political reasons for his Egyptian Campaign, he had his own agenda. He wanted to follow in the footsteps of his hero, Alexander the Great, and said as much: "My glory is declining. This little corner of Europe is too small to supply it. We must go East. All the great men of the world have there acquired their celebrity." Like Alexander, Caesar, and Hadrian before him, Bonaparte was fascinated with Egypt. By conquering Egypt, he would reveal the hidden Orient to Europe and place himself among the pantheon of great conquerors. Less than three months after his proposal, Bonaparte set off for the land of the Pharaohs.

NAPOLEON'S SAVANTS

When he sailed from Toulon on May 19, 1798, Napoleon took with him more than 17,000 troops and 700 horses. The destination was kept secret to all but a few in order to avoid detection by the powerful British navy. Napoleon had been authorized to occupy Egypt, free it from the tyrannical rule of the Mameluke warlords, expel the English from the east, take possession of the shores of the Red Sea, and cut the Isthmus of Suez. It was an ambitious plan, but Napoleon intended to accomplish even more. Along with his troops and machinery of war, he brought a second, smaller army of savants—more than 150 engineers, scientists, and scholars, architects, surveyors, and cartographers— to map Egypt and its monuments. Their mission was to study and describe both ancient and modern Egypt. Many of the savants were distinguished members of the National Institute. The group included Gaspard Monge, a physicist who helped assemble the team and who became its leader; Claude-Louis Berthollet, a chemist; Jean-Baptiste Joseph Fourier, the mathematician after whom the Fourier equations are named; Déodat de Dolomieu, the mineralogist after whom the Dolomite Mountains are named; and a brilliant young naturalist, Geoffroy Saint-Hilaire. There were also artists such as Vivant Denon, who later became the first director of the Louvre.

FIRST STOP: MALTA

On their way, Napoleon and his fleet stopped at the island of Malta, which was strategically located for control of the Mediterranean.

Months before he had sent spies ahead to determine the strength of the fortifications. At the time, the island of Malta was ruled by the Order of the Knights Hospitaller of St. John of Jerusalem, who had existed since the First Crusade in the eleventh century. Bonaparte's intelligence report was clear: The island was held by a mere vestige of the Knights Hospitaller. Most of the 332 knights were old or not inclined to fight, and many were French with strong ties to the motherland.

By the time they reached Malta, Bonaparte's fleet had been joined by three other convoys that had sailed from other ports, swelling the flotilla to 400 ships and 55,000 men, far too powerful for the dusty remnants of the Knights of Malta to resist; within 24 hours the island was in French hands. As part of the terms of capitulation, the Knights surrendered treasures valued at 7 million francs, including 12 life-size silver statues of the apostles. An additional 6 million francs in gold and jewel-encrusted treasures were taken from the Church of St. John. In return, the Knights were promised pensions (which they never received), but they were permitted to keep a splinter of the True Cross. Bonaparte left a garrison of his troops to hold the island and recruited 300 Maltese to come with him to Egypt, to serve as translators. (The Maltese language is derived from Arabic.)

ON TO THE BATTLE OF THE PYRAMIDS

When the fleet finally landed at Alexandria on July 1, 1798, it found a sleepy town in the last throes of decay, unable to resist the invading French. Napoleon met with little resistance and was soon in control of the city. The next few weeks were spent organizing troops and marching south to the capital, Cairo, where they would soon find themselves engaged in a battle that would add to Napoleon's growing legend. At that time the Mamelukes, a fierce warrior class, controlled

Egypt, and they were not willing to give up without a fight. The term "mameluke" is Arabic for "bought man," or slave, and the Mamelukes' history stretches back in time almost as far as the Knights Hospitaller. Around the year 1230, the Ayyubite sultan ruling Egypt brought 12,000 youths from the Caucasus Mountains to form an elite corps for his army. Their status was far above that of ordinary slaves and even free-born Muslims, who were not allowed to carry weapons or perform certain tasks. The young Mamelukes were trained in the art of warfare and given the best of everything. When they matured, they showed their gratitude by killing the sultan and seizing power. The Mamelukes ruled Egypt until the Turkish conquest of 1517, and then they became nominal vassals of the Turks. The Mamelukes governed Egypt as they pleased and paid the Turks only a small portion of the taxes they ruthlessly extracted from the peasants.

When news reached Cairo that the French army was marching from Alexandria, 6,000 mounted Mamelukes and more than 10,000 foot soldiers massed for battle. They faced an even greater number of French cavalry, infantry, and artillery. The Battle of the Pyramids presented a striking contrast in combat styles. In their haste to reach Egypt, the French still wore their woolen uniforms from the Italian campaign. The Mamelukes were dressed in brightly colored silks and wore elaborate turbans. Each Mameluke warrior had several pairs of pistols, as well as scimitars, lances, swords, and other hand weapons, many encrusted with jewels. They were followed into battle by servants running behind the horses to reload the spent pistols.

As the Mameluke horses pranced in the distance, Napoleon, on his white horse, rode in front of his troops, pointed to the pyramids eight miles in the distance, and said, "Soldiers, from these heights forty centuries of history look down upon you." His estimate of the age of the pyramids was remarkably accurate. Hieroglyphs had not yet been deciphered, and the Bible was the only guideline for calculating chronology in the Holy Lands. In the seventeenth century, Bishop Ussher, Archbishop of Ireland, calculated that the world began in 4004 BC, and many people still believed that date. Bonaparte's estimate was much more accurate.

In contrast to the fierce but undisciplined Mamelukes, Napoleon's troops were a well-constructed machine. They formed five battle squares with artillery at the corners, riflemen at the sides, and cavalry inside the squares in case they were broken. The French were instructed to hold fire until the charging Mamelukes were almost on top of them. The first charge was decisive. The French held their fire, the Mamelukes charged, and when the French finally fired, hundreds fell. The Mamelukes regrouped, made several more attempts to break the squares, but suffered even greater casualties. Knowing that another charge would be fruitless, they tried Plan B. Mamelukes often carried much of their wealth with them, and many had gold coins sewn into their turbans. In an attempt to get the French to break ranks, they threw gold coins in front of the French lines, but to no avail. Discipline ruled the day. Finally the surviving Mamelukes rode off in defeat, heading south into Upper Egypt. It was clear they were no match for Bonaparte's army.

THE BATTLE OF THE NILE

The French took control of Cairo, and the officers and savants established themselves in the hastily vacated Mameluke palaces. But peace did not last long. On August 1, England's Admiral Horatio Nelson sailed into Aboukir Bay off Alexandra where Napoleon's ships were anchored. Nelson had been searching the Mediterranean for Bonaparte's fleet ever since it sailed, and it finally paid off.

The French fleet was anchored close to shore to protect the landward side of the ships from attack. The cannons were pointed seaward so that all the firepower would be on the approaching enemy. Admiral Nelson came upon the anchored French fleet in the late afternoon. He then did two unexpected things. First, he decided to fight right then and there. Normally battles were fought during the day. Attacking in the late afternoon guaranteed that the battle would last well into the night. Second, Nelson gambled that there was enough room to sail his fleet between the French ships and the shore. He was right. With all the French guns mounted seaward and the British ships sailing in close landward, the French were sitting ducks for the British guns.

As the Alexandrians watched from the shore, the battle continued into the night with cannon fire and burning ships illuminating the sky. Admiral Brueys on the *L'Orient,* the largest fighting ship in the world, had both legs shot off by a cannonball but refused to be taken below to the infirmary. He was placed in a chair, tourniquets tied around the stumps of his legs, and continued to command on the bridge until he was hit and killed by a second cannonball. Brueys was not alone in his bravery.

The French fought heroically, but throughout the night, the British pounded away at the French fleet, sinking ship after ship. The *L'Orient* had been used to store the army's gunpowder; when it caught fire, it was doomed. When the fire reached the powder magazine, it exploded with a deafening roar that could be heard 50 miles away, a noise so loud that everyone was shocked and stopped fighting for ten minutes.

With the French fleet totally destroyed, Nelson sent dispatches to England announcing his victory. Napoleon was now cut off from France, reinforcements, and supplies. He was in a jam and would not get out of it easily, and Admiral Nelson had no intention of fighting him on land. He simply sailed away. When Bonaparte received the bad news in Cairo, he issued an Order of the Day. It doesn't mention defeat, merely the glory with which his sailors covered themselves at the Battle of the Nile, as it would come to be known.

REDISCOVERING EGYPT

When the *L'Orient* sank, much of the savants' scientific instruments, surveying equipment, and supplies went with it. In spite of this setback, the scholars settled into their tasks. The senior men were housed in the palace of Hassan Kashef in Cairo. The botanists set up their experiments in the garden of Qassim Bey's palace. Saint Hilaire was ecstatic about the space and was soon helping set up chemistry labs and collecting mineral, botanical, and zoological specimens. The Egyptian chronicler Abd al-Rahman al-Jabarti described with wonder the library they organized in the house of Hassan Kashef. Al-Jabarti had never seen anything like this. Hard as it is to believe, the Egyptians had never published a book. The printing presses with Arabic type that Bonaparte had looted from the Vatican were the first ever in Egypt. Certainly a library, a place where people came to do research, complete with library table—what al-Jabarti called "a long wide board"—and a librarian were concepts foreign to Egypt.

On August 21, 1798, Bonaparte founded the Institut d'Égypte, the world's first Egyptological society. There were four sections: mathematics, physics, political economy, and literature and art. Bonaparte headed the mathematics section and took an active part in the meetings of the institute that took place in the palace of Qassim Bey, who had fled to Upper Egypt. Napoleon had a real interest in science, but not in the abstract. He proposed very specific, practical problems for the institute to investigate. Perhaps most urgent were determining if the materials for gunpowder were available in Egypt and the best method for purifying the Nile water that the army was drinking.

The scientists were also free to investigate topics of their own, and even the dullest engineer was more interested in exploring the temple of Dendera than designing bread ovens. One of the youngest, René-Édouard Devilliers, an 18-year-old engineering student, brought his school books along, and in October 1798, Monge tested him and pronounced him a civil engineer. For most of the campaign, he teamed up with Jean-Baptiste Prosper Jollois, a 21-year-old engineer, and as far as one can tell from accounts of their activities, they forgot about constructing bridges and roads and fell in love with antiquity. It was a severe case of Egyptomania, but even more important, it marks the beginning of scientific Egyptology.

TEMPLES, TOMBS, AND SAVANTS

The pair of adventurers headed south and were soon enthralled with the Temple of Dendera and its now-famous zodiac ceiling. They copied it carefully, which was far from easy. Carved on the ceiling were hundreds of details of the sky as the Egyptians saw it, complete with signs of the zodiac that had been blackened by soot from the fires of centuries of squatters who had lived in the temple (Fig. 3.1). The dynamic duo went on to record temples at Philae, Esneh, Edfu, Kom Ombo, and Luxor, but their greatest adventure was in the Valley of the Kings.

Not only did Jollois and Devilliers produce the first professional map of the Valley, they discovered a new tomb. When Napoleon's army entered Egypt, there were 11 open tombs in the Valley. Exploring the Valley's remote western branch, the young engineers found a small hole in the cliff's wall and crept in. Illuminating the cavity with candles, they peered through the darkness and saw vivid paintings of a pharaoh and gods on the walls. They had discovered the tomb of

Fig. 3.1   The Dendera Zodiac, copied by Napoleon's engineers in 1799, created a sensation in Paris.

Amenhotep III, Tutankhamen's grandfather. Small antiquities, such as figurines of servants (*ushabtis*) intended to wait on the king in the next world, littered the tomb's floor, and the two took some home as royal souvenirs. A small green schist head of Amenhotep that they discovered is now in the Louvre. Devilliers's descendants still own four ushabtis that he brought back to France.

Jollois and Devilliers were the youngest of Bonaparte's team of savants. One of the oldest members of the expedition, 52-year-old Vivant Denon, was also falling in love with Egypt's ancient monuments. When Napoleon instructed General Desaix to pursue the Mamelukes retreating south, Denon saw it as a chance to sketch the monuments of Upper Egypt and tagged along.

While in the Valley, Denon spotted a relief of a scribe writing on a scroll. Although Denon was an educated man, he was unaware that Egyptians wrote on papyrus and that travelers had already brought papyri back to Europe. Denon congratulated himself on being "the first who had made this important discovery."[1]

Denon made some reasonable observations about ancient Egypt. Examining a Book of the Dead, a series of spells and prayers intended to ensure that the deceased would be resurrected in the next world, Denon noticed that a section of the text ended in the middle of a line and that the space to the left of the writing had been left blank. From this he correctly deduced that the writing was from right to left. (Right to left was the more common direction of writing, but ancient Egyptian could also be written from left to right.) Denon was excited, but he wasn't alone. In his memoirs, Denon records that while sailing up the Nile with the troops, the soldiers spontaneously applauded as they rounded a bend and saw Karnak Temple for the first time. Egyptomania wasn't infecting just Denon and the savants; it was sweeping through Napoleon's army. Even Bonaparte was not immune.

BONAPARTE PLANS A CANAL

When the Directory sent Bonaparte off to Egypt, one of his missions was to determine if a canal was possible between the Mediterranean and the Red seas. Most trade from Europe to India went around the Cape of Good Hope. A canal would permit ships to sail across the Mediterranean to Alexandria, through the canal to Suez, and then into the Red Sea and off to India. If the French could control such a canal, it would be a great economic defeat for their enemy, England.

Bonaparte loved the adventure of searching for an ancient canal. In late December 1798, he rode out to explore the Isthmus of Suez with his chief engineer and a few other savants. After several days of searching, Bonaparte found the canal and traced it for 15 miles. Excited by his discovery, Bonaparte instructed the chief engineer, Jacques-Marie Le Père, to return with a team to survey the entire isthmus to determine if a canal were possible. Le Père and his team made three expeditions to the isthmus, surveying under harsh conditions. Constantly harassed by Bedouins, they had difficulty obtaining food and supplies and slept out in the cold. In 1800, they finally completed the survey. Le Père sent his report to Bonaparte, who was back in Paris by that time. Le Père reported that a canal was possible but not a direct one. He said that because the Red Sea at high tide was 30 feet higher than the Mediterranean, there would be flooding. He suggested one canal to the Bitter Lakes and a second from the lakes to Suez. He was wrong. His fellow savants Laplace and Fourier correctly understood that sea level is sea level everywhere, and there was no danger of flooding Egypt. Still, the plan for the canal was abandoned and not raised again for decades.

THE BATTLE OF ACRE

Though Bonaparte enjoyed looking for the old canal, he was also fighting a war. The Turks were massing in Syria to reclaim Egypt, and Napoleon was forced to march to Acre to head off the invasion. On the way, the French fought a major battle at Jaffa, where they captured more than 4,000 Turks and Moroccans. By this time Napoleon's army was being ravaged by the plague, and they were having difficulty finding food. There was no way to hold all the captives, so Napoleon ordered them killed.

On March 17, 1799, Napoleon began the siege of Acre. Djezzar Pasha, who was known as "the butcher" because of his cruelty, occupied the fortress, which backed onto the Mediterranean. Normally the siege tactic was to starve out those inside, but the British sent Admiral Sidney Smith to supply rations and expertise from the water, so Napoleon found himself in the unfortunate position of having to attack the fort with inadequate artillery. Trenches were dug, and assaults were repeatedly mounted, but each time the French sustained heavy losses and were forced to withdraw. Finally on May 20, 1799, the French army, many of whom were suffering from eye disease and the plague, retreated to Cairo. It was Bonaparte's first defeat on land.

BONAPARTE ABANDONS HIS ARMY

On the night of August 23, 1799, Napoleon, realizing the campaign was a lost cause, secretly sailed for France. On his arrival he commissioned a series of medals commemorating his victory in Egypt. Bonaparte knew that propaganda was crucial to his legacy. His fleet had been sunk, he had lost a disastrous battle at Acre, and his army was being destroyed by the plague, but that didn't stop him from declaring victory. One medal, commemorating his return to France (remember, he deserted his army in the night), shows Bonaparte as victorious Mercury flying over three rather steep pyramids. The captions read "The Hero Returns to His Country" and on the medal's reverse—"Bonaparte Liberator of Egypt." Separate medals for the conquest of Upper and Lower Egypt were struck. The one for Upper Egypt uses the ancient Roman symbol for conquered Egypt, a crocodile chained to a palm tree (Fig. 3.2). Perhaps the most amusing medal is the one showing Bonaparte in a chariot drawn by two camels!

Fig. 3.2   Napoleon commemorated his "victory" in Egypt with an old Roman image—a crocodile chained to a palm tree.

POLITICAL EGYPTOMANIA

The British were issuing their own propaganda, and it was much closer to the truth. Early in the Egyptian Campaign, the British captured several French ships carrying letters home from Bonaparte's stranded Army of the Orient. Until then, only glowing reports had emerged from Bonaparte in Egypt. The captured letters revealed that the French were desperate, disease was rampant, and all was not going as well as claimed. In a brilliant propaganda coup of their own, the British published the letters, and they soon became the rage of London, going through six editions in a few months. While the English public read of the desperate straits of Napoleon's army, James Gillray, a popular London satirist, published a series of cartoons lampooning Bonaparte.

One of Gillray's cartoons lampoons the French scientists who were constantly being attacked by the natives. The savants are shown trapped on top of Pompey's Pillar in Alexandria (Color Plate 1). To determine the height of the column, the French flew a kite to the top, pulled the string taught, and then measured the string. Gillray shows the savants trapped on top of the pillar while the locals shoot at them. Learned treatises the scientists were writing are shown falling from the pillar. They have titles such as "The Rights of Crocodiles." The British ate it up.

In these early cartoons, we see the beginning of an iconography of Egyptomania. Gillray's cartoon "French Generals retiring on account of their health" contains more icons than you can shake a crocodile at. Suspended overhead is a crocodile, an icon for Egypt, while in back, Bonaparte and General Jean-Baptiste Kléber are depicted as mummies, perhaps the ultimate icons.

When Bonaparte left Egypt, he did not even say farewell to Kléber, his next in charge. Instead, he simply left him a letter appointing him commander in chief of the Army of the Orient. Kléber, a respected general and seasoned veteran of war, knew there was no hope for the Egyptian Campaign and began negotiating an honorable peace. Before that could be achieved, he was assassinated. General Jacques-François Menou succeeded him. Menou had converted to Islam to marry a bath keeper's daughter and had the respect of neither the Egyptians nor the French. The hopeless war dragged on until 1801 when a treaty was finally concluded.

One of the terms of the agreement was that the collections formed by the scientists were to be handed over to the English. The savants refused, declaring they would rather burn them than hand them over. The British permitted the scientists to keep their botanical and zoological specimens, but they insisted that the antiquities go to England, where they eventually ended up in the British Museum. The most famous of all the Egyptian antiquities, the Rosetta Stone, is an enduring legacy of Napoleon Bonaparte's Egyptian Campaign.

THE ROSETTA STONE

The French found the Rosetta Stone in July 1799 when they were strengthening the foundations of the fort at Rosetta in the Nile Delta.

Lieutenant Pierre-François Bouchard, the officer in charge, realized that the stone was important, and by August it was being studied in Cairo. The 47-inch-tall, 30-inch-wide stone slab bore three inscriptions, one in Greek that the savants could read. The stone is basically a thank-you note written in 196 BC from the priests of Egypt to Pharaoh Ptolemy V in gratitude for reducing their taxes. Contrary to what is usually taught in schools, the Rosetta Stone is not written in three languages; there are only two: Greek and Egyptian. The confusion is that there are three *scripts* on the stone: hieroglyphic, demotic, and Greek. Hieroglyphs were used for religious and official texts while the demotic (from the Greek *demos,* meaning "people") was for mundane, daily matters. Both the hieroglyphic and demotic texts are Egyptian; they just use different scripts. When the savants began examining the stone, they immediately realized that it would be the key to deciphering the ancient Egyptian language. The last line of the Greek inscription says that the three inscriptions were the same text in sacred (hieroglyphs), native (demotic), and Greek characters. But deciphering the language was not as easy as scholars had expected, primarily because everyone was making the same mistaken assumption—that the hieroglyphic inscription was purely ideographic, with hieroglyphs standing for concepts. In retrospect, this doesn't make sense. If hieroglyphs were picture writing, then everyone would be able to read them! Further, if the hieroglyphs were pictures of what was being discussed, then the Egyptians would seem to have been always talking about birds and feet. Scholars were convinced hieroglyphs were ideographic and thus concentrated on the demotic text because they believed it alone was an alphabetic script and would provide a close parallel to the Greek text.

The British physician and physicist Thomas Young made the first breakthrough around 1814, when he realized that the demotic was a mixture of phonetic and symbolic signs. (So are hieroglyphs.) He knew from the Greek text that King Ptolemy's name was repeated several times and deduced that it was inside the ovals in the hieroglyphic text. The name for these ovals, *cartouche,* is the French word for "cartridge," given by the soldiers who saw them carved on temple walls and thought they looked like ammunition. Knowing that "Ptolemy" was inside the cartouche, Young was able to figure out the phonetic values of many of the hieroglyphs. Young's discovery was crucial, but it would be another decade before the Egyptian language was truly deciphered. Even Young, who first deciphered the phonetics of the name in the cartouches, was a victim of the entrenched assumption that hieroglyphs were pictorial. He thought the non-Egyptian name Ptolemy was the exception to the rule. Jean-François Champollion's realization that hieroglyphs were both ideographic and phonetic opened the door to understanding how the language really worked. With the cracking of the code, Egyptologists could now read the history of the country they had been studying for decades. Thus began a whole new wave of Egyptomania.

FRENCH EGYPTOMANIA

Even before the decipherment of the ancient Egyptian language, Egyptomania took France by storm. When Denon returned to France with Bonaparte in 1799, a full two years before the rest of the savants, he had a head start on publishing. His *Travels in Upper and Lower Egypt* appeared in 1802. It was a sensation, going through 20 editions in various languages. The drawings Denon had made provided the first accurate depiction of Egypt that Europe had ever seen. Prior to Denon, Richard Pococke's *Description of the East, and Some Other Countries* (1743–1745)[2] and Frederik Norden's *Voyages d'Égypte et de Nubie* (1755)[3] were the only primary references, but Norden and Pococke were ship captains, not artists (Figs. 3.3 and 3.4).

Fig. 3.3   *Richard Pococke sailed up the Nile in 1737 and drew the antiquities as best he could, but he was a ship captain, not an artist.*

Fig. 3.4   *Vivant Denon, seen sketching on the left, was one of the first professional artists to depict Egypt.*

Denon's illustrations generated a wave of interest in Egypt, but the true beginning of the scientific study of Egypt came from the savants. Left behind in Egypt, they measured, surveyed, and drew the monuments with the precision of engineers and architects. Thirty-four of Napoleon's scholars died in Egypt, many of the plague, some in battle. Those who did return produced one of the most remarkable publications in the history of the world, the monumental *Description de l'Égypte*.

THE DESCRIPTION DE L'ÉGYPTE

Soon after Bonaparte left Egypt and returned to France, he was proclaimed First Consul. In that role, he quickly authorized funds for the publication of the savants' work. The publication was to cover everything: the ancient monuments, natural history, and modern Egypt in 1800, including the first comprehensive map of Egypt. Edme François Jomard, one of the expedition's young engineers, was named editor and solicited drawings, paintings, and research papers from his colleagues. As the submissions accumulated and the years passed, it became evident that the project was even larger than anyone had anticipated. A small army of engravers transferred the savants' drawings to copper plates so they could be printed, but eventually they realized that if something was not done to speed the process, the work would never be completed. Nicolas-Jacque Conté, an artist and engineer famous for his talents and resourcefulness, solved this problem as he had past problems. After the savants lost many of their instruments when the *l'Orient* went down, Conté fashioned new ones. Once when lead was in short supply and the artists needed pencils, he used graphite, thus inventing the modern pencil—the *crayon Conté*. According to Napoleon, Conté was capable of creating "the arts of France in the deserts of Arabia." Monge, the leader of the scientific expedition, said Conté had "all the arts in his hands and all the sciences in his head." So when the engraving of the plates for the *Description de l'Égypte* seemed stalled, everyone turned to Conté for a solution. He quickly invented a machine to mechanically engrave the skies for the plates with views of temples, saving thousands of man-hours. The machine even had a little adjustable wheel so it could be programmed for clouds.

Nothing like the *Description* had ever been attempted. One thousand sets of 21 volumes were printed, each containing nearly 1,000 large engravings, so approximately 1 million large sheets of hand-made paper had to be produced. Each page had the watermark *Égypte Ancienne et Moderne.* Creating the *Description de l'Égypte* was far more difficult and costly than anyone had anticipated. In 1804, Napoleon asked for an estimate of how much it would take to complete the project. When he was told 600,000 francs for the engraving alone, he was not pleased but supplied just enough money to keep the project going. It was not until 1809 that the first installment was published, and even then there were ongoing problems. Bonaparte, losing patience, decreed that the entire project had to be completed by 1811. The deadline was missed by two decades.

To speed production, five printers were used to handle the job. Because Bonaparte ordered that the maps of Egypt should remain "under the seal of a state secret," the map volume was the last to be published. Even after his exile, the maps were considered state secrets, which delayed their publication until 1828, seven years after his death on the island of St. Helena. When the *Description* was finally complete, five massive volumes of engravings depicted the antiquities, three volumes told the natural history, and two depicted modern Egypt. Several dozen of the plates were hand colored. The bird plates are especially striking (Color Plate 3).

The representations of the temples fall into three categories. First there were the broad views of tombs and temples that had captivated Europe. Karnak and Luxor temples were shown in all their glory, complete with obelisks, massive gateways, and halls of columns. The architectural renderings were not as showy as the grand temple views, but they were more important to archaeologists. These architectural plans, drawn by the engineers and architects among the savants, provided a precise recording that marked the beginning of the scientific study of archaeological monuments. No longer would the monuments be viewed only as objects of wonder. Now their size, construction techniques, and function were known. The savants also copied the reliefs on temple walls—processions of the gods, the Dendera zodiac, pharaohs in battle, and the religious rituals performed by priests. This recording of the temples would assist in the reconstruction of the ancient Egyptian civilization and religion, which until Napoleon's time had been more speculation than fact (Fig. 3.5).

Fig. 3.5   The interior of Philae temple as illustrated by Napoleon's artists.

In addition to temples and tombs, the antiquities volumes described artifacts that the savants found in their explorations. Here were mysterious papyri (Books of the Dead that no one could read yet), statues of pharaohs, and, perhaps most interesting of all, mummies. Some of the earliest accurate drawings of mummies appear on pages of the *Description de l'Égypte*. The savants found thousands of animal mummies in underground tunnels. The animals had been sacrificed as offerings to the gods, and several engravings of cat, crocodile, and other animal mummies show them both wrapped and unwrapped. Two of the most beautiful engravings portray the unwrapped heads of mummies of a man and a woman. Bonaparte gave the head of the female to the Empress Josephine as a present (Fig. 3.6). When she died and her estate was sold, Denon bought the head, a remarkable souvenir of his adventures in Egypt.

Sometimes the savants produced romantic re-creations of what the temples looked like when they were being used 3,000 years ago, complete with vivid colors and shaven-headed priests in processions. These

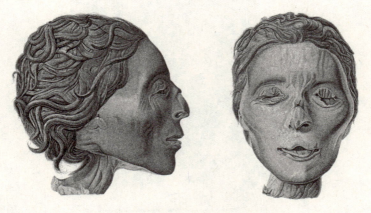

Fig. 3.6 This head of a female mummy recorded in the Description de l'Egypte *found its way into the Empress Josephine's collection.*

atmospheric depictions were the beginning of orientalism—European artists' highly romantic paintings of Egypt and the Middle East.

Those savants involved in the *Description de l'Égypte* knew that this was history, big history. Often the artists and engineers included themselves in their engravings for posterity. One of my favorite artists was curly-headed François-Charles Cecile. In his early engravings, we see him as a tiny figure seated at his drafting table, dwarfed by the temple he is recording. In later illustrations, he's the most prominent feature, usually shown holding his sketchbook (Fig. 3.7).

When the *Description* was finally completed, it was a spectacular academic, aesthetic, and archaeological success but a financial disaster. It was simply too expensive. Only the very wealthy were able to purchase it, so the French government was left with hundreds of unsold sets.

Fig. 3.7   The artist Cecile drew himself into all his depictions of Egypt's monuments. He is usually shown holding his sketchpad.

Many were given to foreign countries and institutions as goodwill gifts that helped to trumpet the glories of ancient Egypt across the world, but this was not the final chapter in the history of the *Description de l'Égypte*.

In 1821, as publication was nearing completion, C. F. Pancoucke, a well-established French publisher, began work on a second edition that was intended to be more affordable—a people's edition. The engravings were the same size as in the first edition, printed from the same copper plates, but because the plates had already been paid for, Pancoucke's expenses were far less so he could offer his set at a much lower price. To cut costs even more, there were no hand-colored plates. Pancoucke's real stroke of marketing genius was to offer his edition on the installment plan. A few engravings were released each week in folders called *livraisons*. You would pay as they were released and thus didn't have to spend a large amount of money all at once. Once you had accumulated all the engravings, you could take them to a binder and have them bound any way you wished. For this reason there is no standard binding for Panoucke's edition of the *Description de l'Égypte*. To house the set, Pancoucke offered a custom-made bookcase modeled after the temple of Dendera, an early piece of Egyptomania furniture.

All subscribers to the second edition received a medal that was a combination of Egyptomania and French propaganda. It showed victorious Gaul (France) uncovering (rediscovering) a buxom Egypt. On the reverse side was the Dendera zodiac that had been so faithfully copied by Jollois and Devilliers. Another fascinating bit of Egyptomania inspired by Napoleon's Egyptian campaign was a remarkable dinner service produced in the early part of the nineteenth century.

THE SÈVRES DINNER SERVICE

Soon after Denon returned to France, he contacted Sèvres, the famous French porcelain factory, suggesting that it might want to use his drawings as the basis for a dinner service. Sèvres agreed and produced one of the most spectacular items of Egyptomania ever. This was not your ordinary dinner service. The decorative centerpiece stretched for 22 feet and was based on Denon's engravings of the temples of Dendera, Philae, and Edfu, complete with pylons and obelisks.[4] An army of Sèvres craftsmen and painters created 72 dinner and dessert plates, each with a different hand-painted scene in the center and gilded processions of Egyptian gods around the edges. The set was created as a present for Tsar Alexander I of Russia and is now in the state Museum of Ceramics in Kuskuvo, just outside Moscow (Color Plate 4). Like the *Description de l'Égypte,* it is a fitting tribute to the Egyptian Campaign, and also like the *Description,* there was a second edition, but this time not for the people.

As the Egyptian dinner service was being made for Tsar Alexander, Josephine visited the Sèvres factory and admired it. Soon afterward, Napoleon divorced her, but as a parting gift, he gave her 30,000 francs in credit to purchase Sèvres porcelain. She ordered a set of the Egyptian dinner service. Three years later it was delivered by twelve men carrying six litters containing the dishes, serving bowls, and the incredible centerpiece. Josephine didn't like it and returned it to Sèvres, where it remained for four years. In 1818, it finally found a new owner, one Napoleon could never have imagined.

In 1815, after the Duke of Wellington defeated Napoleon at Waterloo, he commanded the British army occupying France. With Bonaparte deposed, Wellington intended to replace him with Louis XVIII. At a dinner party, Louis and Wellington found themselves talking about porcelain. Wanting to please the man who would restore him to the throne, Louis gave the Sèvres dinner service to Wellington. Today it can be seen at Wellington's residence, Apsley House, in London.

CROCODILES AND HIEROGLYPHS FOR TEA

The Sèvres Egyptian dinner set was not the only one inspired by Napoleon's Egyptian Campaign. The British produced their own. After all, they were the ones who won the war, not the French. Around 1808, the English pottery firm Wedgwood produced an Egyptian-themed tea service. The lids of the teapot and sugar bowl bore crocodiles while winged sun disks and Egyptian altars decorated the bodies of the pieces (Color Plate 2). This wasn't just Egyptomania, it was a political statement. When an Englishman poured his tea in the morning from an Egyptian-style teapot, he was saying, "We beat Bonaparte!"

Bonaparte's Egyptian Campaign was a monumental event that created an unparalleled wave of Egyptomania. Later waves would follow with the opening of the Suez Canal, the moving of obelisks from Egypt to Paris, London, and New York, and the discovery of Tutankhamen's tomb. Napoleon's savants showed the world, for the first time, what ancient Egypt really looked like, establishing the scientific foundation of modern Egyptology. Napoleon started it all, but that was not the end of French involvement in Egypt. The story continues when Bonaparte's fellow Frenchmen decided to cut the canal through the Isthmus of Suez.

FOUR

How an Obelisk and a Canal Conquered France

As the *Description de l'Égypte* was being published and Europe was enthralled with all things Egyptian, Egypt itself was in turmoil. The British had no intention of staying there after defeating Napoléon, but when they evacuated in 1803, they left behind a power vacuum. Ostensibly the Ottoman Empire was once again in charge with the Mamelukes subservient to them, but after Napoleon, the dynamics changed. The Mamelukes returned to Cairo, and the Ottoman government sent troops to Egypt to reestablish control. Many of these troops were Albanians who had not been paid for months and were grumbling. The decisive moment came when the Sublime Porte (Constantinople), ever short of cash to pay its troops, disbanded the Albanian forces so it could pay its own Turkish soldiers. The Albanians turned on the Turks, beginning a decade of brutal infighting among Turks, Albanians, and Mamelukes. In the end, an Albanian officer named Mohamed Ali firmly established himself as ruler of Egypt in a brutal coup like something out of the *Arabian Nights*.

MOHAMED ALI COURTS EUROPE

On March 1, 1811, during a lull in the conflict, Mohamed Ali invited 470 Mamelukes to the Cairo citadel to take part in the installation of his son as commander of the army. When the Mamelukes arrived, they were served coffee and then formed a procession on their horses. As soon as they reached the citadel's inner courtyard, the gates were shut, and Mohamed Ali's troops began firing down on the unsuspecting Mamelukes, slaughtering them. Legend has it that one Mameluke escaped by leaping on his horse from the ramparts. If true, it would have been an incredible feat; what is certain is that Mohamed Ali was now the undisputed ruler of Egypt.

Yet his ambitions were far grander in scope than mere governor of Egypt. Over the course of his career, he reformed many of Egypt's institutions and military and became known as the father of modern Egypt. In 1811, Mohamed Ali realized how much he owed to the British forces for defeating Napoleon Bonaparte's Egyptian force. He asked Samuel Briggs, the British consul, what would be a proper present for George III. Briggs suggested one of the two obelisks at Alexandria, and Mohamed Ali agreed. The British didn't act on it, and nothing happened.

In 1820 Mohamed Ali again offered an obelisk, this time to George IV who had succeeded George III. When the British government learned that it would cost £15,000 to bring their obelisk to England, again they did nothing. In 1831 Mohamed Ali offered the obelisk to a third English king, William IV, and even offered to move it onto any ship the English sent to pick it up. For the third time, Britain failed to take action.

For Muslim Mohamed Ali, obelisks were pagan monuments that meant nothing to him. If he could purchase influence with an obelisk or two, Mohamed Ali was all for it. England was not the only European power that Mohamed Ali was courting. He also offered the French an Alexandrian obelisk. Unlike the British, they sprang into action. Jean-François Champollion had just made his first visit to Egypt and had seen all the obelisks. He suggested that France ask for one of the two obelisks in front of Luxor Temple, as they were in far better condition than the pair at Alexandria. Mohamed Ali granted the French whichever Luxor obelisk they wanted, and the French began building a ship to bring it to Paris.

THE FRENCH GET AN OBELISK

Transporting an obelisk from Luxor was far more difficult than from Alexandria, as it involved an additional 500 miles up and down the Nile to and from Luxor. Any ship making the journey would have to be designed for both ocean and river voyages. The French built the *Luxor* specifically for this purpose, with a hull large enough to accommodate the 74-foot long obelisk. On July 26, 1830, it was launched on the Seine for trials.

Jean-Baptiste Apollinaire Lebas, the engineer responsible for bringing the obelisk to Paris, left a fascinating account of its journey. Perhaps most remarkable is the first sentence, "The brilliant and rapid conquest of Egypt by the French Army is inscribed in the annals of history."[1] He seems not to know that the French lost! Lebas, however, reveals some interesting details about the French government's zeal for obelisks. Mohamed Ali had given them one obelisk, but the French wanted three. On November 29, 1830, the Egyptian government granted three obelisks to King Louis-Philippe, two from Luxor and one from Alexandria.

Therefore, the *Luxor* was not the only French vessel sent to bring an obelisk to France. On July 26, 1830, the *Dromedaire* landed at

Alexandria, intending to lower the standing obelisk and return with it to France. The French team had not, however, realized that timber was not readily available in Egypt. Because there was not enough wood for the scaffolding needed to take down the obelisk, the plan was abandoned. (It may also be that Mohamed Ali had changed his mind and wanted to save some obelisks for other European powers and merely said there was no wood available.) Now French hopes rested solely on the *Luxor*, which on April 15, 1831, sailed from Toulon for Egypt, just as Napoleon had done three decades earlier. France was still interested in all the obelisks it could procure, and Count Sébastiani relayed the French government's orders to Lebas. "If, as I presume, only one obelisk will fit on the *Luxor*, the operation will be made twice, it will be necessary to begin with the one on the right, which was said to be the more precious, as you will see from the copy here appended of a letter by Mr. Champollion the younger, who has recently seen and translated the inscriptions."[2] Neither Sébastiani nor Lebas realized how difficult it would be to bring even one obelisk home. It would be another five years before the citizens of Paris would see their obelisk erected in the Place de la Concorde.

When Lebas first arrived in Alexandria, he had to wait 20 days for the French consul to return to Alexandria. It would be the first of many delays, but it gave him a chance to visit the two Alexandrian obelisks to assess what he would have to deal with in Luxor. One obelisk still rested on its pedestal, but the second had fallen centuries earlier and was half covered with sand (Fig. 4.1). It is widely believed that it fell during the earthquake of 1301, but that is far from established. Because it was covered in sand, many early travelers believed it was broken.

On June 6 the French consul finally arrived in Alexandria and accompanied Lebas to meet with Mohamed Ali. Lebas was extremely short, and the pasha made a joke of it, pretending not to see him and

Fig. 4.1   *The two Alexandria obelisks. The fallen one was partially covered till the 1870s.*

asking, Where is the engineer? They hit it off very well, and Lebas, armed with permissions from the pasha, was soon on his way to Luxor. Upon his arrival, his first task was to remove ten feet of debris that covered the lower portion of the obelisk. He hired 400 men, women, and children to remove the accumulation of the centuries, the men breaking up the debris with pickaxes, the women and children carrying the rubbish away. Lebas had no trouble finding workers. He paid them a small salary, but this was far better than what they were used to. When Mohamed Ali needed a workforce, he simply conscripted people with no pay and treated them brutally.

Once the debris was removed, Lebas was the first person in modern times to see the pedestal on which the obelisk rested, complete with carvings of sacred baboons that greeted the sun each morning.

On two sides were images of bound foreign captives, silent testament to the might of Ramses the Great, who had erected the obelisk. There is a wonderful detail on the pedestal that tourists can't see because it is too high, but that Lebas recorded in his drawing. Pharaohs frequently chiseled over the names of their predecessors' monuments that they wanted to claim for themselves. Ramses was one of the most enthusiastic practitioners, so he knew it could happen to him. Before he had the pair of obelisks erected in front of Luxor Temple, he had his name carved on the tops of the pedestals. When the obelisks rested on the pedestals, they covered his name so no one could obliterate it after his death. His plan worked.

With the base cleared, the next task was to grade a ramp from the obelisk down to the Nile. Lebas's Egyptian workers removed massive piles of rubbish, cut through two villages, and graded the quarter-mile path. Working 14-hour days, it took four months to complete the slope. Battling intense summer heat, they were also struck by a cholera epidemic that claimed the lives of 15 French crewmen and dozens of Egyptian laborers. The next task was to lower the obelisk.

Lebas had brought his own wood and all the supplies necessary to lower and transport the obelisk. Nothing like this had been done since architect Domenico Fontana moved the Vatican obelisk in 1586. Lebas had read Fontana's description and knew that the architect had used capstans driven by both men and horses to lower the obelisk.

Lebas had an advantage over Fontana. The second Luxor obelisk was standing just 100 feet away from the one he was taking. By employing a system of ropes and pulleys, he could use it to help lower his obelisk (Fig. 4.2). Using his capstans to generate the force to tilt the obelisk off its pedestal, he tied it to the second obelisk to slow its descent. Within 25 minutes, the obelisk had been lowered and was safely

Color Plate 1. British cartoonist James Gillray showed Napoleon's savants trapped by the locals on top of Pompey's Pillar as their scholarly works tumble to earth.

*Color Plate 2.
Wedgwood created an
Egyptian tea service to
commemorate Napoleon's
defeat at the Battle of the
Nile.*

*Color Plate 3.   The engravings
of birds in the Napoleonic
Description de l'Égypte are still
considered some of the finest bird
illustrations ever.*

*Color Plate 4.   The
famous porcelain
manufacturer Sevres
produced a dinner
service of 72 with
hand-painted scenes
of Egypt.*

Color Plate 5. After France got its obelisk, all kinds of household items had Egyptian themes, even barometers.

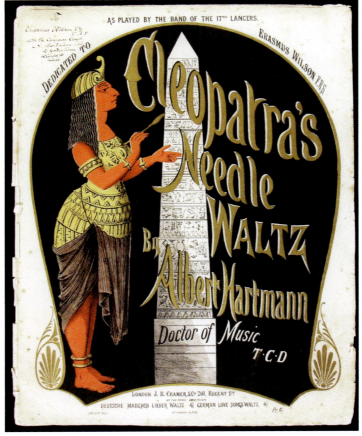

Color Plate 6. "Cleopatra's Needle Waltz" was dedicated to Erasmus Wilson, who paid to bring the obelisk to London.

Color Plate 7.   The bottoms of the cigarette tins often showed the factory in Cairo.

Color Plate 8.   Gianclis was a Greek company, but their package design was pure Egyptian.

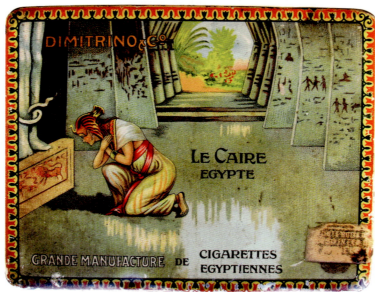

Color Plate 9.   More than 100 companies produced Egyptian brands, and Cairo was a common theme.

Color Plate 10.   In America, Helmar and Murad were popular Egyptian brands.

Color Plate 11. Egyptian cigarette companies had ambitious ad campaigns that often featured an Egyptian beauty.

Color Plate 12.   Because so many colors were used on cigar box labels, lithographers printed special proofs to check color values.

Color Plate 13.   Lord Egypt featured an Indian horseman, and no one seemed to notice he wasn't Egyptian.

Color Plate 14.   Sometimes labels were printed without brand names so small companies could buy them and add their own names later.

REVISED PRICE LIST
FROM
GARDEN CITY BOX CO., 136-140 W. Lake St., CHICAGO, Ill.

100/40	Imitation Cedar Boxes, including Labels, Ins and Outs,				-	$6.00
100/40	Veneered Cedar	"	"	"	-	7.50
100/20	Mixed	"	"	"		7.50
100/40	Cedar Imt. Bottom	"	"	"		8.50
100/20	Cedar	"	"	"	-	9.00

Sample Labels Mailed on Application. Labels also Blank.

Color Plate 16. O'San may sound Irish, but its label combined a lot of Egyptian themes.

Color Plate 17. The ends of cigar boxes were decorated with smaller labels.

Color Plate 18.   *Cigarette cases of the 1920s were inlaid with scenes from the Egyptian* Book of the Dead *in gold.*

Color Plate 19.   *Often cigarette cases with Egyptian themes were made in Japan. This view of Karnak Temple has the feel of a Japanese woodblock print.*

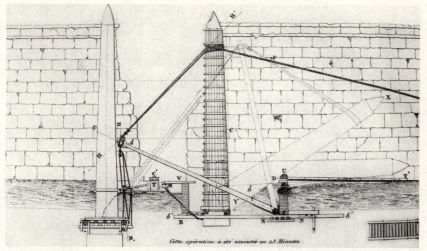

Fig. 4.2   The French used the second obelisk at Luxor to help lower the one they were bringing to Paris.

resting on the ramp built to receive it. This was just about the only aspect of the obelisk's journey that would go quickly.

Workers then hauled the obelisk on rollers down the carefully pre-pared ramp. The bow of the *Luxor* had been specially designed to ac-commodate the obelisk, and that too went smoothly. Then came the long wait. The Nile rises and falls once a year. With the heavy obelisk onboard, Lebas needed a high Nile to sail for Alexandria, and he had just missed it. They had to wait almost a year before sailing for Alex-andria. Finally, on New Year's Day 1833, the *Luxor* reached Alexandria Harbor, but it had to wait in port for another three months due to bad weather. It wasn't until December 1833, nearly a year later, that Parisians got a chance to see the *Luxor* sailing up the Seine. Then came the *very long* wait; the *Luxor* remained moored near the Place de la Concorde for another two years as plans for the erection of the obelisk were worked out. While it rested in the hull of the *Luxor*, Paris went wild with obelisk fever. Debates raged in the newspapers as to the most appropriate site for the obelisk and the design of the pedestal.

Finally, in August 1836, Parisians got their first glimpse of Cleopatra's Needle as it was disembarked in preparation for its placement on a new pedestal in the Place de la Concorde. Carved on the new pedestal were diagrams of the equipment Lebas had used to lower the obelisk in Luxor. On October 25, 200,000 spectators poured into the Place de la Concorde to see the obelisk being raised. The day was cloudy and cold but with no rain, which was important, as rain would affect the ropes and make things slippery. Before beginning the great maneuver, a small cedar box containing French gold and silver coins from 1836 was placed inside a compartment in the pedestal. In addition to the coins was a commemorative medal bearing the king's portrait on one side and on the other the inscription "Under the reign of Louis-Philippe I, King of the French, M. de Gasparin, Minister of the Interior, the obelisk of Luxor is raised on its pedestal on the 25th of October, 1836 by the care of M. Apollinaire Lebas, Marine Engineer." Lebas's place in history was established; now he just had to raise the obelisk.

At 11:30 A.M., Lebas gave the signal, a trumpet blared, and 48 soldiers assigned to each of ten capstans began turning. Ropes from the capstans ran over ten tall masts, five in front of the obelisk and five in back, which continued downward from the masts to chains fixed near the top of the obelisk. As the obelisk moved slowly to an upright position, the pressure on the wood block around which the 250-ton monolith was pivoting was so great that sap from the fresh timbers squirted out. The obelisk continued moving upward when a loud cracking noise from the compressed wood sounded.

Everything stopped so Lebas could check the apparatus. Lepage, Inspector of Works, shouted, "Nothing has moved. You can continue."

The turning of the capstans continued. As the obelisk rose, Lebas realized that they had not adjusted the ropes attached to the chains near its top. He had intended to do this as the tension on the ropes changed, but in the excitement, he had forgotten. Two marines were called upon to climb up the obelisk and readjust the rigging. But now there was a new problem.

The carpenters had made a mistake when they converted the measurements from feet and inches into the new metric system. As a result, the wooden pivot on which the obelisk was turning was too high. Two hundred thousand fascinated spectators looked on as ten strong men with axes hacked through the wood so the obelisk could be raised while a band played the Isis Suite from Mozart's *Magic Flute*.

Finally, with the king and queen looking on from their decorated balcony, the obelisk was erected on its pedestal where it stands today. Lebas was honored and generously rewarded by his grateful country, and France was launched onto a fresh wave of Egyptomania. Soon there were pens in the shape of obelisks, obelisk confections, and songs about obelisks.

The French basked in their obelisk's glory, but the English still didn't have one, and it bothered them. As recently as 1831, they had been offered an obelisk, but still, they seemed frozen, unable to act. It would be nearly 50 years before England would get an obelisk. The major event that would set things in motion was the building of the Suez Canal.

DE LESSEPS DIGS A CANAL

The idea of digging a canal across the Isthmus of Suez, connecting the Mediterranean with the Red Sea, goes back to the time of the pharaohs. Napoleon's disastrous Egyptian Campaign had revived the idea most recently, but there was little progress. With the invention of steamships in the 1830s, sea trade increased, and the utility of a Suez Canal became obvious. At that time the British were using an overland railway route through the Sinai Peninsula to the Red Sea and were not interested in a canal, but a French former consul to Egypt, Ferdinand de Lesseps, saw the advantage and pushed hard for France to build it.

As consul, de Lesseps had been a close friend of Mohamed Sa'id Pasha, one of Mohamed Ali's sons. When he heard that his old friend had been made viceroy of Egypt, he went to Cairo to reconnect and discuss the canal. Sa'id was enthusiastic; it would be the jewel in his reign and establish him as a world leader. In November 1854 Sa'id signed an agreement that the Suez Canal Company would be funded by foreign shareholders. Egypt would supply the land and labor and receive 15 percent of the annual profits. Even with the viceroy on his side, though, de Lesseps had a difficult time getting the canal going. The British did everything they could to sabotage the project, telling the Turkish sultan it was a plot for Egypt to gain independence (Egypt was still nominally under Turkish rule), even telling the viceroy that French colonies would spring up along the canal. The English efforts failed, and finally, with the support of Emperor Napoleon III, the project began to move forward. In 1857, with the viceroy supplying 20,000 conscripted workers, digging began.

England continued to try to sabotage the canal, starting a campaign against the "slave labor" used in its construction. In response, de Lesseps correctly pointed out that he paid the laborers and treated them well. Work on the canal continued, but Sa'id never saw its completion. He died in 1863 and was succeeded by his nephew, Isma'il Pasha. The new viceroy was even more enthusiastic about the canal than Sa'id had been, seeing it as a way to increase his power in the world, but ambition and debt eventually cost him his throne.

As the work continued, England put so much pressure on the sultan to stop the canal that the Sublime Porte told Ismail that he could no longer use conscripted labor and that he had no right to give Egyptian land to the Suez Canal Company. Under pressure, Ismail stopped supplying the labor, but an arbitration committee forced him to pay for the labor he was contractually obligated to supply. It was a staggering fee that he could ill afford. In addition, in an attempt to appease the Porte, he bought back all the land Sa'id had given to the Suez Canal Company. To do this, he mortgaged the cotton crop for the coming year, a risky proposition.

De Lesseps solved the labor problem by importing huge steam-powered dredging machines. After 1865, these monsters were digging most of the canal. By 1869 the canal was nearing completion. Finally realizing they could not stop progress, the British were now eager to participate rather than be shut out by France. De Lesseps accompanied the Prince of Wales on a tour of the canal, and the prince confided that he was sorry his government had fought construction and wished they had an interest in it. Soon the prince would get his wish. Although Isma'il had now been given the loftier title of khedive by the Porte and was a major stockholder in the Suez Canal Company, he was about to lose everything.

The khedive planned spectacular celebrations for the grand opening of the canal. He built a palace for the Empress Eugénie of France so she would be comfortable during her visit. Later, when she returned to France, Isma'il commemorated her visit with murals painted on the palace walls. The building, which still retains much of its original grandeur, is now a Marriott Hotel. In the lobby are the murals commemorating the opening of the canal, complete with the khedive and Empress Eugénie at a banquet and later on a dais at the opening of the canal. The opening was a great social success, followed by an even greater economic disaster. The Nile had failed to rise high enough to inundate the crops. With no harvest, Khedive Isma'il could not pay Egypt's debts. He had no alternative but to sell his shares in the canal to England.

It is a little-known fact but without the khedive's bankruptcy, America would not have the Statue of Liberty. The khedive had commissioned sculptor Frédéric Auguste Bartholdi to create a colossal statue for the entrance to the canal that would dwarf ships as they entered. Bartholdi's creation was intended to be an Egyptian woman holding a torch aloft. It was never completed because the khedive and Egypt were bankrupt. The resilient Bartholdi sold the idea of the colossal statue to France. With some minor alterations, the French people could give it to America, renaming it "The Statue of Liberty."

FRENCH EGYPTOMANIA

For most of the nineteenth century, France had close relationships with Egypt. Its savants published the *Description de l'Égypte,* Lebas brought the obelisk to Paris, and de Lesseps dug the Suez Canal. Thus, it is not surprising that it was France that produced the current wave of Egyptomania: clocks with Egyptian designs, cigarette tins with Egyptian motifs, and barometers supported on the backs of sphinxes (Color Plate 5). Now that England was involved with the canal, it too jumped on the Egyptomania bandwagon and finally decided to pick up their obelisk.

FIVE

The Amazing Voyage of Cleopatra's Needle

In the summer of 1872, engineer Waynman Dixon was dispatched to Cairo by his older brother, John, to build a bridge across the Nile at Giza. In October, John visited Waynman, and the brothers went to see the two Alexandrian obelisks. They knew that one had been offered to England years before, but nothing had been done about it. Immediately they began discussing how to transport the fallen obelisk. From talking to local fishermen, they determined the depth of the coast in front of the obelisk. Waynman immediately devised the plan that would bring England's obelisk home. He would encase the fallen obelisk in an iron cylinder, roll it into the sea, and tow it to England.

THE REMARKABLE DIXON BROTHERS

John was so excited at the prospect of finally bringing the obelisk home that he wrote to several newspapers, telling of the plan and offering to subscribe £500 toward the cost. He invited all patriotic Englishmen to join him. John wrote to Waynman, telling him to clear more sand from the obelisk to determine its condition. In the past, support for the project had been repeatedly held back by a rumor that the obelisk was in poor condition and that most of the hieroglyphic inscriptions were worn away. This was not true. The problem was that the Alexandria obelisk was being compared with the Luxor obelisk, which was nearly perfect. The rumor was due to Sir John Gardner Wilkinson, one of the founders of modern Egyptology who lived in Luxor in the 1830s. Wilkinson watched when the French lowered their obelisk from the front of Luxor Temple. He then made comparisons between the Luxor and the Alexandria obelisks. This led to his comment about the Alexandria obelisk: "from its mutilated state, and the obliteration of many of the hieroglyphics by exposure to the sea air, it is unworthy [of] the expense of removal."[1] If England's most prominent Egyptologist said it was not worth the expense, who would contribute to the project?

Waynman immediately hired some workmen who uncovered three sides of the obelisk and even dug out the middle section of the underside. It was, in fact, in quite good condition. Waynman took photographs that he sent to his brother so John could show potential donors that the obelisk was worth bringing to England. Armed with the photographs, John once again began knocking on doors. His idea of a national subscription to pay for transporting the obelisk never took hold. Fortunately, though, Sir Erasmus Wilson, a famous surgeon and philanthropist, became interested in the project.

In November 1876 Wilson, curious to learn about the plan for transporting the obelisk, visited John Dixon in his London office. Wilson had never met the elder Dixon but knew of his reputation as a reliable and resourceful engineer who had recently built the first railway in China. Wilson entered Dixon's office with optimism for the project, but what seems to have clinched the deal was that they were both Freemasons. As Wilson put it, "I soon found that Mr. Dixon was a Freemason, hence all formality and ceremony were at once banished."[2] All ceremony may have been banished, but there was still a contract to work out. John estimated that he could bring the obelisk to England for £7,000; Wilson wanted to think it over. At their second meeting, Wilson presented John with an offer that was both generous and risky. "The undertaking is not an easy one; you say you can do it for 7,000 pounds; will you undertake to set it up safely on the banks of the Thames for 10,000 pounds; no cure no pay?"[3] The phrase "no cure no pay" meant that John would have to fund the project himself. If he failed, the loss would be his alone. He would receive the £10,000 only when the obelisk was standing upright on a site to be determined. Dixon would have two years to complete the project. He was a very successful engineer, but £7,000 pounds—the amount he estimated it would take to bring the obelisk home safely—was more than he could afford to lose. He accepted his fellow Freemason's offer without hesitation. The Dixon brothers would bring Britannia an obelisk.

THE OBELISK AND THE CYLINDER

John began by taking Waynman's plans for the cylinder to the Thames Ironworks Company. He entrusted the job of constructing the cylinder to a brilliant young engineer named Benjamin Baker, who 20 years later would be elected president of the Institution of Civil Engineers. At the time, Waynman was in Somalia erecting a prefabricated cast iron lighthouse. His drawings were not finished blueprints, so Baker had to make many important decisions in designing the cylinder. Baker studied previous attempts to move obelisks, including Fontana's repositioning of the Vatican obelisk.

Five months after signing the contract for the cylinder, all the parts of the cylinder, 60 tons of it, had been shipped to Alexandria

Fig. 5.1　An iron cylinder was built around England's obelisk so it could be towed to London.

for assembly. The plan was to tow the cylinder, with its own crew on-board, to England by steamer. Captain Henry Carter, an experienced and highly respected seaman from the P&O Company, accompanied the parts. He was going to supervise the small crew who would live inside the cabin fitted on top of the cylinder.

The first step was to assemble the cylinder around the obelisk. Six bulkheads inside the cylinder formed individual watertight compartments so that if one sprung a leak, the others would not fill with water (Fig. 5.1). Once this work was completed, the cylinder now had to be rolled down to the sea. Large stones from ancient temples blocked the cylinder's path and had to be laboriously removed by Egyptian workmen. Finally, an old seawall was demolished, removing the cylinder's last obstacle on shore.

DOWN TO THE SEA

The seabed still had to be prepared to receive the cylinder. When divers were sent down, they found the remains of a huge wall with blocks weighing up to 20 tons. They used dynamite to blow up the blocks so they could remove the shattered stones. For all we know, they dynamited the remains of Cleopatra's palace!

On August 28 two small steamboats began slowly pulling the 300-ton cylinder down to the sea. When the cylinder was in seven feet of water, the two tugs, with their cables attached to the cylinder, headed out to sea, but the cylinder would not budge. A diver was sent down and found an 18-inch gash created by a huge ancient building block firmly lodged in the hull. After the torn iron plate was replaced, the cylinder, now named *Cleopatra,* was once again seaworthy.

CLEOPATRA FLOATS

When the cylinder was towed to Alexandria's dry dock, the seas were particularly rough. The tugs bobbed up and down violently, but the cylinder took the waves easily, barely rising or falling, a reassuring sight for the *Cleopatra*'s captain and three engineers.

The cylinder received its final fittings in dry dock in preparation for its voyage on open seas. The twelve tons of counterballast that had been placed on top to roll the cylinder to the sea were removed and transferred to the bottom of the vessel as ballast. Then a steering deck with an iron catwalk around it was riveted in place. Beneath the cylinder two 40-foot-long keels were riveted in place to make sure the *Cleopatra* didn't roll in high seas. A mast was fitted, to be used in an emergency, and a third keel was attached to the stern. These final preparations took ten days with Captain Carter and Waynman Dixon overseeing every step.

Waynman had designed the *Cleopatra* so the obelisk would lie below the geometric center of the cylinder; the low center of gravity gave it more stability on open seas. In dry dock, an additional 20 tons of scrap iron railings were laid in the bottom of the *Cleopatra,* lowering the center of gravity even more. With this additional ballast, two-thirds of the *Cleopatra* would be submerged during the voyage. The ballast was held in place by wood flooring laid over it.

Captain Carter hired seven men for his crew: a second in command (boatswain), five Maltese seamen, and a carpenter to make any necessary repairs at sea. Carter had to pay a bit above the going wages; many men were hesitant about signing onto such an unusual vessel for a four-week voyage on the open seas.

A British steamer, the *Olga,* was about to sail from Alexandria with a load of grain destined for England. Captain Carter thought the *Olga* suitable for towing the *Cleopatra.* Powered by a 130-horsepower steam engine, she was 251 feet long and commanded by an able captain. Carter struck a deal with Captain Booth who agreed to tow the *Cleopatra* to Falmouth for £900, half to be paid in advance, half upon arrival.

CLEOPATRA SETS SAIL

The *Cleopatra*'s odyssey began on September 21, when the *Olga* slowly towed her out of Alexandria Harbor and into the open Mediterranean. On the deck of the *Olga* was Waynman Dixon, who intended to accompany his cylinder all the way to England. Captain Carter and his crew were onboard the *Cleopatra.* Several systems had been worked out so the two captains could communicate. A megaphone could be used during calm seas, but for rough weather, Captain Carter would stand on the steering bridge and use a blackboard to communicate his needs. At night, a system of lights was employed. The *Cleopatra*'s early behavior greatly reassured everyone. She moved calmly through the water with her steering house splitting the waves that washed over her.

Every six hours Carter checked the bulkhead compartments to make sure there were no leaks. First he would open a small hatch in the floor of his cabin and, carrying a candle, would slip down into the darkness. He would check the first compartment, open a tiny door to the second, and, holding the candle in his teeth, squeeze through and inspect that bulkhead. He repeated this process for each of the six bulkheads, and then he made his way back to the first compartment and the hatch to his cabin. Once, he held the candle in his mouth while using both hands to push himself through one of the doors, and it began to burn his nose. The candle fell and went out, and Carter was stranded in the dark with a singed nose. It took him more than half an hour to feel his way back to daylight. After that experience he took a crew member along to hold the candle.

The first week was uneventful, with clear skies and calm seas. All England followed the progress of their obelisk in the *Illustrated London News.* Off the coast of Algeria they hit bad weather. They were using more coal than Captain Booth had anticipated, so he put in to port. The men on the *Olga* were given shore leave (they got drunk), but Carter, fearing his *Cleopatra* crew would jump ship, kept them on board. In less than 24 hours, the *Olga* had taken on coal, and the two vessels were on their way. They reached Gibraltar, their first scheduled stop, on October 7, and put in to port for supplies. Waynman wrote letters home telling of their progress. The *Cleopatra* was performing admirably, but he was worried about Captain Carter, who was exhausted from his lack of sleep. At Gibraltar, Carter had his first full night's rest in two weeks. Refreshed and refueled, the armada of two pressed on.

TRAGEDY AT SEA

On October 9 they headed north into the Atlantic. The waves were larger than in the Mediterranean, but the *Cleopatra* took them easily. Continuing north, they passed the northern coast of Spain and entered the Bay of Biscay, notorious for its bad weather. They needed only three more days of reasonable weather to reach the English Channel, but on October 15, their luck ran out.

At 9:00 A.M., rains began out of the south southwest. Within a few hours, the winds reached gale force. The waves were building rapidly, and for the first time the *Cleopatra* was going to be tested. Waynman watched her anxiously from the *Olga*'s deck. At 10:40 A.M. he wrote in his log:

> "Olga" rolling 10 times per minute 10 degrees to port 5 degrees star'd.
> It is really wonderful how "Cleopatra" rides out the heavy sea—hardly
> a roll in her!

For the next few hours the barometer continued to fall, and the winds were now at hurricane force. Captain Booth continued to steer the two ships into the wind. Amid thunder and lightning, the wind suddenly shifted, and waves and wind came at right angles to the *Cleopatra*'s steering house. The winds and waves were so strong that Carter feared they would rip the deckhouse right off. He signaled Captain Booth: "Prepare to Heave-to, Head to Wind." He wanted some slack so they could turn into the wind. Booth replied: "Greater Risk to Tow-Line if Hove-to." He was afraid the cable connecting the two vessels would snap.

For an entire day, gale and hurricane force winds tossed them about, and now it was getting dark. It seemed almost impossible, but the weather was worsening. Carter, fearing that the next wave might wash him off the deck, again signaled "Heave-to." Captain Booth, this time sensing Carter's desperation, complied, skillfully moving the *Olga* into the wind. As Carter tried to steer the *Cleopatra* to follow the *Olga*'s lead, a tremendous wave hit the deckhouse, capsizing the *Cleopatra*. As the cylinder rolled onto its side, Carter, clinging desperately to the railing, felt and heard something moving deep inside the *Cleopatra*. He immediately knew what it was: The ballast had shifted.

The captain knew they could not reposition the ballast. He decided their best hope was to abandon the *Cleopatra*. He lowered the little lifeboat, but before the eight men could get into it, a huge wave sent it crashing into the hull, smashing it to bits. On the *Olga,* Captain Booth slowed engines and tried to maneuver closer to the *Cleopatra* when he heard "Foundering, send a boat." Booth said to his men, "What can we do, no boat will live in such a sea." William Askin, the second mate, replied, "We must lower a boat and try, we can't leave the poor fellows to drown."[4] Five other brave crewmen volunteered and with great difficulty descended in a lifeboat to rescue the *Cleopatra*'s crew.

The lifeboat slowly fought its way toward the *Cleopatra*. As it neared the cylinder, Booth lost sight of it in the darkness. The *Cleopatra*'s crew was on deck clinging to the railings. It took Askin and his crew over an hour to reach the *Cleopatra*. *Cleopatra*'s crew threw them a line, but it was pulled out of the sailor's hands as the lifeboat was battered by the waves. Then, before the line could be thrown again, a giant wave reared up and crashed down on the little boat, and it vanished.

Those six brave men were never seen again. On board the *Cleopatra,* Carter and his terrified crew would have to survive the night on their own. He brought the crew inside, and they descended below the flooring for one last attempt at repositioning the ballast. For several hours, they worked in incredibly cramped conditions, all the while being thrown around by the waves. By midnight the *Cleopatra* was almost upright, and, amazingly, she was headed into the wind. It looked as if they might succeed. Then a huge wave crashed into the side of the *Cleopatra*, scattering the ballast and capsizing the cylinder once again.

Captain Booth on the *Olga* could see little, but by now he knew his six crewmen were probably lost.

On the *Cleopatra*, Carter's spirits were extremely low. His log entry reads:

> The swells high and confused, and the *Olga* seems determined to tow us through the water or under it. I wish she would break down, for the quick pitching motion is almost unbearable.

Still, he encouraged his men to keep trying to reposition the ballast, but one by one they fell to exhaustion. In such heavy seas, there was the horrible possibility that both vessels would collide. Around 1:00 A.M. Captain Booth cast off the towing cable, setting the *Cleopatra* adrift. Waynman Dixon volunteered to take a second lifeboat to the *Cleopatra*, but no one volunteered to accompany him. Captain Booth kept his ship as close to the *Cleopatra* as possible. At 2:00 A.M. he steamed around the *Cleopatra*, dragging 100 fathoms of line so it would cross on top of the cylinder and could be grabbed, enabling the men to be hauled on board the *Olga*, but the sea was too rough. Booth signaled that they would have to wait for daylight, and Carter replied he didn't think the *Cleopatra* would float that long. They made one more attempt that also failed, but finally it was getting light.

Booth tried to maneuver the *Olga* close enough to the *Cleopatra*, but he was still worried that a wave could send him crashing into the cylinder, sinking both ships. He got as close as possible and heaved a line. It missed. Twice more he tried with no success. Finally a line went across the *Cleopatra*'s stern and was grabbed and made fast. The

Fig. 5.2   *Rescuing the crew of the* Cleopatra *involved lowering them into the small wooden boat shown in the foreground.*

Cleopatra's crew closed all bulkhead doors, hatches, and manholes in preparation to abandon ship. This was their last chance at rescue.

Using the line they had thrown, the *Olga* sent an unmanned lifeboat to the foundering *Cleopatra* (Fig. 5.2). In high seas, one by one the *Cleopatra's* crew members jumped into the boat, Captain Carter last. The boat was quickly hauled in to the *Olga*. Finally all hands were on board.

Booth now began searching for his six missing sailors. About 1:00 P.M., he gave up and returned to where they had left the *Cleopatra*. He still intended to bring the obelisk home, and he was also concerned that the 300-ton cylinder would be a hazard to navigation. But it was gone. Everyone concluded it must have filled with water and was now at the bottom of the Bay of Biscay.

What began as a wonderful patriotic adventure had ended in disaster. Six brave men were dead, and the object for which they had lost their lives presumably lay beneath the sea. Captain Booth reset the *Olga's* course for Falmouth, reaching it two days later to deliver their sad news. John Dixon had been waiting there anxiously. He had received a telegram that the *Olga* had been sighted—without the *Cleopatra* in tow. He rushed on board and was relieved to see Captain Carter, but his spirits fell when his brother told him of the six drowned sailors and the lost obelisk.

CLEOPATRA, LOST AND FOUND

As they stood onboard, none of the sad company had any inkling that the *Cleopatra* was still afloat. As Captains Carter and Booth were battling the hurricane, several other captains on the Bay of Biscay were doing exactly the same thing. One was Captain Evans of the *Fitzmaurice,* who had sailed from Middlesborough bound for Valencia, Spain, with a cargo of pig iron. As he entered the bay he hit the same strong winds that the other ships encountered. Just like Carter and Booth, he fought the hurricane, keeping his ship into the wind for a full day. When the storm finally died down, Evans and the *Fitzmaurice* resumed course for Valencia. Carter and Booth had lost the *Cleopatra,* but she was about to be found.

About 4:00 P.M., the *Fitzmaurice*'s lookout spotted what looked like a capsized ship. Through his binoculars, Captain Evans made out the letters on the hull: CLEOPATRA. He had read of the *Cleopatra*'s voyage in newspapers and knew exactly what she was. Getting as close as possible, he hailed her but was not hailed back. There was no sign of her crew; she had been abandoned.

Evans knew that if he could secure a line to the *Cleopatra* and tow her to a port, according to maritime law, he would be entitled payment for his work and also the value of the ship and its cargo. The *Cleopatra* was salvage, and given her unique cargo, it could be worth a fortune.

The problem was going to be getting a line on her. Although the gale had subsided, the *Cleopatra* was partially submerged and rolling from side to side in rough seas. Some of the *Fitzmaurice's* crew would have to be lowered in a lifeboat onto the churning seas, then someone would have to jump onto the half-submerged bucking cylinder, catch a line thrown to him, and tie it to the *Cleopatra*. It was a dangerous proposition and no one volunteered, but when Captain Evans offered a share in the prize, four men agreed to attempt it. Lowering the boat in swells was difficult, but boarding the *Cleopatra* proved nearly impossible. One man tried to jump from the boat onto the *Cleopatra's* steering deck, the only place with railings to hang on to. But in the rough seas, he missed and fell into the water. His comrades pulled him back in by the rope they had tied around his waist, but now he was cold, shivering, and not eager to try again. Several other men made the attempt until, finally, one succeeded in securing a towing rope to the *Cleopatra*. The prize was theirs; now they just had to tow it to port.

It was a difficult tow with the *Cleopatra's* steering deck half submerged, but Captain Evans managed. On the second day, the winds built to gale force and the towropes came free. But by now they were within sight of Ferrol, and the captain and crew weren't going to give up their prize. By heroic efforts they managed to reconnect the towropes and brought the *Cleopatra* into the safety of the harbor.

Captain Evans immediately contacted the British vice consul and left the *Cleopatra* in his custody. The vice consul telegraphed London, and soon all of England knew their obelisk had not been lost after all. The two illustrated newspapers of the day, *The Graphic* and the *Illustrated London News,* ran articles about the recovery of the *Cleopatra* and the death of the six crewmen. England would be getting its obelisk, but at a terrible price.

RANSOMING THE OBELISK

When Captain Evans docked in Liverpool, Captain Carter was waiting to ask about the condition of the *Cleopatra*. Evans had brought Carter's log book and some of his navigation instruments, but almost everything else was gone, including a collection of ancient Greek and Roman coins Carter had assembled while in Alexandria. Carter was told that with some refitting, the *Cleopatra* would be seaworthy, but before they could begin, the salvage claim had to be settled.

Carter returned to London and, with John Dixon, set off to Scotland to deal with the owners of the *Fitzmaurice*, Burrell & Son of Glasgow. Mr. Burrell demanded £5,000 to release the *Cleopatra*, an extraordinarily high figure. John Dixon countered with an offer to write a check for £600 pounds on the spot. Burrell wouldn't budge; the matter would have to be settled in court.

The judge assigned a total salvage value of £25,000 for the *Cleopatra* and her cargo. Now he had to determine what portion of that should be given to the salvors. He awarded a total of £2,000 plus costs, with £1,200 going to the owners, £250 to Captain Evans, and the rest distributed among the crew according to their rank, with double shares to the four brave sailors who first boarded the *Cleopatra*.

With the salvage claim settled, Captain Carter set out to repair the *Cleopatra*. It was now mid-December. With a new crew hired in Liverpool, he headed out to the disabled *Cleopatra* at Ferrol. As soon as they arrived, Carter inspected the vessel. Internally it was in remarkably good condition. It had remained watertight throughout its battering, so aside from repositioning and securing the ballast, there was little to be done. The exterior was another matter. For three weeks the crew worked to replace the mast, install a new tiller, repair the smashed rudder, and refit the steering deck. When everything was in order, John

Dixon hired the *Anglia,* one of the largest and most powerful deep-sea tugs, to tow the *Cleopatra.* The *Anglia* specialized in towing distressed ships and had a crew of 17 plus two captains, one to steer the *Anglia* and one to supervise the ship being towed. Dixon wasn't taking any chances on losing the *Cleopatra* again.

AT SEA AGAIN

At 7:00 A.M. on January 15, the *Anglia* gingerly moved out through Ferrol harbor with the *Cleopatra* in tow. For two days the weather was unusually fair for the Bay of Biscay in January. On the morning of the eighteenth they rounded the tip of France and entered the English Channel. They were halfway home with only 350 miles to go.

On January 21 at 10:00 A.M., they reached Gravesend. Mr. and Mrs. John Dixon were waiting to greet the two ships. The two vessels cleared customs and slowly sailed up the Thames. As the sun was setting, the tug *Mosquito* gently guided the *Cleopatra* into her berth at the East India Docks. The long journey was over at last.

LOCATION, LOCATION, LOCATION

Although Cleopatra's Needle was finally in London, it still hadn't been decided exactly where the obelisk would be erected. Some favored the middle of a public square, like France's obelisk at the Place de la Concorde. Others felt that because the ancient Egyptians put obelisks at the entrances to temples, it should be in front of a building. The two men who had paid for the obelisk's journey, John Dixon and Sir Erasmus Wilson, got to make the final decision. Their original contract stipulated that it would be on the Thames Embankment, but now both agreed that a better site would be in front of the Houses of

Parliament. John went so far as to erect a full-scale wood model of the obelisk to show how it would look. Some unexpected players—the directors of the Metropolitan District Railway—vetoed the proposed site, which was above an underground train route. The directors were afraid the train's vibrations would topple the obelisk, and it would fall through the top of the tunnel and onto a train. Dixon suggested that iron beams could be used to reinforce the tunnel, but the directors were not convinced. They wanted a perpetual indemnity, and no insurance company would take the risk.

Dixon and Wilson then returned to the original idea of the Thames Embankment. John quickly dismantled his wood obelisk and erected it again at the Adelphi Steps of the embankment to show Londoners how it would look. For the next four weeks, the *Cleopatra* remained docked, and curious Londoners were permitted to go on board. London was caught up in obelisk fever.

While London was meeting and greeting its obelisk, the site at the embankment was being readied to receive the city's newest and oldest inhabitant. It was now time for the *Cleopatra* to make her last voyage.

On May 30, Captain Carter supervised the towing of the *Cleopatra* to the Adelphi Steps, where an ingenious dry dock awaited her. A wood cradle was anchored to the riverbed so that when the tide rose, it would just barely be submerged. The *Cleopatra* was floated above the cradle, and when the tide went out, she came safely to rest in dry dock. The dock's anchor was then pulled up so the *Cleopatra* would be permanently out of the water, enabling a swarm of ironworkers to dismantle her. First the steering deck that Captain Carter and his men had clung to in the hurricane was stripped off for its scrap value. Next the uppermost iron plates were removed, and workers descended into the hull, removing the cabins and flooring, exposing the obelisk to sunshine for the first time since it left Egypt.

The tops of the bulkheads were removed so the obelisk could be lifted out of what remained of the *Cleopatra*. Four pairs of hydraulic jacks were placed beneath the obelisk and slowly lifted the granite monolith, a few inches at a time. As the obelisk inched upward, timbers were placed beneath it, the jacks were raised a bit, and the process was repeated until the needle was hovering on timbers and jacks above the *Cleopatra*.

It took nearly two weeks to elevate the obelisk 30 feet up to the embankment, but finally it rested horizontally on a bed of timbers. The last challenge was to raise the obelisk onto its new pedestal of granite blocks.

RAISING CLEOPATRA'S NEEDLE

Throughout the summer, teams of carpenters nailed and bolted together a giant scaffold to support the obelisk and its turning mechanism as it was raised aloft. Now they had to raise the 300-ton combination of granite and iron 50 feet into the air.

The same hydraulic jacks that lifted the obelisk out of the *Cleopatra* and up the Adelphi Steps were now placed beneath the iron beams supporting the obelisk. Using the same system of jacks and wood beams, the obelisk rose 4 inches in ten minutes. Then the lifting was halted, timbers were placed under the obelisk, the jacks were repositioned, and another 4 inches could be gained. This process continued throughout August. By early September, the obelisk, like a magician's assistant, hovered 50 feet above the ground, ready to be swung to the vertical and placed on its pedestal.

John Dixon announced to the public that he would lower the obelisk onto its pedestal at 3:00 P.M. on September 12. This gave him a few days to test his system and make sure everything would go smoothly.

Fig. 5.3   Preparing to turn the London obelisk upright.

The day before the big event, he removed the iron pins that locked the obelisk into a horizontal position (Fig. 5.3) and discovered that he had calculated the obelisk's center of gravity so accurately that with just his own muscle power, he could pull on a cable and move the obelisk toward vertical. Satisfied, he replaced the pins and waited for the next day.

People started gathering around the obelisk early in the morning to get a good viewing spot. For months Londoners had been following the saga of Cleopatra's Needle. Both the *Graphic* and the *Illustrated London News* had chronicled building the cylinder, the loss at sea, and the deaths of six seamen. Now that the obelisk was finally in London, everyone wanted to be part of its history. Hawkers sold a variety of souvenirs; one of the most popular was a lead pencil in the shape of an obelisk that ladies could wear on a chain around their necks. Pamphlets with translations of the obelisk's hieroglyphs were sold for a penny. There was even a song called "Cleopatra's Needle Waltz" that was dedicated to Erasmus Wilson (Color Plate 6).

As the crowd grew, so did anticipation. By noon, everyone was eager to see the obelisk finally on its pedestal. Then, as if the obelisk hadn't had its fair share of bad weather, the rains came. Heavy rains at 1:00 P.M. scattered the crowd, forcing everyone to seek cover. Finally, after an hour, the rain stopped, the sun broke through the clouds, and the crowds gathered again.

A few minutes before 3:00 P.M., John Dixon gave the signal to remove the pins that held the obelisk horizontal. Steel cables running from the obelisk to two pairs of winches on either side steadied the stone shaft. At John Dixon's signal, four men on each winch started turning, drawing in the cables, and the 230-ton obelisk began slowly rotating toward the vertical position. The packed, wet crowd stood transfixed, amazed at how gracefully the massive stone moved. After ten minutes of breathless silence, the shaft of granite was at 45 degrees—halfway to vertical. A few minutes later it was at 60 degrees. When Big Ben sounded 3:30 P.M., the obelisk was upright, hovering just 4 inches above its pedestal.

Dixon had calculated that the obelisk could balance on its pedestal with nothing fixing it to the base, just as the ancient Egyptian engineers had done it. As the engineers looked at the suspended monolith, one of them felt it didn't look quite right; it didn't appear to be perfectly vertical. They decided to wait until morning to check the angle of the obelisk and then lower it if all seemed well. When they announced to the crowd that the day's work was over, everyone burst into applause. It had been an exhausting day for Dixon, Wilson, and everyone else involved in the obelisk's erection, but it had been a rousing success.

The following day the obelisk, found to be perfectly vertical, was lowered the final 4 inches onto its pedestal. For the next few weeks, the site was cleared. The iron jacket around the obelisk's middle was removed, the huge scaffolding timbers were taken down, and the iron-turning mechanism was dismantled. Commemorative plaques were added to the pedestal that can still be read today. One tells the obelisk's ancient history and then recounts its more modern adventure:

TRANSPORTED TO ENGLAND AND

ERECTED ON THIS SPOT

IN THE FORTY-SECOND

YEAR OF

QUEEN VICTORIA.

BY

ERASMUS WILSON, F.R.S., AND JOHN DIXON, C.E.

Most visitors to the obelisk see this plaque, but there is another, on the side facing the Thames, that they usually miss. There is an ancient Egyptian expression, "To say the name of the dead is to make him live again." Whenever I visit the obelisk, I walk around to the riverside and read the plaque.

WILLIAM ASKIN, MICHAEL BURNS,

JAMES GARDNER, WILLIAM DONALD

JOSEPH BENBOW, WILLIAM PATAN

PERISHED IN A BOLD ATEMPT TO SUCCOR THE CREW

OF THE OBELISK SHIP "CLEOPATRA" DURING

THE STORM, OCTOBER 14th, 1877

Although there was a deep sadness associated with England's obelisk, there was also a national pride and a growing interest in Egypt. Egyptomania was about to consume Victorian England.

SIX

Egypt for Sale

VICTORIAN EGYPTOMANIA

When Cleopatra's Needle arrived in London, Britain was very much the upstairs, downstairs society, as depicted on the British TV series *Downton Abbey*, which was filmed at Highclere Castle, home of Lord Carnarvon, who financed the excavation of Tutankhamen's tomb. The British upper classes were expected to live in a style appropriate to their status.

The 1882 catalog of Silber and Fleming, suppliers of fine china and glassware, offered a variety of items for the well-appointed home. Item No. 5055, Etched Crystal Table Glass, includes 15 different styles of glasses, each with delicately etched sphinxes and lotus flowers. His lordship needed to have his wine, port, sherry, claret, and brandy in different shaped glasses.[1]

EGYPTOMANIA MEETS THE INDUSTRIAL REVOLUTION

It wasn't only England's gentry that embraced Egyptomania. The Industrial Revolution made the production of items associated with

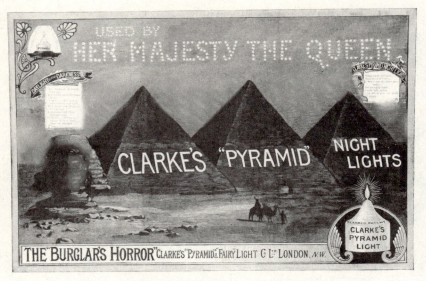

Fig. 6.1   Not quite pyramid-shaped candles were sold as Pyramid Night Lights "The Burglar's Horror." Her Majesty used them.

Egypt affordable for the masses. Clarke's Pyramid Night Lights advertised that if you burned them all night they would be "The Burglar's Horror" (Fig. 6.1). On the high street of any town you could buy Reade Brother's Egyptian Salve, good for "sores, wounds, ulcers, abscesses, burns . . . eruptions and skin diseases." It had no connection to Egypt except for the name, but who cared? Egypt sold.

One industry that quickly connected itself with Egypt was tobacco, which all classes indulged in.

SPHINXES, PYRAMIDS, AND THE TOBACCO CONNECTION

Many industries used a connection to ancient Egypt to market their products, but none so enthusiastically as tobacco companies. Tobacco actually is native to the Americas, not the Middle East. When

Columbus's sailors discovered Indians smoking tobacco, they spread the practice when they returned to Europe.

It didn't take long for the smoking craze to spread across Europe. In England, seventeenth-century aristocrats hosted parties where the art of smoking was taught. Smoking then spread to the Middle East, and by the nineteenth century, countries around the Black Sea had discovered that their soil and climate were perfect for growing tobacco. Because these countries were part of the Ottoman Empire, the tobacco produced there was called "Turkish tobacco."

The government in Greece saw the thriving new industry as a source of revenue. Under the cigarette monopoly, they controlled and taxed every aspect of cigarette production. Burdened by heavy taxes in Greece, many factory owners moved their operations to nearby Egypt, where a bankrupt government welcomed the new industry. In 1885, the three Kyriazi brothers—Ioannis, Efstathios, and Epaminondas—formed Kyriasi Freres. They were soon employing 500 workers in their Cairo factory, which produced about half a million cigarettes each day. The Kyriasi packets and tins often show two Oriental potentates identified as "Trade" and "Mark." Cigarette manufacturers were so proud of their new operations that they often printed pictures of their factories on the bottom of their cigarette tins (Color Plate 7).

The youngest of the Greek cigarette entrepreneurs at that time, Nestor Tsanklis, came to Egypt at the age of 14, and by the time he was 19, he had his own factory. Housed in an 1870 Mameluke-revival building, it was expanded several times. "Nestor Tsanklis" became the brands Nestor and Gianaclis—pure Greek, but the package design was pure Egyptian (Color Plate 8). In 1908 the building was taken over by Cairo University. Today it houses the American University in Cairo. Few students know that the beautiful building in which they attend classes was once a cigarette factory.

One of the largest Greek manufacturers in Egypt was Dimitrino & Co., established in 1886. By 1905 it was producing more than 50 million cigarettes a year. Sold under a dozen different brand names, most tins had Egyptian designs (Color Plate 4).

It wasn't only in Egypt that Greeks produced cigarette packets and tins with Egyptian motifs. In America, S. Anargyros imported Egyptian Deities cigarettes. The company then went on to produce Murad, Helmar, and Mogul, all extremely popular brands with Egyptian designs (Color Plates 9 and 10). Not to be outdone by a fellow Greek, the Stephano Brothers produced Ramses II, cigarettes that can still be purchased in tobacco shops today.

Cigarette manufacturers proudly displayed pharaohs, sphinxes, and gods on their cigarette packets and tins, so it was inevitable that Egyptomania would make its appearance in advertising campaigns. At the beginning of the twentieth century, Egyptian Deities cigarettes mounted an extensive, Egyptian-themed advertising campaign. Almost every month a new Egyptian Deities ad would appear in national magazines or on the back of theater programs. Sometimes the image would be a flapper dressed in a pseudo-Egyptian headdress; other times the ad's Egyptian architectural border associated the product with Egypt.

Mogul cigarettes produced the strangest Egyptian-themed tobacco ad of all. Mixing up three cultures, its ads had authentic Egyptian architectural borders with papyrus columns and winged solar disks. Moguls, however, were definitely not Egyptian. In addition, the people wear Assyrian costumes. The ad shows happy Assyrian smokers cavorting on a boardwalk while the caption proclaims, "Just like being in Cairo!" (Fig. 6.2)

Even today we have Egyptomania in cigarette advertising. Quick question: How many pyramids are on a pack of Camel cigarettes? Two. Cigarette ads were often beautifully produced, but they cannot compare with what manufacturers put on cigar boxes.

Fig. 6.2 Mogul cigarettes had the distinction of confusing three civilizations in one ad. Moguls were not Egyptian; the persons shown on the boardwalk are Assyrian; and the caption says "Just Like being In Cairo!"

CIGAR LABELS ROCK

Cigar smoking reached its peak in the early twentieth century. In 1905, there were 70,000 cigar factories in the United States, each with its own label. By 1920, 8.2 billion cigars were smoked each year. Tobacco shops displayed cigars in boxes with the lids open to show off the beautifully designed labels. By the end of the nineteenth century, lithographs with realistic shading and vivid colors could be produced cheaply, and this is where cigar box labels enter the picture. The Pride of Egypt label is a proof, pulled by the lithographer to check color values (Color Plate 12).

Often the labels were embossed to give the images a three-dimensional effect, then gilding was added. The labels had Egyptian images of the pyramids, sphinxes, and camels, but in the O'San label (Color Plate 16), the crescent that frames a veiled woman is decidedly Turkish.

At the beginning of the last century, few people knew what Egypt really looked like, so the Indian rider on the Lord Egypt label probably didn't seem out of place (Color Plate 13).

One image repeatedly used on cigar labels was a pharaoh wearing the royal *nemes*-headdress. Fashioned of folded cloth, the nemes was synonymous with pharaoh. No name appears on the label at the bottom of Color Plate 14 because it was a stock label, intended for the small manufacturer that couldn't commission its own label. The purchaser would print his own brand's name on it by hand letterpress. Such labels weren't very expensive. The label for Royal Queen shows the prices for different quantities of labels (Color Plate 15).

The label that combines the greatest number of Egyptian elements into a single tableau is O'San, printed by the Consolidated Lithography Co. In the background are the pyramids, palm trees, and camels. The center sports a beautifully drawn winged scarab, and to the left is a half-naked Egyptian maiden playing a harp for a reclining queen Cleopatra (Color Plate 16). This striking pose is taken directly from a famous painting of the day, "Cleopatra Testing Poisons on Condemned Prisoners" by Alexandre Cabanel (1887).

The cigar box label was only part of a set. Smaller labels were glued on the outside of the boxes. These labels weren't as elaborate because the boxes were stacked side by side in the store where the sides wouldn't be seen (Color Plate 17).

As smokers became accustomed to their cigars and cigarettes packaged with Egyptian motifs, they wanted smoking paraphernalia to go with them. In the 1920s, fashionable ladies carried a series of beautiful cigarette cases with Egyptian scenes inlaid in 24-karat gold. I doubt if the flappers knew they were scenes from the ancient Egyptian *Book of the Dead* (Color Plate 18).

The *Book of the Dead* is a collection of magical spells illustrated by vignettes intended to help the deceased be reborn in the next world. The central scene on the case was always Chapter 125, where the deceased's heart is weighed against the feather of truth. If the scale balanced, the deceased went on to the next world; if not, the heart was thrown to Ammit, the Devourer, a creature with the head of a crocodile, front legs of a lion, and hind legs of a hippo. Thoth, the ibis-headed god of writing, recorded the verdict for all eternity.

On top of one spectacular compact/cigarette holder we see Anubis, god of mummification, taking the deceased by the hand to lead him to the next world. These cigarette cases were produced in Japan for export to Europe and America, and one even has the look of a Japanese woodblock print. It depicts one of the gates to Karnak Temple, and on the back is a delicate vignette of a camel and rider in front of palm trees (Color Plate 19). These cigarette cases were clearly designed for women, but there was something for men as well.

At about the same time that the Japanese were crafting their beautiful inlaid cigarette cases, Austrian craftsmen were producing a variety of orientalist-themed bronze smoking accessories. They recognized a new market for orientalism in the decorative arts, and in the 1920s, a series of exotic themes—camels, rug merchants, and palm trees—appeared on the scene. Brightly colored figures were created using a popular new method called cold painting whereby each figure was finished with enamel paint. There was enough demand to keep the workers busy for decades. One cigarette lighter features a rug merchant and his boy assistant perched on top of a camel. A flint was located on the side of the camel. A striker protrudes out of the camel's saddlebag. When the striker ignites, it flames long enough to light a cigarette (Color Plate 20).

Another cigarette lighter depicts a man praying; the striker is in the jar next to him (Color Plate 21). One bronze object shows a man smoking his pipe. The small box next to him contained matches, and you could put your burned matches on a tray in front of him (Color Plate 22).

For pipe smokers, an Egyptian tobacco humidor in the shape of a canopic jar (one of the vessels that held the mummy's internal organs) was available (Color Plate 23). One delightful cigarette dispenser featured a mechanical Egyptian ibis. Push the button on top of the dispenser, the lid opened, the ibis dipped down to pick up a cigarette in its beak, and then popped up to offer it to the smoker (Color Plate 24). The tobacco industry wasn't the only one to cash in on Egyptomania. England, with its long tradition of silversmithing, produced some fabulous jewelry with Egyptian motifs.

BAUBLES, BANGLES, AND MUMMIES

Throughout Egypt's long history, men and women adorned their bodies with necklaces, earrings, bracelets, and rings. Egyptian archaeology, although barely 200 years old, has revealed spectacular caches of ancient jewelry. At the end of the nineteenth century, Jacques de Morgan, excavating in pyramids at Dashour in Egypt, found a fabulous trove of royal jewelry that was heralded to the public in the *Illustrated London News* and the *Graphic* (Fig. 6.3). Soon Victorian ladies were clamoring for Egyptian jewelry.

Silversmiths recognized a new market and answered the call with Egyptian-themed jewelry. Among the many pieces that they designed, the chatelaine, a chain suspended from a ladies belt, was most popular. One elaborate chatelaine had a pharaoh's head, a winged solar disk, a cartouche with pseudohieroglyphs, and lotus blossoms (Color Plate 25).

*Fig. 6.3   Jacques De Morgan's discovery of spectacular jewelry inside a
tomb at Dahshur caused a sensation. The orientalist painter, Philippoteaux,
recorded the find for* The Graphic.

A crystal perfume bottle encased in sterling filigree depicts a pharaoh presenting his beloved with a lotus blossom (Color Plate 26). Even mundane objects, such as a pair of scissors, lent themselves to Egyptian themes (Color Plate 25).

Ancient Egyptians often wore amulets around their necks for magical protection, but fashionable ladies during the 1920s and 1930s took it one step further; they wore little mummy cases around their necks. These little silver enameled anthropoid coffins were hinged so they could be opened to reveal a tiny wrapped mummy inside (Color Plate 27).

One of the most popular forms of Egyptian jewelry was the winged scarab pin. These pins came in a dizzying variety of styles; some even utilized real beetles that had been varnished. Many pins substituted the head of a pharaoh for the scarab, but my favorite is one that substituted a fossilized trilobite (Color Plate 30). A popular variant was the winged vulture—again a symbol of protection. Many scarabs look decidedly Egyptian, but some look more like the American eagle, complete with red, white, and blue feathers (Color Plate 29).

In ancient Egypt, wings were a symbol of protection; the goddess Isis is often shown with outstretched wings protecting the pharaoh. In ancient Egyptian, the word for "beetle" was *kheper,* which also meant "to exist." Thus, beetle jewelry would protect your existence. A pin might combine the scarab with wings and thus offer double protection (Color Plate 28).

England was thoroughly enjoying Egyptomania, and America refused to be left behind.

SEVEN

New York Gets Its Obelisk

Bringing the obelisk to London cost England the lives of six brave men, but America was now determined to have its own obelisk. Rome, Paris, and London had them; why not New York? The idea of an American obelisk was not new. In 1869, when the world powers gathered in Egypt for the opening of the Suez Canal, an obelisk was offered to the United States, not out of generosity and friendship but out of desperation. Egypt was bankrupt, but the preparations for the canal's opening had been made, the invitations to the world's rulers sent, and Empress Eugénie's palace completed. In spite of the country's financial difficulties, the festivities went forward. The only problem was that Egypt no longer owned the canal. It was in the hands of receivers, European financiers who had lent the funds for the project. It was under these difficult circumstances that William H. Hurlbert, editor of the *New York World,* was introduced to the khedive at the canal's opening ceremonies. Khedive Isma'il, eager for an ally to save him from his European creditors, suggested to Hurlbert that America might want an obelisk. Nothing was done at that time, and the offer was forgotten. Ten years later, in 1878, after London erected its obelisk, New York was suffering from obelisk envy. Hurlbert would have gladly accepted the khedive's offer, but did it still hold?

CAN AMERICA HAVE AN OBELISK, PLEASE?

Yes, it did, and E. E. Farman, American consul-general in Cairo, spear-headed the effort to obtain it. However, there were numerous obstacles and much confusion to be overcome. Egypt and the khedive were slid-ing toward hard times. The country was bankrupt, and thousands of peasants had died of starvation the previous year. Once again, Egypt could not pay its debts. England and France notified the khedive that they would insist on payment for the debt coupons they held. The khedive was still the nominal head of Egypt, but an Anglo-French ministry controlled the country's purse strings and internal workings. If Farman was to secure an obelisk, it was this ministry that would have to give it, and it was headed by Europeans. Émile Brugsch, a high-ranking official in the Antiquities Service, was strongly opposed to another obelisk leaving Egypt.

Brugsch was joined by Auguste Mariette, the director of the An-tiquities Service, who sent a memorandum to the ministry stating that he also opposed another obelisk leaving Egypt. The memoran-dum explained the uniqueness and importance of the obelisks under consideration. Certainly at this point things were bleak for America's obelisk. The Europeans and the two highest-ranking Egyptologists in Egypt were striving to keep Egypt's heritage in Egypt. The khedive, who didn't care about pagan relics, was in favor of giving the obelisk but was powerless. Just as things seemed utterly hopeless for New York getting its obelisk, sunlight entered through an unexpected crack.

The head of the Anglo-French–controlled ministry, Nubar Pa-sha, acting prime minister, had recently reformed Egypt's antiquated

judicial system. Nubar told Farman that he was fully aware of his negotiations for an obelisk and that America could have the one in Alexandria. Farman was elated. Nubar was the most powerful man in Egypt.
But then the political balance of power shifted again.

When reports of famine in the south reached Cairo, the people
were furious because Nubar's commission had sold the grain to pay the
European debt. Now Egyptians were starving. A mob, led by former
officers and soldiers who had been fired without pay, attacked Nubar
and other government officials and held them prisoner until the khedive personally came to free them. The khedive took advantage of the
anti-European sentiment and moved quickly.

He disbanded the commission and appointed a new, entirely Egyptian, ministry headed by Ali Pasha Sherif, a man admired by all for his
honesty and intelligence. Soon, under his stewardship, the government
began to stabilize and function again. Farman and Sherif knew and
respected each other, and after a few weeks of political calm, Farman
screwed up his courage to ask about the obelisk. Sherif's reply was that
he would have to speak to the khedive; Farman could check with him
the next day and he would have an answer.

The next day Farman called at the palace and was told Sherif was
in a meeting with the khedive. Farman dropped in on the khedive's
seal bearer and found him chatting with the khedive's two brothers.
The three invited the consul-general to join them for coffee, and just as
Farman settled in, a very agitated Pasha Sherif strode in. Farman sensed
there were governmental problems again. Pasha Sherif said something
in Arabic to the seal bearer and then nodded to Farman to follow him
outside. Pasha Sherif walked silently with Farman down a long hall-
way and then descended a grand staircase leading to the door, where
Farman's carriage was waiting. As they walked through the doorway,
Pasha Sherif asked, "It is the obelisk in Alexandria that you prefer, is

it not?" The consul-general explained that it would be the easiest to remove. "Well," said the pasha, "we have concluded to give it to you."[1]

Farman was pleased but not elated. He had been promised the obelisk several times—by the khedive, by Nubar Pasha, and now by Sherif. Sherif was an honorable man, but how long would *he* stay in power? Farman thought quickly and suggested he should have something in writing. He also requested that the obelisk be given directly to the City of New York, not to the United States. William H. Vanderbilt was paying for the obelisk's transportation to New York. If it were given to the United States, Congress would have to decide which city got it, and funds for transport would have to be appropriated. "We give you the obelisk, do as you wish with it." Pasha Sherif paused and then added, "Write me a note, indicating what you wish to have done. State that all the expenses of removal are to be paid by the United States or by the City of New York, if you prefer. Hand the note to my Secretary-General, and tell him to prepare an answer confirming the gift in accordance with the suggestions you give, and bring it to me for my signature."

FINALLY THE DEAL IS DONE

New York would have its obelisk. It was wise that Farman acted so quickly. France had been insisting that the khedive resign, and England reluctantly seconded this motion. Soon other European nations joined the call for abdication. On June 27, just one month after Farman had secured the obelisk, the khedive resigned and passed the throne to his son, Muhammad Tewfik Pasha. Three days later, when the former khedive sailed into exile, Farman had the letter giving the obelisk to New York—from a government that no longer existed. Immediately foreign powers began pressuring the new ministry to negate the gift of the former regime. The matter was debated twice. Finally the Council of

Ministers decided that the gift held; it had been given by a legitimate government. New Yorkers would have their obelisk; all they had to do was pick it up.

HENRY HONEYCHURCH GORRINGE STEPS UP

The June 17, 1879 issue of the *World* carried the announcement that America had been given an obelisk, funds were available for its transport from Egypt, and all that was needed was the man to do the job. Lieutenant-Commander Henry Honeychurch Gorringe was convinced that he was the man. Gorringe had little formal education, but he was smart and ambitious. He had served under Admiral David Farragut in the Civil War and had been promoted three times for gallantry in action. By the time he was 26, he was a lieutenant commander in the U.S. Navy.

After the Civil War, Gorringe was dispatched to map the coast of the Levant. It was his first taste of antiquity, and he was enthralled. When he read the announcement in the *World* asking for someone to move the obelisk, he couldn't believe it. He had visited the Alexandrian obelisks during his hydrographic surveys and had thought about moving one to America. He thought the obelisks were unappreciated where they were, amid the garbage of a squalid neighborhood. Some locals made money by taking sledgehammers to the fallen obelisk to chip off souvenirs for tourists. Gorringe could rescue the standing obelisk and bring it home to New York, but he had to submit a plan that would convince Hurlbert he could do it.

When Gorringe began planning how to move the obelisk, he studied the methods the French and English had used to transport their obelisks. The French didn't have to navigate the open seas. Once the *Luxor* reached Alexandria, it was a straight sail across the Mediterranean to Toulon, so the *Luxor* could be towed. Also, the *Luxor* had been specially constructed to hold the obelisk and navigate the shallow Nile. Gorringe wasn't going to have the luxury of constructing a special ship for his obelisk. He would have to buy one inexpensively and then re-configure it.

The British also didn't have to cross the Atlantic Ocean; they towed their obelisk to England. Still, even with a special vessel con-structed to house the obelisk, the *Cleopatra* had been lost at sea. Despite the details available, a limited amount was pertinent to what Gorringe would be attempting. Transporting the New York obelisk across the Atlantic was far more daunting than what the French and English had faced. Towing it was not an option. Gorringe was sure of only one thing: He was going to need a ship that was self-powered and could navigate heavy seas with a 250-ton obelisk in its hold. Until that time, the largest object ever put in the hold of a ship was a 100-ton cannon manufactured in England and shipped to Italy. Hydraulic cranes had been constructed to put the gun on board, and they cost a fortune—more than the entire sum available to move the obelisk. Since these super cranes were out, Gorringe could not lift the obelisk onto the ship. His plan was to open the hull, slide the obelisk into the ship's hold, and then replace the planks that had been removed.

HOW TO MOVE A VERY LARGE ROCK

This ingenious solution created another problem to be solved. How do you slide a 250-ton obelisk into a ship? Gorringe would also have to move the obelisk over land, first from where it stood in Alexan-dria to the transport ship, and then from the dock in New York to its final site in Central Park. As he searched previous attempts at mov-ing heavy weights over land, he found an earlier engineering feat that would become his model, but it wasn't an obelisk that was moved. It was something even heavier—the immense base for a statue of Peter the Great in Russia.

In 1768, Empress Catherine the Great of Russia was planning a massive equestrian statue of Peter the Great on his horse galloping up a steep craggy rock. It was decided that the base of this statue should be a single stone. The task of finding and transporting such a stone was entrusted to Count Marino Carburi, who had a reputation for engineering skills. For the base, Carburi found a 600-ton rock that was approximately 42 feet long, 27 feet wide, and 21 feet high. Like the Egyptian obelisks, it was granite, but it was more than twice the weight of the obelisk Gorringe would be moving a century later.

Carburi had to move the 600-ton rock over uneven terrain. Something that large couldn't move on wheels. There was no material strong enough for an axle, and wheels would collapse under the heavy load. Carburi's solution was parallel iron grooves containing metal balls that rolled freely—essentially giant ball bearings.

When Gorringe read of Carburi's method, he decided to use cannonballs to move the obelisk. Now his plan was taking shape. He knew how to move the obelisk on land, and he knew that he would have a self-propelled ship that could navigate high seas with a 250-ton obelisk in the hold. The last major part of his plan was how to lower the obelisk from its pedestal in Alexandria.

GORRINGE SUBMITS HIS PLAN

Gorringe designed a structure similar to what the Dixon brothers had used for the London obelisk: two towers that stood right next to the obelisk on opposite sides. An iron belt fitted around the obelisk's center of gravity would be bolted to clamps (trunnions) projecting from the towers. The obelisk would then be pivoted around its center of gravity until it was parallel to the ground. Once in this position, it would be lowered to the ground by hydraulic jacks at both ends of the obelisk. All this ironwork would be fabricated in the United States, shipped to Alexandria, and assembled. Once the obelisk was down, the equipment would be disassembled and brought back to New York so it could be used to erect the obelisk in Central Park. It was a well-thought-out plan based on years of experience; now Gorringe just had to convince those in charge that it would work.

Gorringe had several things going for him. He was a decorated naval commander who had never failed in any task that his government had given him. Those who worked with him had nothing but praise, and he exuded a calm, reassuring confidence. Aside from his personal qualities, his plan impressed those who saw it. It seemed realistic and well thought out, so they quickly concluded that Gorringe was up to the task.

With his plan accepted, Gorringe went full steam ahead. He immediately contacted Seaton Schroeder, his former navigator, who was now a lieutenant in the U.S. Navy, to see if he would help on the project. Schroeder was delighted. The State Department arranged for both men to be given leaves of absence to bring America's obelisk home. Gorringe contracted with John A. Roebling's Sons to manufacture the iron parts for the turning mechanism. The company had supplied the ironworks for the Brooklyn Bridge and clearly had the capability to produce large iron parts, some weighing as much as 12,575 pounds.

LET MY OBELISK GO!

As soon as Gorringe and Schroeder arrived in Alexandria, the European community began a campaign opposing the removal of the obelisk. Petitions were circulated for signatures, angry editorials appeared in the newspapers, and Gorringe was called names as he walked through the streets. The opposition that Consul-General Farman had encountered was intensified as it became clear that the Americans were serious about taking an obelisk. Gorringe thought it best to get the support of the new khedive, Isma'il's son Tewfik, so they took the train to Cairo for an audience with his highness.

The khedive was gracious and welcoming, and the men talked frankly about the pressures that the European powers were putting on the khedive. Tewfik was concerned that if the obelisk were damaged during removal, it would be a political disaster for him. Gorringe's calm demeanor and detailed plan reassured him, and he ordered the governor of Alexandria to formally hand over the obelisk and assist Gorringe in every way possible.

As work began on the site, an Italian appeared claiming that the land was his and they had no right to be on his property. The Italian didn't dispute that America now owned the obelisk; he was merely pointing out that they couldn't take it. Gorringe offered to lease the land, but the Italian refused. Gorringe responded with a letter to the governor, a remarkable document showing diplomacy and restraint while making it very clear that he would not back down.

Soon after he received the letter, the governor explained that although the Italian's claim to the land was far from clear, court proceedings to settle the matter could take years. Gorringe took matters into his own hands and informed the Italian consul-general that he would sue anyone attempting to hinder his work for £15,000 in damages. He then offered to lease the land and added that the offer would expire at 4:00 P.M. that day. The offer was accepted. Gorringe had cleared the first hurdle, but the race was far from over.

A SHIP AT LAST!

In Alexandria, Schroeder and Gorringe continued to look for a suitable ship to transport the obelisk across the Atlantic. Their timing was perfect. The Egyptian government was bankrupt. Because it could not afford to maintain a full postal service, it was decommissioning several of its postal steamers. Gorringe spotted one, the *Dessoug,* at dock and went on board to inspect it. The good news was that the hull was in perfect condition and was just large enough to admit the obelisk belowdecks. The bad news was that the engines and boilers were in poor condition. Gorringe and Schroeder decided to make an immediate offer of £5,000 for the ship, calculating that it would cost an equal amount to refit. Schroeder could work on refitting while Gorringe focused on the obelisk itself.

The assistant postmaster-general notified Gorringe that he could have the ship for £5,100. On December 3, Gorringe transferred the funds. Soon after, he boarded the ship with a representative of the postal service who lowered the Egyptian flag. Gorringe quickly raised the American flag, making it clear to all who owned the ship. As Schroeder began refitting the *Dessoug,* Gorringe turned his attention to the obelisk.

Gorringe erected scaffolding around the obelisk so it could be sheathed in wood planks to prevent damage during transport. The planks were held together by iron barrel hoops. On top were several loops through which cables could be run to control the obelisk as it was turned. At the very top, a large American flag was flown, to emphasize ownership of the obelisk (Fig. 7.1). Gorringe hired local workers to clear the rubble and prepare the site, which he treated like an archaeological excavation. When fragments of bronze statues, ancient coins, scarabs, and amulets turned up, he paid bonuses to those who discovered them. He also sent men to the shore to search the beach for objects that might have escaped detection, been dumped, and later washed ashore.

While the turning mechanism was being manufactured in New Jersey, Gorringe prepared the foundation on which it would rest. Two masonry piers were constructed, then wooden derricks were erected to lift the pieces of the turning mechanism onto the piers for assembly.

Fig. 7.1   The Alexandria obelisk was encased in wood for protection before being lowered.

HOW TO TURN AN OBELISK

Once the prefabricated pieces were on the site, they were quickly assembled on top of the masonry piers. When the obelisk was fixed to the trunnions, it was supported by the turning mechanism. By means of turnbuckles and screws (much like the mechanism in an automobile jack), the obelisk was raised straight up a few inches. Steel cables were run from both ends of the obelisk over the top of the scaffolding and into the masonry piers to take some of the weight off as it turned. Gorringe was afraid that when the obelisk went horizontal, it might break under its own weight. By his estimate, the cables supported only 60 of the obelisk's 230 tons.

On December 5, Gorringe tested the machinery. The obelisk swung effortlessly. When it reached an angle of about 12 degrees off the vertical, Gorringe stopped the obelisk's motion, tied the cables, and left the 230-ton shaft of granite suspended in air overnight. He was making a statement. The system was clearly strong enough to hold the obelisk.

On December 6 he ordered his men to pull on the cables to bring the obelisk horizontal. Surrounded by a teeming crowd of protesters, the obelisk slowly and silently moved toward the horizontal, then disaster. A creaking came from the turning mechanism followed by a loud *snap.* One of the cables had separated. For a moment the obelisk's movement stopped, but just for a moment. Then it began moving again toward the horizontal, picking up speed as it went. With the obelisk out of control, spectators began running in all directions, but Gorringe had planned for such a situation. He had stacked timbers almost as high as the obelisk would have been when it was horizontal; if the obelisk for any reason went past horizontal, continuing toward

Fig. 7.2   When a cable snapped as the obelisk was being turned, it came crashing onto the pile but did not damage the obelisk.

the ground, the timbers would stop it. Indeed, that is exactly what happened. As the obelisk went past the horizontal, it crashed into the timbers, bounced up a few feet, then moved downward again, only far more slowly, and came safely to rest on the timbers (Fig. 7.2). Once the obelisk was safely horizontal, the spectators sent up a great cheer, as if they had never opposed the project.

GETTING THE PASSENGER ONBOARD

Next the obelisk had to be lowered to the ground. Gorringe positioned a stack of timber beneath its bottom end to match the one by the point that had saved the obelisk. The two jacks were then raised a few inches so they supported the full weight of the obelisk. Workers could remove the top layer of timbers and lower the obelisk onto the stacks again, lowering the obelisk by four inches. Slowly and methodically this cycle was repeated so that the obelisk was lowered about three feet each day. While it was being lowered, another very difficult operation was being conducted.

Gorringe had to move the obelisk overland to the port by floating it there through the same treacherous waters that had previously ripped a hole in England's iron caisson. He immediately hired professional divers to clear an underwater route for the obelisk. Because of his interest in archaeology, Gorringe knew that the bottom of the shore was littered with blocks from Cleopatra's sunken palace. He built piers in the water on which he positioned lifting cranes. When the divers found a block that was a navigational hazard, it was lifted out of the water and placed onshore. As all this was going on, Gorringe dismantled the masonry on which the turning mechanism had stood and then focused his attention to moving the 50-ton pedestal on which the obelisk had rested.

An iron bar was inserted beneath the pedestal, and with the help of hydraulic jacks, it was raised off the three steps on which it rested. Iron channel rails with rows of cannonballs were positioned near the elevated 50-ton pedestal, and it was lowered onto the rails. The channels and cannonballs formed giant skids, like the ones supermarkets use to transport crates of goods from trucks being unloaded into the basements beneath stores. The pedestal slid off to the side with the greatest of ease on these rails, which must have been a great relief to Gorringe. This was the same method he was going to use to transport the obelisk, which was five times the weight of its pedestal.

THE MASONIC PUZZLE

With the pedestal out of the way, Gorringe began removing the three steps on which it had rested. These steps were formed of several dozen large, rectangular limestone blocks and four granite ones that fit together like a jigsaw puzzle. When the last step was removed, Gorringe made a surprising discovery.

The foundation beneath the steps had been filled with large sandstone blocks and three granite blocks. Two of the granite blocks were polished; the third was rough. One block was a perfect polished cube, and next to it was a limestone block on which rested a metal trowel and lead plumb bob. Gorringe, a Freemason, thought he had found emblems of Freemasonry. He proceeded to remove the foundation blocks, carefully numbering and recording their original positions. A committee from the Grand Lodge of Egypt was asked to inspect the stones. Their report would eventually lead to one of the most incredible parades New York had ever seen.

The committee, headed by Masonic grand master S. A. Zola, examined the blocks Brother Gorringe had unearthed and concluded they were indeed the handwork of fellow Masons. The polished cube looked like the Masonic perfect ashlar (Man in his educated, refined state), with the rough blocks representing Man in his uneducated, rough state. Another block had two snakes carved on it, representing Wisdom. The trowel and plumb bob were clearly Masonic, seemingly left behind to be found by brother Masons in the future. Gorringe immediately decided he must bring all of it back to New York for his brother Masons to marvel at. Neither the French nor the English had brought their obelisk pedestals home. Because it was a Masonic monument, however, Gorringe felt New York should have the pedestal.

Gorringe's belief that Freemasons could trace their origins to ancient Egypt was widely accepted in his day. Obelisks, Freemasonry, and Egyptomania had always been closely related. Many of our founding fathers—George Washington, Benjamin Franklin, John Hancock, and Paul Revere—were Masons. In 1836, when Robert Wills designed a monument to commemorate the life of George Washington, it was in the shape of an Egyptian obelisk. The obelisk symbolized America, an emerging world power, associating itself with a great ancient power. On July 4, 1848, when the cornerstone to the Washington Monument was laid, Washington's brother Freemasons conducted the ceremony.[2] Gorringe felt the pedestal and steps belonged with the obelisk, cementing the link between American Freemasonry and ancient Egypt.

DOWN TO THE SEA

With the obelisk nearly on the ground, a caisson—an 83-foot-long wood box resembling a giant coffin—was built to receive it. Once the obelisk was secured inside the caisson, the plan was to launch it down a gangway that had been built right up to the water. Divers had continued the gangway underwater to protect the bottom of the caisson until it floated. The hope was that with an initial shove provided by the hydraulic jacks, the caisson with the obelisk inside would slide down the well-lubricated gangplank and into the water. Once afloat, it would be towed to Alexandria's port. On March 18, they attempted to launch the caisson. It wouldn't slide and had to be inched along by jacks. This process took nearly two weeks, and at 10:00 A.M. on March 31, the caisson was towed to the port.

While the obelisk was being lowered and the pedestal was being removed, Schroeder oversaw the refitting of the *Dessoug*. First he strengthened the interior of the hull with steel beams to distribute the weight of the obelisk over the entire ship. Existing internal beams had to be cut out to make room for the obelisk and bolt-holes drilled so they could be fitted again once the obelisk was inside. Thirty plates in the hull were removed as well as some above the waterline. A foreman shipwright from Glasgow was brought to Alexandria to oversee the boiler and engine repairs and the final opening and closing of the hull. The massive and time-consuming job involved three teams of 30 Arab boilermakers working around the clock.

TAKE THE PEDESTAL TOO

The obelisk was not the only heavy cargo the *Dessoug* had to be prepared to receive. There was also the pedestal weighing in at 50 tons. Bringing the pedestal to the port where the *Dessoug* was waiting was relatively easy. A lighter—a small barge—was brought to the coast, following the path that had been taken by the caisson, only in reverse. With the lighter beached, Gorringe used the hydraulic jacks to lift the pedestal and set it on the lighter's deck. Then the lighter was launched down the gangway with a push from the jacks. The lighter was then towed to the port easily; Gorringe knew that loading the pedestal on the *Dessoug* was going to be difficult.

To keep the pedestal from shifting during the ocean voyage, it had to be secured to an iron frame that Schroeder had constructed. To get it onto the frame, the pedestal had to be raised 30 feet above the deck and lowered through a hatch. Again, weight was the problem. The pedestal weighed 50 tons, and the largest crane in Alexandria could lift only 30 tons. Gorringe's solution was complex and risky. In addition to the 30-ton shore crane, a local floating steam derrick could lift 25 tons. If the weight of the pedestal could be precisely distributed between the crane and the derrick, the pedestal could be lifted above the *Dessoug* and placed in the hold. If, however, something went wrong and the pedestal fell on the *Dessoug,* it would destroy the ship.

The delicate balancing act required four steel cables, the derrick, and the crane all working in tandem, but Gorringe was confident. The next day the pedestal was lifted off the lighter, swung above the *Dessoug,* and lowered through the hatch and into the frame designed to hold it. The pedestal was the largest object ever maneuvered onto a ship at Alexandria. Next up was the obelisk, weighing nearly five times its pedestal.

LOADING THE NEEDLE

After the obelisk was towed to the port, it was moved onto the floating dock, and the caisson was removed. It awaited the *Dessoug* sheathed only in its protective wood casing. It had been calculated that the obelisk must enter the hold at a 21-degree angle, so it was placed at this angle on the dock, and the *Dessoug* was brought in. A wood gangway was laid down from the bottom of the obelisk, which would enter the ship first, through the aperture, and into the hold. On this gangway carpenters anchored the iron channels with their five-and-a-half-inch balls that would form the skids on which the obelisk would slide into the ship (Fig. 7.3). These skids proved so efficient that the two hydraulic jacks that pushed the obelisk into the hold never had to exert more than five tons of force.

When the obelisk was completely inside the hold, the hydraulic jacks were repositioned to lift it a few inches so the channels and iron balls could be removed. Once the obelisk was securely resting on its bed of soft wood, teams of carpenters began wedging it in on all sides so it couldn't shift during the voyage. As the carpenters worked inside, ironworkers replaced the plates over the aperture. On June 1, 1880,

Fig. 7.3   The New York obelisk was slid into the ship's hull on cannon balls.

the *Dessoug,* with its precious cargo stowed in the hold, was almost ready to sail.

WHAT'S AN OBELISK WORTH?

The blocks from the steps beneath the pedestal were stowed belowdecks and secured as ballast, as were the parts to the turning mechanism. On June 8, the *Dessoug* took on 500 tons of coal, twice the weight of the obelisk, but just enough to get it as far as Gibraltar, where it would refuel. The last arrangement was for the ship's insurance. Like every other part of the project, it was stressful. The usual rate for insurance of a vessel was 2 percent of its value, but when the underwriters heard about the obelisk as cargo, they wanted 25 percent. Gorringe refused, and by June 11, the rate was down to 5 percent—better, but still more than twice the going rate. Gorringe told his London agent to inform the underwriters that he would sail the next day without insurance if the rate was not 2 percent. Offers of acceptance came flooding in; the *Dessoug* was insured. But now there was a problem with the crew.

A PIRATE CREW

The chief engineer was a Scotsman who had worked for the Egyptian Postal Service. He knew the *Dessoug* well and oversaw the refitting of the boilers and engines. The officers were all British. The first and second mates were alcoholics, and the second officer got so drunk that he fell overboard twice before they ever left port and had to be fired for his own safety. Forty-eight of the locals who had signed on deserted before the ship even sailed. In addition, Gorringe's description of the quartermasters wasn't encouraging: "They would do credit to a pirate crew."[3]

The ship couldn't be registered as an American vessel because of legal technicalities, and Gorringe wasn't about to sail under the Egyptian flag or under the flag of a European country. When the *Dessoug* finally entered international waters, Lieutenant-Commander Gorringe was commanding an unregistered ship with no nationality. This meant that any man-of-war could seize it while at sea, and any country could confiscate it when in port. It was a risk that Gorringe was willing to take.

Even with all the problems they faced, Schroeder and Gorringe felt a great sense of relief as they watched the coast of Alexandria recede. They had overcome great obstacles in Egypt, and now they were together again, in their element, the open sea, confident they could overcome any future hurdles. The *Dessoug* behaved beautifully, pitching and rolling only slightly, like any other merchant steamer.

The first problem they encountered was that the refitted boilers still leaked. When they put in at Gibraltar, they stayed for three days, allowing the boilers to cool so they could be properly repaired. Again they took on 500 tons of coal, enough to reach New York, and left at midnight on June 25–26 in good weather. On July 10, they got the biggest fright of the trip.

TROUBLE AT SEA

They encountered squalls, which should have been no problem for the *Dessoug*, but Gorringe could see waterspouts forming in the distance. Usually these spouts form and dissipate quickly, rarely reaching a height of more than 20 feet. The crew watched in horror as a spout formed directly in front of the ship and kept growing until it was 50 feet high. The weight of so much water landing on the *Dessoug* could crush the deck, and it was heading straight for them. Normally ships fired a cannon to dissipate waterspouts, but the Dessoug was unarmed. All they could do was batten down the hatches and wait. For nearly five minutes the spout slowly moved toward them; then, just as it was upon the ship, it turned and crashed back into the sea. A gale blew for the next three days, but the ship behaved beautifully, and New York was straight ahead.

HOME AT LAST

On July 19, they sighted New York and were met by the pilot boat *A.M. Lawrence, No. 4.* After anchoring overnight off Fire Island, they were escorted to the Staten Island Quarantine Station, given a quick once-over, and released. Then they steamed around the southern tip of Manhattan, up the Hudson River, and docked at 23rd Street. Gorringe gave the officers leave and opened the ship to visitors. The *Dessoug* and its ancient, distinguished passenger were a New York sensation with more than 1,700 visitors in one day. New Yorkers had been following the ship's progress in the newspapers. Now that it had arrived, it was like a Broadway star. As New York's curious traipsed through the ship to see the obelisk, Gorringe made plans for erecting it.

For logistical reasons, the pedestal and obelisk had to be disembarked at different locations. The ship sailed north to 51st Street, where a huge dock crane lifted the pedestal out of the hold and swung it onto shore with the greatest of ease—a marked contrast to the difficulties encountered loading it at Alexandria. It was next loaded on a truck specially rebuilt to bear the 50-ton load. Pulled by 16 pairs of horses, the pedestal-bearing truck started east on 51st Street toward Fifth Avenue. Several times along the way the procession had to halt because the wheels of the truck sank into the soft pavement. After reaching Fifth Avenue, the truck turned north and proceeded up to

Fig. 7.4   The pedestal was pulled to New York's Central Park by 16 pairs of horses. It was the heaviest object ever moved on wheels in the city.

82nd Street, where it entered Central Park (Fig. 7.4). The park terrain was too uneven for the wheeled vehicle so the pedestal was placed on greased skids and hauled to Greywacke Knoll, the site where the obelisk was to be erected.

Earlier, there had been some debate about where to place the obelisk. Some favored prominent sites in the middle of the city, such as Columbus Circle. However, there were concerns that tall buildings would eventually be erected nearby, obstructing the view of the obelisk, so the park site was agreed on. Greywacke Knoll was the park's highest point, provided a solid foundation, and was near the city's new Metropolitan Museum of Art. On August 5, Department of Parks workers began preparing the site by removing young trees and leveling the surface. Throughout September the site was prepared, but a great deal more had to be done.

MASONS MARCH

The Masons were going to preside over the ceremony for laying the foundation. Thousands of members of various lodges and their officers participated. On October 9, 1880, dressed in top hats, black coats, and white gloves, 500 commanders of the local Masonic lodges formed ranks on 15th Street on the east and west sides of Fifth Avenue. As they converged onto Fifth Avenue in the cool October air, they marched north, six abreast with four-foot intervals between ranks, resembling a giant, black millipede with white legs. When the last row passed 16th Street, the marchers were joined by 500 more commanders converging onto Fifth Avenue, lengthening the parade to nearly a quarter of a mile. On 17th Street, members of the Brooklyn Masonic lodges and lodges from Suffolk and Richmond Counties joined them, and so it went, street after street adding to the flow up Fifth Avenue. At 21st Street, members of French-, Italian-, Spanish-, and German-speaking lodges joined in until more than 8,500 Masons filled Fifth Avenue. Many of the lodges were preceded by their bands, so the 30,000 spectators who lined the route were treated to music as well as pageantry. It was the greatest congregation of Masons the world had ever seen.

As the column marched north toward Central Park, three horse-drawn carriages left the Grand Masonic Temple on 23rd Street and Ninth Avenue. The carriages contained the officers of the Grand Lodge and Supreme Grand Master Jesse B. Anthony, who carried a baton of gold and amethyst specially crafted for the occasion. It was a thing of wonder with gold obelisks decorated with mysterious hieroglyphs incised into the gold, just like the hieroglyphs on the obelisk that Brother Gorringe, Anglo-Saxon Lodge No. 137, had brought all the way from Egypt to New York (Color Plate 31).

An amazing sight greeted the 8,500 Masons as they marched north, passing by the Statue of Liberty's torch. When Bartholdi sold the French on the idea of converting "Egypt Enlightening the World" to the "Statue of Liberty," funds to build the entire statue were unavailable. They hoped to deliver the statue in time for America's Centennial in 1876, but by 1880 only the torch and a hand were completed. Thus, the torch was sent on a fundraising tour of the United States. The Masons were passing a little-known link to Egypt.

As the parade neared 40th Street, the Masons had one last Egyptian encounter—an Egyptian temple complete with 30-foot-high walls and even taller entrance pylons. The Croton Reservoir had been built in "the Egyptian style," and when it opened on July 4, 1842, it was the pride of New York City. No longer would people have to rely on rainwater caught in cisterns and barrels. Fresh, clean water flowed from the upstate Croton River via two aqueducts to serve the growing population. The reservoir remained operational until 1911, when it was dismantled, the land filled in, and New York's famous 42nd Street Public Library was erected on the site.

After passing the reservoir, houses and buildings began to thin out. Northern Manhattan was still mostly pastoral. At 82nd Street, the column paused. By now it stretched more than a mile back to 60th Street, where the ranks opened their center and faced inward, permitting the Anglo-Saxon Lodge and Grand Lodge to march up the center to be the first to enter Central Park. To their right was the newly constructed Metropolitan Museum of Art. Behind the museum, a large elevated deck had been constructed for the grand master, grand officers, masters, and wardens of the lodges. Once they took their places on the platform, the other marchers closed ranks on the north, east, and west sides of the platform. The grassy knoll on the south, left open for visitors, quickly filled to capacity, swelling the crowd to more than 20,000.

A MASONIC RITUAL

In front of the crowd, on Greywacke Knoll, the ancient limestone blocks of differing sizes and shapes had been fitted together, forming the steps that would support the obelisk's pedestal. This unique assemblage of blocks had drawn the thousands of Freemasons to this spot. Months earlier, and 8,000 miles away, in Alexandria, Egypt, Brother Gorringe had noticed that the unusual arrangement of blocks suggested it was a Masonic monument. Gorringe and other brother Masons concluded that 20 centuries earlier, brother Masons had prepared the obelisk base as a time capsule for future Masons.

Now he and his brothers crowded around this Masonic wonder to fit its last stone into place. The stone was several inches smaller on all four sides than the void that would receive it, and Gorringe had ideas how to fill the space. His choices give us a rare insight into his personality. Gorringe intended to transform the base of the obelisk into a time capsule. He asked the American Bible Society for copies of the Bible in various languages. They told him where he could buy them, and he did. He tried to get an example of an amazing new invention, the telephone, but couldn't. He asked the United States Coast Guard and Geodetic Survey for samples of weights and measures. They refused, but he did have some successes. The Treasury Department contributed a set of medals of the presidents of the United States and a proof set of 1880 coins. The Department of State gave a facsimile of the Declaration of Independence and a Congressional Directory for 1880. The Navy supplied a silver medal given to seamen and officers for Arctic exploration by Queen Victoria. The Society for the Prevention of Cruelty to Animals provided some of their literature. Gorringe's Anglo-Saxon Lodge No. 137 gave a complete set of silver emblems and jewels of the Order of Freemasons. But this wasn't all. Into the base went *Webster's Unabridged Dictionary,* the works of Shakespeare, a New York City Directory and map, an *Encyclopedia of Mechanics and Engineering,* and even a hydraulic jack like the two that had lowered and moved the obelisk in Alexandria. William Hurlbert, the editor of the *World* newspaper, who had helped so much to bring the obelisk to New York, supplied the most intriguing of the items placed in the time capsule. He "contributed a small box, the contents of which is known only to himself."[4]

Grand Mason Anthony now stood before the stone, now in place, and said, "I, Jesse B. Anthony, Grand Master of Masons of the State of New York, do find this stone plumb, level, and square, well formed, true and trusty, and duly laid." Deputy Grand Master Taylor placed a handful of grain, the emblem of plenty, on the stone. The grand senior warden poured wine on the stone to symbolize joy, and the junior warden poured oil, representing peace.

Lieutenant-Commander Gorringe, the man whose heroic efforts had brought them all to this spot, was formally presented to the grand master, who declared, "In the name of the Grand Lodge of the State of New York I now proclaim the corner stone of this obelisk, known as Cleopatra's Needle, duly laid in ample form." He then repeated these words three times on the south, west, and east sides of the stone. When this was done, 8,500 Masons clapped in unison three times, and the voices of 20,000 people rose in one great cheer. Cleopatra's Needle had been officially welcomed to New York.

THE MASONIC MASTER SPEAKS

It was now 5:00 P.M. and the sun was just beginning to cross the Hudson River to the west, a half-mile from the gathering. Grand Master Anthony stepped forward to formally address the crowd. The speech was a bombshell. It began by praising the ancient Egyptian builders for their skill and insight. Okay so far. Then Grand Master Anthony launched into a discussion of the Great Pyramid and how a record of past history had been coded into the measurements of its blocks and passageways. If one measured carefully, perhaps one could use the pyramid to predict the future. This was a theory recently put forward by Charles Piazzi Smyth, Scotland's Astronomer Royal, who was a fine astronomer but a bit of a new-ager when it came to the Great Pyramid. He had surveyed the pyramid and declared it a repository of ancient wisdom inspired by God. Soon he would be labeled a pyramidiot by scientists and archaeologists, but when Grand Master Anthony gave his speech, there were still plenty of people who believed the theory. The references to coded messages and prophecies were nothing new. Then, toward the end of his speech, came his real message.

Referring to the committee of Alexandrian Masons who declared the base had been built by fellow Freemasons, Grand Master Anthony proclaimed that many people believed there were Freemasons in ancient Egypt, but they were wrong. The grand master explained that modern Freemasons do share many principles in common with the ancient Egyptian builders, but when one looked at the timeline of Freemasonry, it simply didn't go back that far. There were no Freemasons in ancient Egypt.[5]

Grand Master Anthony was right. The Masons had always believed their origins went all the way back to ancient Egypt. This was a holdover from the Renaissance when it was widely believed that Egypt was a repository of all lost or mystical knowledge. Freemasonry actually dates back to medieval stonemason guilds; originally it was not a fraternal order. Masons were unlike other craftsmen, such as carpenters or weavers. They didn't sell their products or engage in trade because stone buildings were reserved for castles and cathedrals. Houses and other ordinary buildings were constructed of wood. The Middle Ages was the golden era of cathedral building. It often took a century to complete a cathedral, so there was plenty of work for masons of all types and skill levels. Two kinds of stone were needed for a cathedral: hard stone used for the structure and softer freestone used for carving the facing. The freestone masons were the elite, needing artistic ability on top of basic stone-working skills. Eventually freestone masons became known as freemasons, the origin of the modern term.

Masons of all levels worked long days, often 14 hours during summer, with only two breaks for meals. On the worksite, they built lodges in which to take their meals, thus the tradition of the Masonic Lodge. Later, in the eighteenth century, the masons evolved into a fraternal order that had nothing to do with building in stone.

Grand Master Anthony's presentation was carefully reasoned, thoughtful, and with a clear conclusion: Ancient freemasons did not build the monument they were inaugurating. There is no record of the reaction of Lieutenant-Commander Gorringe or his fellow Masons. Were they shocked? Disappointed? We just don't know. All indications are that they were thrilled to be conducting the ceremony and delighted to be part of such a historic event.

LANDING THE OBELISK

On the following day, October 11, the 50-ton pedestal was lifted into place on top of the three steps, awaiting the obelisk's arrival. Before Gorringe reached New York, he had planned how to offload the obelisk from the hull of the *Dessoug*. The ship would go into dry dock, then the loading procedure would be reversed. All the wood struts that held it in place would be removed, the obelisk would be jacked up a few inches with hydraulic jacks so the channel irons and iron balls could be slipped under it, and then it would be hauled out of the aperture in the hull. As soon as he arrived in New York, Gorringe set out to find the right dry dock. Unfortunately, only one was suitable, and

Color Plate 20. This Austrian bronze sculpture is a cigarette lighter. The striker is in the saddlebag and the flint is on the camel's saddle.

Color Plate 21. The striker for this oriental cigarette lighter is in the jar next to the praying man.

Color Plate 22. The small box next to the pipe smoker contains his matches.

Color Plate 23. A tobacco humidor shaped like a canopic jar (a container for the internal organs of a mummy).

Color Plate 24. The ibis on this cigarette dispenser dipped down, picked up a cigarette in its beak, and offered it to the smoker.

Color Plate 25.   Chatelaines were decorative chains suspended from Victorian ladies' belts. They could hold keys, silver pencils, and scissors all at once.

Color Plate 26.   A crystal perfume vial to be suspended from a chatelaine.

Color Plate 27.   Ladies wore charm mummy cases with tiny mummies inside.

Color Plate 28.   Winged scarab pins were especially popular.

Color Plate 29. *Some winged scarab pins looked more like American eagles.*

Color Plate 30. *One "winged scarab" pin used a trilobite fossil rather than a scarab.*

Color Plate 31. *Masonic gold and amethyst baton used at the installation ceremony for the New York obelisk. Illustration courtesy of the Chancellor Robert R. Livingston, Masonic Library of Grand Lodge, New York, NY.*

THE GREATEST THREAD AND NEEDLE IN THE WORLD.

Color Plate 32.   Because the obelisk was called "Cleopatra's Needle," sewing goods manufacturers used the obelisk connection to sell their products.

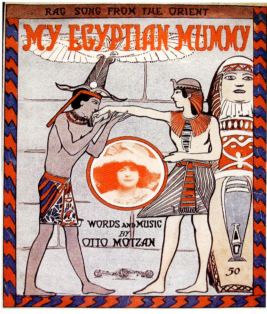

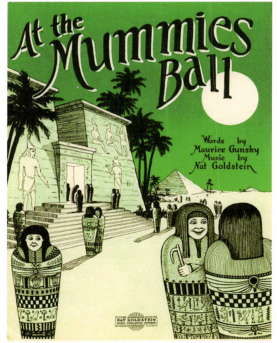

Color Plate 33.   Mummies were not always viewed as objects of horror.

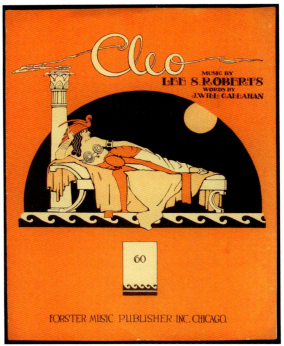

Color Plate 34.
Cleopatra was a recurring
theme for 1920s songs.

once the owner heard about the obelisk, he requested an exorbitant rate. Gorringe walked out. Now he needed a new plan.

There was an alternative to a dry dock—a marine railway at Staten Island. A marine railway is basically a cradle on pilings next to the shoreline. A ship is sailed into the cradle and the cradle lifted above the high tide level so the ship can be worked on and repaired. The obelisk had gone into the *Dessoug*'s hull at an angle of 21 degrees, and it would have to come out at that angle. Gorringe sank pilings into the water and built what looked like a boardwalk right next to the marine railway, at a 21-degree angle. When the obelisk exited the hull, it would go onto the boardwalk. After two weeks, everything was ready. The hull was opened, the iron railings and balls were placed under the obelisk, and 50 minutes after the hydraulic jack began tugging on the obelisk, it was resting safely on the boardwalk. Now came the hard part.

The obelisk was resting safely on its pier, but the 230-ton monolith still had to be lifted onto some sort of barge that could be towed to Manhattan. The question was how to lift it. Gorringe's solution was as brilliant as it was simple: Let the tide do the work. He had designed the pier pilings so that two pontoons could be brought under the pier and thus under the obelisk. When the tide came in, the pontoons rose, lifting the pier's crossbeams with the obelisk on them. The two pontoons were towed free of the pier and lashed together to form a kind of catamaran with the obelisk fixed to the deck. The plan was to tow it 12 miles around the southern tip of Manhattan, up the Hudson River to 96th Street, where a landing stage had been prepared. On September 6, the obelisk began moving slowly toward its new home. All along the way boats tooted their steam whistles welcoming New York's newest and most celebrated resident.

The obelisk reached the loading stage during high tide, just as planned. The pontoons were floated between pilings that had been sunk into the water so that the crossbeams on which the obelisk rested formed a boardwalk, like the one he had built at Staten Island. Because of high tide, they were floating a few feet above the pilings. As planned, valves in the pontoons were opened to fill them with water. As the pontoons sank lower in the water, the crossbeams and obelisk settled on the pilings. The obelisk had now officially landed on Manhattan Island and was about to begin its remarkable journey to Central Park.

THE OVERLAND JOURNEY

Gorringe had already planned the route the obelisk would take to the park and knew the first few hundred feet would be the most difficult. The Hudson River Railway ran along the riverside, so its tracks were between the obelisk, as it lay on the boardwalk, and 96th Street, where the obelisk would begin wending its way through New York City streets. The obelisk would have to cross the railroad tracks quickly to avoid the frequent passenger trains that traversed them. Gorringe had a team of workers lay timbers from the boardwalk across the tracks and onto 96th Street. On this he would lay the iron channels that held the cannonballs on which the obelisk would roll. The wood pathway was designed so it could be taken apart and reassembled rapidly. For days the workers practiced the maneuver until they knew every timber and its place intimately. Finally, on September 25, it was ready.

Fortunately, William H. Vanderbilt, who was paying to move the obelisk, also owned the railroad. Railroad officials were instructed to stop all incoming trains at 11:00 A.M. Soon after, the workmen frenetically assembled the wood path, laid the iron channels on top of it, and attached the obelisk by an enormous iron chain to an engine of one of the pile drivers, which had been repositioned to pull the obelisk over the tracks. The men had been so well prepared that the entire operation, including disassembling the iron channels and wood path, took a

Fig. 7.5   The obelisk crossed the Hudson River railroad tracks in less than two hours, hardly disrupting passengers.

mere 1 hour and 20 minutes (Fig. 7.5). This was the last time the iron channels and cannonballs could be used. The channels would split under the enormous weight. For the two-mile journey to Central Park, something even stronger was needed.

The obelisk would sit in a steel cradle with rollers attached underneath, and a pile driver engine would winch the cradle with the obelisk in it. Tracks were laid along the first leg of the route on 96th Street from the Hudson River to West Boulevard, today's West End Avenue. There was a 60-foot climb from 96th Street by the Hudson River to West Boulevard. Engines can't pull heavy loads up steep grades, so tracks were laid to make the grade as gentle as possible. Holes were drilled into boulders as attachments for cables to anchor the tracks. This difficult piece of engineering required considerable precision to complete. It took over a month for the obelisk to travel its first quarter mile in a straight line to West Boulevard.

Because of steep grades and difficult terrain, the obelisk couldn't go directly to the pedestal; it had to go all the way east through the park to Fifth Avenue. Even with the longer, gentler route, the trip across Central Park soon became a battle with the forces of nature.

The trek worsened as a bitter December cold wave hit New York and heavy snows fell for days. Soon members of Gorringe's handpicked team began dropping out, victims of exposure to the elements. Gorringe formed those who remained into two teams that worked round the clock, replacing each other at 6:00 A.M. and 6:00 P.M. Each day the foreman estimated a reasonable distance that could be covered; if the men exceeded it, they received bonuses. To encourage his crews and show solidarity, Gorringe spent six hours with each day crew and five with the evening crews. After 19 brutal days exposed to the elements, the obelisk had completed the half-mile journey across the park and turned south on Fifth Avenue. The goal was almost within sight.

The final leg of the journey to the pedestal was just 890 feet but required tremendous advance preparation. The obelisk had to be lowered onto the pedestal that rested on the highest point in Central Park. This meant that it had to gain about 50 feet of elevation. In October, Gorringe had begun constructing a railroad trestle from Fifth Avenue to the final location of the obelisk. While his workers were fighting the elements, hauling the obelisk through the park in November and December, another team of workers was building the massive trestle out of timbers as thick as 17 inches. On December 28, just as the obelisk was to begin its journey on the trestle, a blizzard hit New York, and all work was suspended for several days. When the snows finally let up, the obelisk continued its odyssey, arriving at Greywacke Knoll on January 5, 1881. It was positioned so that its center of gravity was directly above the pedestal. Now all that remained was to turn the obelisk vertically and lower it onto the pedestal.

SECRET REHEARSAL

Just beneath the trestle Gorringe had previously reassembled the masonry base on which the turning mechanism used in Alexandria had rested. The obelisk was scheduled to be moved onto its pedestal at noon on January 22. On January 20, near midnight, Gorringe and a small team of trusted workers quietly entered Central Park. In the frigid cold, under the light of a quarter moon, the obelisk floated, suspended horizontally over its pedestal. Gorringe wanted to test whether it would turn easily. The team stealthily went to work. Several workers pulled on the cables attached to the obelisk's base while others gave slack to the cables at the tip. The obelisk began to pivot on its center of gravity, silently coming to rest in the vertical position above the pedestal. Reassured, the men returned the obelisk to the horizontal position and left.

The next day a violent storm tore through New York, causing extensive damage throughout the city, but the obelisk remained unmoved, suspended high above its pedestal. Throughout the morning of January 22, New Yorkers filed into Central Park, seeking good vantage points to see the obelisk erected. The park was covered in snow with punishing winds blowing, but by 11:30 A.M., more than 10,000 people crowded the site. A grandstand had been built for dignitaries, and a little before noon, a Marine band marched into the park and took its place. Soon after, the carriages of William M. Evarts, the secretary of state; William Hurlbert, the editor of the *New York World*; and others pulled up to the grandstand. They descended and took their seats in the stands.

ERECTING THE OBELISK

Gorringe had arranged a signal to turn the obelisk with the workmen; when he raised his hand, they would begin working the cables to turn the obelisk and would continue turning it until he lowered his hand. With no fanfare—it was bitter cold—Gorringe raised his hand. As the massive shaft of granite began to move effortlessly, an

unnatural silence fell over the crowd. When the obelisk reached 45
degrees, Gorringe lowered his hand to allow the famous photographer
Edward Bierstadt to record the moment. After a very brief pause for
the photo, the obelisk continued turning. The spell of silence broke,
and the crowd began cheering until the obelisk was perfectly vertical,
suspended above its pedestal. The turning and photography took only
five minutes, and at its completion the military band played patriotic
tunes. The crowd, eager to get out of the cold, quickly dispersed. As
everyone happily headed indoors, Gorringe still had a long cold day of
work ahead of him.

The obelisk was vertical, but it still had to be lowered onto its
pedestal. Gorringe's method of seating the obelisk was the third tech-
nique that the obelisk had experienced in its 3,000-year history. In the
time of Tuthmosis III, when it was carved and erected in Heliopolis,
the Egyptian masons placed it directly on its pedestal with no support other than gravity. Fifteen hundred years later, when the Romans
moved the obelisk to Alexandria, they crafted four bronze crabs with
poles protruding from their bodies that slipped into slots cut in the
pedestal and the bottom of the obelisk. We do not know why they
chose this method, but a clue may be the corners of the obelisk—or,
more accurately, the lack of corners. The four corners at the bottom are
missing, broken in antiquity. The bottom of the obelisk now had only
about two-thirds of its original surface area. Perhaps the Romans were
afraid that this reduced surface area was not enough for the obelisk to
balance on safely, and thus they added the extra support of the crabs.
This gave the obelisk a slightly different look because it now rested on
the crabs, not the pedestal. This is how the obelisk remained for nearly
2,000 years until it was moved again, this time to Central Park. Gorringe began to implement a combination of the ancient Egyptian and
Roman methods of placing the obelisk on its base.

His plan was to spread a thin layer of cement on the pedestal and then lower the obelisk onto it by using the turning mechanism. Cement, however, doesn't pour in freezing weather. The team of workers had to heat the surface and spread the cement repeatedly before one pour finally set. It wasn't until 8:00 P.M. on January 22 that the obelisk was finally balancing on its pedestal, looking much as it had in ancient Egyptian times. Completing the process of fixing the obelisk to the pedestal would take an additional 10 days of hard work. To ensure the stability of the obelisk, Gorringe used the Roman method of bronze crabs. Over the previous months, craftsmen at the Brooklyn Navy Yard had made plaster casts of the broken crabs, carved the missing parts, and cast four replica bronze crabs weighing more than 900 pounds each. Working in the bitter cold, it took Gorringe's workers more than a week to install the crabs at the corners of the obelisk. The New York obelisk now rested directly on its pedestal, anchored by crabs at the corners. Finally Gorringe could relax; his job was done.

EGYPTOMANIA, POLITICS, AND THOMAS NAST

New Yorkers had followed the obelisk's journey across the Atlantic and through Central Park with growing fascination. Among them was a 39-year-old political cartoonist named Thomas Nast, who capitalized on New York's new interest in Egypt. *Leslie's* weekly magazine employed the best engravers and artists of the time, and it was in this atmosphere that young Nast learned the techniques that would make him famous. During the Civil War, Nast's patriotic cartoons helped sustain the war effort in the North. Abraham Lincoln said, "Thomas Nast had been our best recruiting sergeant. His emblematic cartoons have never failed to arouse enthusiasm and patriotism, and have always seemed to come just when these articles were getting scarce."[6] Nast then moved on to the more influential *Harper's Weekly*, where he created the familiar images of Uncle Sam, the Republican elephant, and the Democratic donkey. As New York's obelisk was steaming toward New York, America was embroiled in a great political scandal, and Nast, the political reformer, jumped in, but with an Egyptian twist.

Nast's main target was Samuel J. Tilden, leader of the Democratic Party. Tilden and his running mate, Governor William Hendricks of Indiana, had been caught in the 1876 presidential election trying to buy votes, but this did not end his career. Later, a Senate committee obtained copies of telegrams sent during the Democratic convention by Tilden to his nephew and secretary, Colonel Pelton. These telegrams were in code but were printed by the *New York Tribune* with suggestions as to their meaning. Each day more code was revealed, and each day thousands of readers bought papers for the next thrilling installment. Finally, when the full cipher was broken, it was clear that Tilden had attempted to buy the presidency. Nast went after Tilden with his pen. Tilden is shown as a mummy, but instead of the striped-cloth nemes-headdress that the pharaohs wore, Tilden's is decorated with dollar signs. Above his head, where in ancient times there might be a winged scarab, there is a winged bag of money.

On the central panel of the coffin are the actual cipher telegrams that had been published in the *Tribune*. The address on the first telegram is 15 Gramercy Park, Tilden's address, and it also appears as a keyhole beneath the mummy's chin. Tilden's chief conspirators were C. W. Woolley, whose code name was "Fox," and Manton Marble, whose code name was "Moses." Both names appear on the mummy's shoulder.

The first telegram, when deciphered, read:

Have just received a proposition to hand over
at any hour required Tilden decision of board
and certificate of governor for $200,000

While $200,000 was the amount for the payoff, other amounts had
been discussed, and bargaining had been going on. The second telegram on the coffin reads:

Board may make necessary expenses on half
a hundred thousand dollars. Can you say
will deposit in bank immediately if agreed?

The last telegram on the coffin is the reply:

Telegram received. Will deposit dollars agreed.
You cannot however draw before vote [of]
member[s] received.

Incredibly, Tilden remained a political force for another decade. When
the 1880 presidential election was near, the Democratic Party was in
trouble. It couldn't nominate Tilden because he couldn't win, but not
to nominate him would look like an admission of guilt for bribery.
John Kelly, the Democratic leader of Tammany Hall, even declared
that he would rather a Republican were elected than Tilden. Rumor
had it that Tilden would withdraw his candidacy. Fearful that Tilden
might still resurrect at the Democratic convention in Cincinnati,
Nast depicted a pharaonic Democratic Party laboring under the heavy
weight of Tilden's coffin.

Tilden, still very much alive and attempting to gain the nomination, sent a letter of withdrawal to the convention, in the misguided

hope it would draw him the nomination by acclaim. The ploy did not work; the convention elected General Hancock as its candidate. Always ready to ridicule Tilden, Nast showed Tilden and his running mate Hendricks as mummies, suggesting that they stay that way. Hendrick's name is written with a pseudohieroglyphic hen on his coffin (Fig. 7.6).

New Yorkers now had a double dose of Egyptomania. They were thoroughly enjoying Nast's Egyptian-themed political cartoons while at the same time they were enthralled with Gorringe's heroics erecting the obelisk in Central Park.

OBELISK MANIA

The official ceremony to welcome the obelisk to New York was held on February 22 in the Grand Reception Gallery of the new Metropolitan Museum of Art. The event was by invitation only, but by 2:00 P.M., more than 20,000 people crowded around the museum, wanting to be part of the festive occasion. The installation of New York's obelisk began a wave of Egyptomania, producing all kinds of collectibles. In the 1880s, merchants frequently gave their customers trade cards, the equivalent of today's baseball cards. These colorful cards had various pictures on the front—the Taj Mahal, a Japanese pagoda, or perhaps an opera star. When you made a purchase, you were given a card that you could put in your album at home. Since the obelisk was called "Cleopatra's Needle," it was natural that sewing goods stores created cards capitalizing on the obelisk's fame. The John English Needle Co. produced a beautiful card showing Cleopatra threading a needle that's an inverted obelisk. Stores selling their needles received these cards, and the stores then printed their addresses and advertisements on the back (Color Plate 32). J. P. Coats produced a card showing the obelisk being towed to New York using Coats threads. The reverse is a calendar

Fig. 7.6 Cartoonist Thomas Nast used pharaonic themes to lampoon Samuel Tilden, who was caught trying to buy votes for his presidential election. Even after the scandal Tilden hoped for the presidential nomination. Nast showed him and his running mate, Hendriks, as mummies. Hendriks's name is spelled with a hen, a pseudohieroglyph. On Tilden's coffin is a windmill, a symbol of New York.

for 1880–1881 (Color Plate 32). One of the most inventive is Corticelli's Spool Silk card showing the obelisk being erected by angels using silk threads (Color Plate 32).

Gorringe released a new wave of Egyptomania by bringing the obelisk to New York, but he did not live long to enjoy his accomplishment. A few years after placing Cleopatra's Needle on its pedestal, he tripped while boarding a moving train, hit his head, and died from his injuries. Only 45, Gorringe didn't live long enough to see the explosion of Egyptomania in popular culture and the forms it would take in the twentieth century.

EIGHT

The Mummies Sing Songs of the Nile

At the close of the nineteenth century, the London and New York obelisks had established Egyptomania on both sides of the Atlantic. The great British Egyptologist Sir Flinders Petrie was excavating all over Egypt, and the illustrated newspapers trumpeted his finds to an eager audience. Petrie's finds were interesting, but in 1881, there was a spectacular find unequaled in the annals of Egyptology: The pharaohs themselves had been discovered.

A CACHE OF ROYAL MUMMIES

Before this, not a single pharaoh's mummy had been uncovered despite 100 years of assiduous searching. All the pyramids had been robbed in antiquity, and all the royal tombs had been thoroughly looted—as least as far as anyone knew or was saying. But someone was *not* saying because in the 1870s, spectacular objects once belonging to pharaohs started appearing on the antiquities market. It could only mean one thing: a great royal find.

Auguste Mariette, director of the Egyptian Antiquities Service, had purchased a papyrus of the *Book of the Dead* belonging to Queen Henettowey of the Twenty-first Dynasty from a Luxor antiquities dealer. The book was in remarkable condition, the colors of the vignettes accompanying the spells to ensure resurrection remained vibrant and bright, suggesting that the book had been found recently. During the next few years other royal copies of the *Book of the Dead* appeared on the market, all from kings, queens, princesses, and princes of the family of Henettowey. In addition to the papyri, beautiful jewelry also surfaced, and it became clear to Mariette that an intact royal tomb of the Twenty-first Dynasty had been discovered, and its contents were being sold off piecemeal. Mariette was determined to find the tomb before everything was looted, but he died in 1881 before he could complete his search. His successor, Gaston Maspero, made this his top priority.

When Maspero arrived in Luxor, he enlisted the help of a former student, Charles Edwin Wilbour. Wilbour, an expatriate American businessman and politician, became interested in Egyptology in his 40s. He studied in Paris under Maspero and became one of the most dedicated recorders of ancient texts. Wilbour's passion was collecting antiquities, and today many of his purchases reside in the Brooklyn Museum. He was copying inscriptions in Luxor when Maspero came to find the tomb.

Maspero asked him to keep his ears open, and Wilbour soon heard rumors that the el Rassoul family was plundering a newly found tomb. The family lived in Qurna, the village adjoining the Valley of the Kings. For generations its inhabitants had followed the vocation of tomb robbing, and now it appeared as if they had made their greatest find. Wilbour was offered the leather straps that encircled the mummy of King Pinedjem I. In a letter to his wife dated March 8, 1881, Wilbour writes that he thinks the brothers will lead him to the tomb. He was wrong.

With Maspero in Luxor, the el Rassoul family was justifiably nervous. They knew that the "Grand Moudir (master) of Antikas" had come to find their tomb and take away the fortune in antiquities that the village of Qurna viewed as theirs. Maspero sent for Ahmed el Rassoul, who denied everything. When his house was searched, only a few worthless antiquities were found.

Maspero sent two of the Rassoul brothers, Ahmed and Hussein, to Qena for questioning by Daud Pasha, who was a brutal interrogator. Neither man confessed, but one of the brothers limped for the rest of his life. Maspero then had to leave for France, but the Rassoul brothers knew this would not be the end of the questioning. Muhammed, the eldest, went to Daud Pasha and confessed that he knew where the tomb was and that it contained 40 mummies. Daud sent word to the museum at Boulaq (the Egyptian Museum in Cairo had not yet been built), and Émile Brugsch, Maspero's assistant, went to Qurna immediately.

Daud had reasoned that the Rassouls would make one last trip to the tomb before revealing its location, so he searched their house a second time and found three copies of the *Book of the Dead*, which he presented to Brugsch. Two days later, the brothers were leading Brugsch along an elevated, winding path overlooking the Valley of the Kings.

FACE-TO-FACE WITH PHARAOH

The path wound through the area known as Deir el-Bahri, site of Queen Hatshepsut's mortuary temple. As they walked, Brugsch, his two assistants, and the Rassouls must have had quite different thoughts. The Rassouls were about to lose a fortune; Brugsch and his party could only imagine what they were about to find. The Rassouls stopped at the base of a chimney-like outcropping. They found a shaft eight feet by ten feet, descending forty feet down into the rock. Muhammed placed a palm log across the opening and let himself down by a rope so he could clear the sand blocking the small entrance at the bottom. Brugsch followed. When he squeezed through the entrance, the first thing he saw was the huge coffin of Nebseni, a priest of the Twenty-first Dynasty. Behind it were three more coffins, and past these, on the right, ran a corridor more than 70 feet long. Littering the floor were bright blue faience *ushabtis*—servant statues—faience cups, canopic jars and chests, and all the other equipment an ancient Egyptian needed for the next world. At the corridor's end stood a room 17 feet square. Almost every foot of space was covered with splendid coffins, with inscriptions naming their inhabitants. Here lay the greatest pharaohs of ancient Egypt: Amenhotep I, Tuthmose I, Tuthmose II, and Tuthmose III of the Eighteenth Dynasty. Next to them were the Nineteenth Dynasty pharaohs, Ramses I, his son Seti I, and his son, Ramses II. It was more than Brugsch could have ever imagined.

Farther back in the tomb was another room, much higher than the others and 20 feet long. It was here that the search came to an end. The room held the Twenty-first Dynasty royal family whose *Books of the Dead* had initiated the quest. The mummies of Pinedjem I and Pinedjem II, Queen Henettowey, and others of this family of priest-kings all rested in this room. It was a stupendous find.

The question was, how had the kings of the Twenty-first Dynasty come to be buried with the kings of the Eighteenth and Nineteenth dynasties? The answer was security.

WHAT'S A ROYAL MUMMY LIKE YOU
DOING IN A TOMB LIKE THIS?

Toward the end of the Twentieth Dynasty, a succession of pharaohs named Ramses lost their grasp on the throne. Near the end of the dynasty High Priest Hrihor wrote his name in a cartouche and declared himself king. His descendants formed the Twenty-first Dynasty. Knowing that the previous dynasty had been weak and that there had been robberies in the Valley of the Kings, the Twenty-first Dynasty priests inspected and inventoried the royal tombs. They found that most of the tombs had been violated, treasures stolen, and many of the royal mummies damaged by thieves looking for jewelry. They rewrapped the mummies, labeled them, placed them in new coffins, and moved them to a safe place. They recorded the steps taken to preserve the royal mummies in black ink, both on the coffins as well as the walls of the original tombs.

Finally, the priests moved all of the mummies to the secret cache in a high tomb at Deir el-Bahri, where they remained undisturbed for 3,000 years. This was the answer to the question of how mummies of different dynasties came to be buried in the same tomb. After two hours in the tomb, Brugsch realized that the candles they had brought might set fire to the dry coffin wood, so they left quickly. Brugsch knew that the mummies and their funerary equipment had to be moved to Cairo as quickly and quietly as possible. For centuries the inhabitants of Qurna had made their living by robbing tombs. There was no telling what they would do once they realized that they were about to lose the riches that had supported the village. In six frantic days, 300 workers from nearby villages wrapped all the coffins and funerary goods for transport, hoisted them to the surface, and carried them across the blistering desert to the west bank of the Nile.

OFF TO CAIRO

There the treasures of Deir el-Bahri were loaded onto the museum's steamer. On June 15, the steamer began its journey to Cairo. When word of its royal cargo became public, peasant women lined the banks of the Nile and wailed, just as their remote ancestors must have mourned the passing of the pharaohs. When the mummies arrived safely at the Boulaq Museum, Brugsch unwrapped only one, that of Tuthmosis III, the greatest of the Eighteenth Dynasty warrior pharaohs. Brugsch and his colleagues became the first people in modern times to gaze on the face of a king of ancient Egypt. The Royal Cache, as it became known, created a sensation (Fig. 8.1). The *Illustrated London News* devoted

QUEEN MATHOR HONT-TAUI, TWENTY-FIRST DYNASTY.   KING THOTHMES II, EIGHTEENTH DYNASTY.   THE PRIEST NEBSENI.

Fig. 8.1   The discovery of a cache of royal mummies in 1881 was covered by all the newspapers. It created a sensation, and mummies became all the rage.

four pages to the incredible discovery, complete with beautifully drawn illustrations.

MUMMY MANIA

Mummies have always fascinated the public, but the discovery of the Royal Cache at Deir el-Bahri put mummy mania in high gear. Over the next decade, Gaston Maspero unwrapped the remaining 40 royal mummies, and each new pharaoh's face created a sensation. The mummy with the greatest impact was Ramses II, who was almost certainly the pharaoh of the biblical Exodus—the pharaoh who refused to let Moses and his people leave until the ten plagues forced him to relent. His is the only face from the Bible that anyone will ever see. The public was enthralled with Egyptian mummies so it was only a short time until they entered popular culture.

MUMMY MUSIC

At the end of the nineteenth century, a song's success was measured by how many sheets of music were sold. Every home that could afford it had a piano in the parlor and a stack of sheet music. More often than not, that stack contained an Egyptian song, and if the lyrics were about a mummy, so much the better.

Thousands of sheets of music were produced in Tin Pan Alley, on 28th Street between Broadway and Sixth Avenue in New York. Here, in brownstone buildings, music publishers had printing presses in the basements, offices above, and, on the third floor, piano rooms where the musicians and composers banged out their latest songs. With this concentration of composers and lyricists on the premises, it was inevitable that if one publisher had a hit song, another could quickly commission a spin-off, and they all wanted mummy songs. The mummies in tunes were not the grisly fiends that would later be created for the movies. In song lyrics they were usually female and objects of romance.

"Mummy Mine" (1918) was typical of this genre (Color Plate 33).

> Mummy, a million years you have been sleeping, friendlessly.
>
> Mummy, a million years I've used in weeping endlessly.
>
> I've waited thro' the years just sighing,
>
> Oh can't you hear me again crying, Waken?
>
> Your love no more denying,
>
> Mummy mine, mine.[1]

The million years is a bit long; she'd be a fossil, not a mummy, but the sentiment is typical of Tin Pan Alley. "My Egyptian Mummy" (1913) laments the same concept of love lost over many years (Color Plate 33).

> My Egyptian mummy from the land of the pyramids,
>
> We were sweethearts years ago.
>
> That's why I know, though you were turned to stone,
>
> I almost hear you moan.
>
> I'm in love with you, I'm in love with you.[2]

Even in novelty mummy songs, they never were viewed as horrible creatures. In "At the Mummies Ball" (1921), we see mummies portrayed as party animals (Color Plate 33).

> Dressed in magnificent style,
>
> They were dancing all the while.

Great and small, high-steppers all,

Dancing at the Mummies Ball.

Cleopatra made them stare,

Vamped each old mummy there.

I do declare, Old King Ramesses shook himself to pieces,

Dancing at the Mummies Ball.[3]

Cleopatra was another natural topic for Egypt-themed pieces of music, and she was almost always associated with romance. The cover of the sheet music "Cleo" (1919) shows a rather sultry art nouveau Cleopatra reclining on her couch, but "Cleopatra Had a Jazz Band" was a light-hearted combination of the new music sensation (jazz) and history (Color Plate 34).

Cleopatra had a Jazz Band, in her castle on the Nile,

Every night she gave a jazz dance,

In her queer Egyptian style.

She won Marc Antony with her syncopated harmony.

And while they played, she swayed . . .

Egypt got the dancing craze, so the wise men say, And when they

heard that music start, The natives began to sway.

Caesar came from Rome to learn, to dance the latest step.

And when he heard those Jazzers play, he sure was full of pep.[4]

As mentioned, at the beginning of the twentieth century, few tourists had been to Egypt. Movies and television were in the future, so Egypt was very much a place of mystery and romance, the perfect subject for love songs. "'Neath the Shadow of the Pyramids" (1914) was typical of the genre. Its cover has all the iconic Egyptian imagery—the pyramid and sphinx, the camel caravan—but most prominent is the maiden proclaiming her love.

> River Nile, please flow away,
>
> Carry a message to my own and say
>
> That my love shall last until the Sphinx has passed,
>
> 'Neath the shadow of the pyramids, 'neath the pyramids.[5]

Some of the writers of these romantic lyrics seem to have been geographically challenged. "My Sahara Rose" (1920) sports an attractive girl on the cover in front of the pyramid and sphinx, but the song's first line is a surprise: "I saw her face, 'twas in the market place in old Bagdad."[6] Perhaps our Sahara Rose was on a road trip (Color Plate 35).

The cover of "Ilo" (1921) shows another Oriental beauty and proclaims we shall hear a "Voice from Mummyland" (Color Plate 35). The first line: "I am on my way again to Madagascar Bay."[7] Wrong again, but this is far from the worst of the mix-ups. My favorite is a nicely designed cover showing the sphinx flanked by two Egyptian falcon gods holding ancient Egyptian symbols of power (Color Plate 37). Here we don't even have to wait for the first line for the geographical surprise. The title? "Aphrodite" (1919). What's a nice Greek goddess like this doing in an Egyptian love song?

Egyptian songs were all the rage at the beginning of the twentieth century, but the 1920s would see Egyptomania explode with the discovery of Tutankhamen's tomb.

NINE

Tutankhamen, Superstar

Ask anyone to name an Egyptian pharaoh, and the answer will probably be "King Tut." Tutankhamen's fame isn't due to anything he did while alive; it comes solely from the discovery of his fabulous tomb, the only intact pharaoh's tomb ever found in the Valley of the Kings. Before the tomb was discovered, Tutankhamen was unknown to the public and hardly known by Egyptologists. His name first appears toward the end of the nineteenth century when British Egyptologist Flinders Petrie began excavating Tell el-Amarna. Amarna was the sacred city built by the monotheistic pharaoh Akhenaten to worship the solar god, the Aten. Among Petrie's finds were small objects inscribed with the names Tutankhamen and Tutankhaten, variants of Tut's name. Who this unknown king was, and where he fit into the Egyptian royal family, remained a mystery for decades until Howard Carter discovered the tomb in the Valley of the Kings. The discovery did not come easily.

PREFERABLY NOT A GENTLEMAN

Carter's introduction to Egyptology came via his talent as an artist. His father, Samuel John Carter, made a living painting animal portraits.

Howard, the youngest of 11 children, inherited his father's artistic abilities. The elder Carter had been the portrait painter for Lord Amherst's family, so as a young boy, Howard often accompanied his father to Didlington Hall, the Amherst family estate, and was fascinated by the collection of Egyptian antiquities there. The Amhersts were patrons of the Egypt Exploration Fund, Britain's recently formed organization for excavating and recording the monuments of Egypt. One of the fund's excavators requested an artist, "preferably a non-gentleman," to copy scenes from the tomb walls. The Amhersts recommended 17-year-old Howard Carter, who, with virtually no formal schooling, fit the bill perfectly. Soon Carter was on a steamer bound for Egypt.

Carter quickly proved to be both competent and hardworking, living happily in the simple surroundings of an expedition camp. He learned excavation techniques from Flinders Petrie at Amarna, skills that would later serve him well. Petrie, the most skilled excavator in Egypt, had begun uncovering clues to the life of Tutankhamen at Amarna, but neither Petrie nor Carter could have any idea that a quarter century later, Carter would discover the tomb of Tutankhamen and become the most famous Egyptologist of all time. Indeed, as Carter worked on the site, he probably handled objects inscribed with Tutankhamen's name but had no idea who the boy-king was.

Carter worked on other excavations as well, and by the age of 26 had mastered the techniques of archaeology so well that the Antiquities Service appointed him chief inspector of Southern Egypt. Carter was energetic, diligent, and concerned about preserving Egypt's monuments. In addition to supervising excavators, he had iron gates installed on tomb entrances to prevent vandalism, and he had electric lights mounted inside so tourists could see the wall paintings.

At the beginning of the twentieth century, a wealthy American, Theodore M. Davis, appeared on the scene. Carter arranged for him to excavate in the Valley of the Kings, under Carter's supervision. In the first year, they found the plundered tomb of Tuthmosis IV. For some reason, the ancient tomb robbers had abandoned many objects, including beautiful blue faience servant figures as well as part of the pharaoh's chariot, decorated with battle scenes. Davis was elated, and although Carter and Davis worked well together, it was not to last. In 1904, Carter was transferred north to oversee the monuments at Saqqâra, 14 miles south of Cairo. Carter became involved in an incident that ended his career in the Antiquities Service.

An unruly group of French tourists forced their way past a tomb guard and refused to leave. Carter was called to the scene. When the French assaulted the tomb guards, Carter told the guards to defend themselves, and a melee ensued. The French were outraged that the Egyptian guards had hit them, but Carter took the guards' side and wanted to prosecute the French. In colonial Egypt, it was unheard of for an Egyptian to strike a European. The matter reached the highest diplomatic levels in Egypt, and Carter was ordered to apologize to the French. He refused. Gaston Maspero, director of the Antiquities Service, sympathized with Carter but was forced to reprimand him. The outraged Carter resigned, never to return to the Antiquities Service. He was now a free agent.

IN SEARCH OF TUTANKHAMEN

Back in Luxor, Davis, now without the services of Carter, employed 22-year-old Edward R. Ayrton to continue the excavations in the valley. Like most of Petrie's disciples, Ayrton was well trained and served Davis well. He discovered the plundered tomb of the pharaoh Horemheb. He also found the first clue to Tutankhamen's tomb lodged under a rock—a faience cup bearing the pharaoh's name. Excited by this find,

Ayrton and Davis continued their search for Tutankhamen's tomb. In 1907, they discovered a small pit containing the remains of an ancient meal. Mixed with the food, cups, and wine jars were floral garlands and mummy wrappings that bore the name of Tutankhamen. Davis didn't understand the meaning of his find—he thought he had uncovered reburied plunder from Tutankhamen's tomb. What he actually found were the remains of the ritual funerary meal eaten by Tutankhamen's mourners on the day of his burial. Along with this meal were remnants of materials used to mummify the king. Davis made his second Tutankhamen-related discovery in 1909, a small unfinished tomb that contained some broken furniture and gold foil with the name Tutankhamen. He concluded he had found the plundered tomb of Tutankhamen. He was wrong.

Each year Davis self-published his finds in a series of sumptuous books containing a description of the excavation and objects found. Some of these books included watercolor illustrations by Howard Carter, who was then unemployed and grateful for the work. In the preface to the volume on the Tutankhamen findings, Davis concluded, "I fear the Valley is now exhausted."[1] He would soon give up his concession to excavate in the Valley of the Kings, clearing the path for Howard Carter to obtain the concession.

THE EARL AND THE ARCHAEOLOGIST

While Davis was excavating in the valley, George Edward Stanhope Molyneux Herbert, the fifth Earl of Carnarvon, a wealthy aristocrat and art collector, began excavating. He also had a passion for racehorses and automobiles and has the unfortunate distinction of being involved in the world's first near-fatal automobile crash. His accident had injured his lungs, and he went to Egypt to recuperate. He developed a keen interest in archaeology, and he thought he would enjoy excavating, but he was too frail to play an active role.

When Carnarvon applied to Maspero for permission to excavate, Maspero, seeing a chance to help the impoverished Carter, suggested that Carnarvon employ him. In 1907, Lord Carnarvon and Howard Carter formed a partnership; Carnarvon would finance a series of excavations, and Carter would direct the work.

They were an odd couple. Lord Carnarvon had grown up with immense wealth, had great personal charm, and exhibited all the social graces. Carter came from a hardworking, middle-class family where he developed a no-nonsense attitude toward life, viewing issues as either black or white, right or wrong. He was a bachelor and a loner with few social skills and little personal charm. Although an unlikely team, Carnarvon and Carter developed a lasting friendship. Their relationship was always that of the lord and his vassal, but they cared for and protected each other.

THE SEARCH CONTINUES

For several years, they excavated near the Valley of the Kings and made modest finds. When Theodore Davis relinquished his concession for the Valley, Carter and Carnarvon took it over. Carter was sure Tutankhamen's tomb was there, waiting to be found. In 1914, he set out on a systematic and exhaustive search of the Valley that was interrupted by World War I. After the war, the search resumed in earnest. Carter was convinced that Tutankhamen's tomb lay somewhere within a triangle formed by the tombs of Merneptah, Ramses II, and Ramses VI, the only area in the Valley that had not been fully excavated. Carter worked down toward the base of the well-known tomb of Ramses VI, clearing thousands of baskets of debris. He uncovered the remains of a group of ancient workmen's huts. In order to proceed, Carter needed to clear the huts, but doing so would have closed Ramses VI's tomb, one of the most popular tourist sites in the Valley. So Carter decided to search elsewhere.

Five years went by as Carter assiduously scoured the Valley of the Kings, with no success. Lord Carnarvon came to believe that Davis had been right, that the Valley was played out. In 1922, he invited Howard Carter to Highclere Castle (site of the television series *Downton Abbey*) to inform the archaeologist that he had decided to end the excavation. Doing so must have been difficult for Carnarvon, given the bond that had developed between the two men. After so many years with no results, Carter was not surprised, but he was not yet ready to give up. He made a counterproposal. They would continue for one last season for which Carter would pay the expenses, and Carnarvon could keep anything they found. Carnarvon, touched by this bold gesture from the unmoneyed Carter, agreed to finance one last season.

A TOMB AT LAST

In 1922, Carter returned and began clearing the huts in the triangle formed by the tombs of Merneptah, Ramses II, and Ramses VI. On November 4, one of the waterboys discovered a step cut into the valley floor. After another day of clearing, a stairway going down into the bedrock lay exposed. At sunset on November 5, after the twelfth step was cleared, workers uncovered the upper part of a plastered entrance with the royal necropolis seal still in place. Carter knew they had discovered a king's tomb, but which one? Through a small hole near the top of the entrance, Carter could see a passageway filled with rubble to deter tomb robbers, indicating that the tomb was intact. Somehow able to keep his excitement in check, Carter filled in the stairway with sand and rubble and cabled Lord Carnarvon in England: "At last have made wonderful discovery in Valley; a magnificent tomb with seals intact, re-covered same for your arrival; congratulations."[2]

Carter waited almost a month for his friend, who arrived in Egypt the last week in November. During this time he made preparations for the opening of the tomb. The stairway was cleared again, and this time Tutankhamen's cartouche was revealed on the lower part of the sealed door. When the door was opened, the excavators could see an ancient narrow path through the rubble, almost certainly made by tomb robbers. The tomb had been entered before.

WONDERFUL THINGS

Workers devoted an entire day to clearing the 30-foot-long descending passage. Strewn among the limestone chips were alabaster jars, pottery, and workmen's tools. Finally they reached a second sealed door. This one clearly showed evidence of having been breached and sealed again. Carter made an opening in the upper left corner of the doorway to insert a candle to test the air inside. At first the flame fluttered in the escaping hot air. Carnarvon, behind Carter, asked, "Can you see anything?" Carter replied, "Yes, wonderful things."

The room, called the antechamber, was packed with all the possessions Tutankhamen would need in the next world. Chariots, statues, game boards, linens, jewelry, beds, couches, chairs, even a throne were all piled up on top of each other (Fig. 9.1). Because little had been disturbed, it is a good bet that the ancient robbers had been caught in the act or frightened away. The tomb was virtually intact.

The antechamber Carter peered into was only the first of four rooms, and it would take him more than a year to excavate it. Every object had to be photographed in place before it was removed.

Fig. 9.1   Tutankhamen's tomb was packed with everything he would need for the next world.

Often the wood objects were so fragile they had to be conserved before they could be moved. The public was frantic to learn more about Tutankhamen, the unknown pharaoh. Photographers and reporters camped outside the tomb to report each object as it emerged. The illustrated newspapers published weekly reports from the "Special Correspondents in the Valley of the Kings," and schoolchildren created scrapbooks with clippings chronicling Carter's progress.

Throughout the excavation, there were enough surprises and twists and turns for a murder mystery. Who was Tutankhamen? Who were his parents? (Nothing in the tomb mentioned his parents, and his parentage is still debated today.) Soon after the opening of the tomb, Lord Carnarvon died in Cairo of an infected mosquito bite. Reporters eager to sell papers created "The Curse of the Pharaoh."

Every day there was a new discovery. New objects meant new opportunities for hawkers to create postcards and souvenirs to sell to the

Exploitation of Tout-Ankh-Amon's Tomb

*Fig. 9.2   This Tutankhamen postcard has an interesting typo—
"exploitation" for "exploration"—not far from the truth.*

tourists who were flocking to the Valley of the Kings (Fig. 9.2). Tutankhamen was good business, and the music industry jumped on the bandwagon.

MAKING THE BOY KING SING

Soon after the discovery of Tutankhamen's tomb was announced, sheet music titled "Old King Tut" (1923) appeared for sale. A year after the song's publication, the excavators entered the burial chamber and finally gazed on the face of the long-dead pharaoh. Then the world discovered that Old King Tut wasn't old at all. Tutankhamen was a boy king who died at the age of 18 or 19. But no one knew this when "Old King Tut" was written, so Tut is depicted with a wrinkled face, smoking a cigar. As a matter of fact, so little was known that the lyric writer went for pure fantasy.

Three thousand years ago,
In history we know

King Tut-an-ka-men ruled a mighty land.

Mid laughter, song and tears,

He made a record that will always stand.

They opened up his tomb the other day and jumped with glee.

They learned a lot of ancient history:

His tomb instead of tears,

Was full of souvenirs.

He must have traveled greatly in his time.

The gold and silverware that they found hidden there,

Was from hotels of every land and clime.

While going through his royal robes they found up in his sleeve,

The first love letter Adam wrote to Eve.[3]

"Old King Tut" was a hit, and other publishers soon jumped on the bandwagon. J.W. Jenkins Sons Music Company thought, why waste a good title? So they merely added a few words when they created "Old King Tut Was a Wise Old Nut." The cover illustration shows a wrinkled pharaoh wearing a crown that looks like a teapot shaped like a swan (Fig. 9.3). The cover of the original "Old King Tut" had a female servant carrying a wine jar, and the new version borrowed that imagery. The lyrics indicate that some details of the tomb's contents were known by the time this version was written.

Along the valley of the Nile, tonight a torch is flamin'

Because two excavators found the tomb of Tut Ankh Hamen.

They searched and searched for years and years at last they found the

    king

And as they Jesse Jamesed his tomb, these royal ghouls would sing.

Old King Tut was a wise old nut, to snooze away in peace.

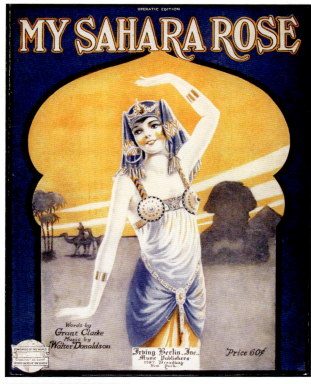

Color Plate 35. *In the 1920s songwriters often got their geography wrong. My Sahara Rose was discovered ". . . in the market place in old Bagdad," and Ilo is reached ". . . on my way again to Madagascar way."*

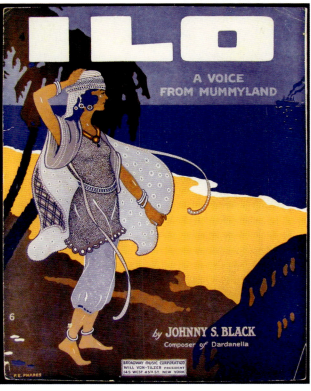

Color Plate 36. *Egyptian songs reflected the increase in Egyptian tourism at the beginning of the twentieth century.*

Color Plate 37. *Sometimes sheet music got it wrong. The images are Egyptian, but Aphrodite is a Greek goddess.*

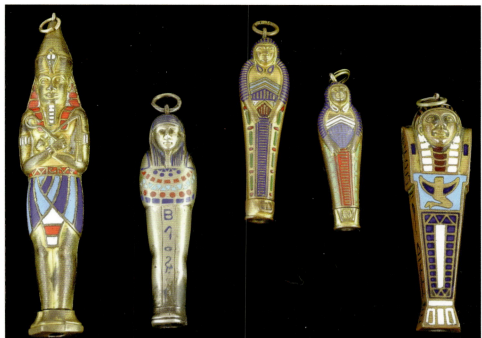

Color Plate 38.
Caught up in
Tutmania, flappers
started wearing
mummy-shaped
mechanical pencils
around their necks
and on charm
bracelets.

Color Plate 39.   A
1920s pocketknife
decorated with a replica
of one of the guardian
statues discovered in
Tutankhamen's tomb.

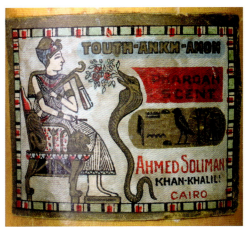

Color Plate 40. Soon after the discovery of Tutankhamen's tomb, merchants in Cairo's Khan el Khalili Bazaar were selling Touth-Ankh-Amon perfume to tourists.

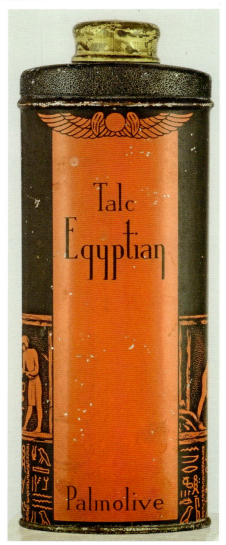

Color Plate 41. Not long after Tutankhamen's tomb was discovered, the Palmolive company was selling Talc Egyptian.

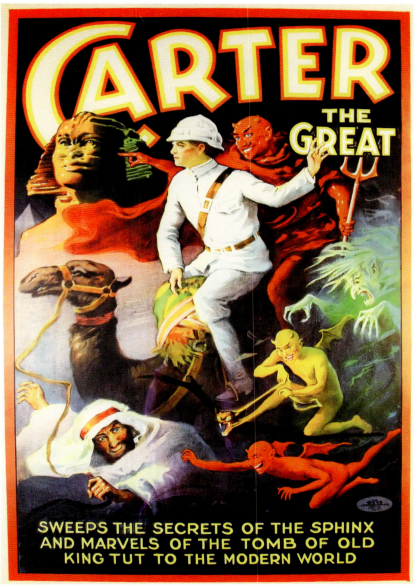

Color Plate 42.   Carter the Great's name really was Carter, and when Howard Carter discovered Tut's tomb, the magician quickly capitalized on his namesake's fame.

Color Plate 43.   Theda Bara was the original film icon for Cleopatra as a vamp.

Color Plate 44.   The Ten Commandments, *with its all-star cast, was one of the most successful movies ever made.*

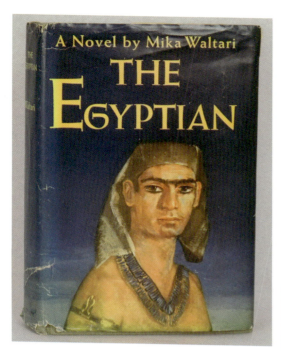

Color Plate 45.   Mika Waltari's best seller The Egyptian *was the basis for the also successful film by the same title.*

Color Plate 46.   All kinds of Tut-related products appeared when the Tutankhamen exhibition began touring the United States.

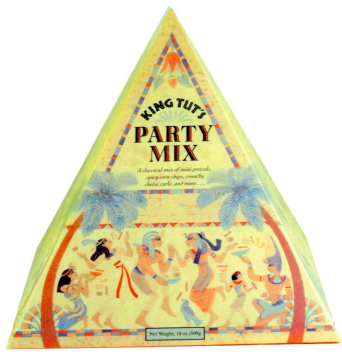

Fig. 9.3 Old King Tut Was a Wise Old Nut *was rushed into print before the excavators discovered that Tutankhamen was a teenager.*

No landlord ever chased him there,

He had a good long lease.

They stored his tomb with beef and wine to help his journey on.

Today we find the beef is there but all the wine is gone.[4]

Indeed, meat and wine were found in Tutankhamen's tomb. Carter discovered three dozen wine jars; as the song says, the wine had dried up centuries ago.

Many of the Tutankhamen songs were intended to be performed by vaudeville acts. The duo of Murray and Alan came up with "3000 Years Ago" (1923).

> I met two Egyptian mummies from King Pharaoh's tomb.
> They dug them up three weeks ago but they don't know by whom.
> They told me all about King Tut and everything they knew,
> And all the things they spoke about I'll now translate for you . . .
> Then every woman wore a veil to hide her face from view.
> I saw a lot of girls today who ought to wear them too.
> The ladies would salaam the men or else they'd get the sack.
> If you salaam the girls today you bet they'd slam you back.[5]

Few of the Tutankhamen songs were related in any way to the actual discovery or even made much sense. "Tut-Ank-Hamen (In the Valley of the Kings)" (1923) is no exception, but it did correctly describe the Tut craze.

> When he was king, for fame he always was craving,
> Now he's dead, the whole world is raving,
> Down in the Valley of the Kings . . . Kings.[6]

Songs weren't the only Tutankhamen tie-ins.

MUMMIES, PENCILS, AND PERFUMES

Manufacturers around the world began to cash in on Tutmania. There were wonderful mechanical pencils in the shape of mummy cases (Color Plate 38). Pull on the top ring, and the pencil extended from the bottom. Mummy-case pocketknives came in different sizes. It didn't matter that some looked more like medieval knights than Egyptian mummies, people still loved them. One elaborately crafted pocketknife copied the guardian statues found in Tutankhamen's tomb (Color Plate 39).

It seemed as if everyone was cranking out Tutankhamen souvenirs. In Cairo's Khan el Khalili bazaar, Ahmed Soliman was selling Touth-Ankh-Amon perfume (Color Plate 40). In Paris, it was Parfume de la Nubie, and in America, the Palmolive Company was hawking Talc Egyptian (Color Plate 41). Tutankhamen was providing a bonanza, and the magician Charles Joseph Carter, known as Carter the Great, was especially lucky. Carter the Great took advantage of his namesake's discovery, and his magic act quickly took on a decidedly Egyptian theme. His 1923 poster proclaimed: "Carter the Great Sweeps the Secrets of the Sphinx and Marvels of the Tomb of Old King Tut to the Modern World" (Color Plate 42). Looks like our magician didn't yet know that Tut was a boy king.

THE FICTIONAL TUTANKHAMEN

The first novel about Tutankhamen, *The Kiss of Pharaoh: The Love Story of Tut-Anch-Amen,* appeared in 1923, soon after the discovery of the tomb. The book jacket proclaims:

> Those who have read of the finding and opening of Tutankhamen's luxuriously appointed tomb or who have seen newspaper pictures of the treasures will especially enjoy this novel of the young pharaoh's brilliant reign and of his death. When all of Thebes stretched out across the desert in colorful procession of the magnificent tombs in the Valley of the Kings.[7]

When the book was published, very little was known about Tutankhamen, not even his queen's name, Ankhesenamen. So in the
book, Tutankhamen is married to Rana, but only after suitable trials
and tribulations. At the end of the novel, a soothsayer prophesizes
that Tutankhamen shall rule for only seven years and that 3,000 years
after his death, a foreign race would come and plunder his tomb.
A nice literary twist, but nothing like what Théophile Gautier pre-
dicted in his novel 50 years *before* the discovery of Tutankhamen's
tomb.

Gautier's 1857 *Romance of a Mummy* predicts Carter and Carnarvon's discovery of Tutankhamen's tomb by more than half a century
and is remarkably accurate. "'I have a presentment that we shall find a
tomb intact in the Valley of Biban-el-Molook,' said a young Englishman of haughty mien to an individual of much more humble appearance."[8] The humble individual was a hired archaeologist, and, just like
Carter and Carnarvon, the duo discover an intact tomb in the Valley
of the Kings.

The Romance of a Mummy is remarkable for several reasons. It is
the first historically accurate novel set in Egypt, displaying an impres-
sive knowledge of ancient Egypt and providing numerous details of
the customs, clothing, furniture, flowers, and food of pharaonic times.
It is also the first story to touch on the theme of the living falling in
love with a mummy.

In the prologue to the novel, Lord Evandale, a wealthy Englishman, discovers the intact tomb of an Egyptian queen, Tahoser. When
unwrapped, the mummy appears remarkably well preserved.

As he stood beside the dead beauty, the young lord experienced
that retrospective longing often inspired by the sight of a marble or
painting representing a woman of past time celebrated for charms:

it seemed to him that he might have loved her if he had lived three thousand five hundred years ago, this fair being that the grave had left untouched.[9]

When the mummy and the rest of the tomb's contents are transported to England, the excavators find a papyrus in the sarcophagus that tells the story of the beautiful Tahoser. The daughter of a high priest during the time of the Exodus, Tahoser adored an Israelite who did not return her love. She is, however, loved by Egypt's pharaoh. When the Israelite's true love, Rachel, learns of Tahoser's love for her fiancé, she suggests, in true biblical style, that he marry both of them. This cozy arrangement was not to be, for the Exodus, complete with plagues and curses, intervenes, and Tahoser is left behind. Of course, pharaoh never returns from the parted Red Sea, so Queen Tahoser becomes ruler of Egypt. Soon she dies and is entombed, only to be found 3,000 years later by Lord Evandale. At the end of the *Romance of a Mummy,* we are told,

> As for Lord Evandale, he has never cared to marry, although
> he is lord of his race. The young ladies cannot understand his
> coldness towards the fair sex, but would they in all likelihood
> ever imagine that Lord Evandale is in love retrospectively with
> Tahoser, daughter of the high-priest Pelamounoph, who died
> three thousand five hundred years ago?[10]

At the time Gautier was writing this, there were very few excavators in the Valley of the Kings, certainly no one like Howard Carter, so his premonition of the discovery is quite remarkable.

It took Carter ten years to clear Tutankhamen's tomb, and the public's interest in the work continued throughout. Toward the end of the excavation, the film industry joined the parade, creating a film classic modeled on the discovery.

TUTANKHAMEN TAKES TO THE SCREEN

The 1932 movie *The Mummy,* starring Boris Karloff, did not start out as a mummy film. Unlike other horror films, such as *Dracula* or *Frankenstein, The Mummy* wasn't based on a book. Originally the screenplay, called *Cagliostro,* was about several reincarnations of the heroine. Later it was rewritten as *Im-Ho-Tep* and only became *The Mummy* just before release.[11] The author, John L. Balderston, was a journalist who had been to the Valley of the Kings to cover the excavation of Tutankhamen's tomb. Many of the props in the film are replicas of artifacts found in the tomb, and the name of Tutankhamen's wife, Ankhesenamen, was used for the Egyptian princess in the movie. The mummy of Imhotep, however, was visually patterned after that of Seti II in the Egyptian Museum in Cairo.

In the movie, Princess Ankhesenamen dies and is buried by her father, the pharaoh. Her lover, the High Priest Imhotep, risks his life to steal the Scroll of Thoth, which could bring her back to life, but he is caught and buried alive in an unmarked grave. His grave is found by a museum expedition, and Imhotep comes to life when the Scroll of Thoth is read in his presence.

Because several scenes were dropped from the final cut, it was never made clear that Helen Grosvenor, the heroine, is the reincarnation of Ankhesenamen. Imhotep, now resurrected as Ardath Bey, recognizes her. When Ardath Bey magically calls Helen to the Cairo Museum, she goes willingly, happy to be reunited with her lost lover. She balks only when he explains that he must kill her first so she can be resurrected and join him for eternity.

In the original screenplay, Helen had many lives, first as an Egyptian princess, then a first-century Christian martyr, next an eighth-century barbarian queen, a medieval lady, and then a French aristocrat. But as the film neared completion, it became clear that to capitalize on the discovery of Tutankhamen's tomb, the focus should be on the mummy, so these scenes of previous lives were cut. They may still exist somewhere in the vaults of Universal Studios, but one vestige of them appears in the list of characters at the beginning of the movie, where "the Saxon Warrior" is played by Henry Victor. The scene was cut, but not the credit.

The filming of *The Mummy* pioneered new techniques for movie production. The shooting schedule was only 23 days, and much of the filming was done 100 miles north of Los Angeles in Red Rock Canyon, which resembled the Valley of the Kings. Because it was too expensive to transport actors to shoot in Egypt, a small crew was sent over to shoot background scenes, which were then projected on a "process screen." The actors performed in front of this screen while the process camera synchronized with the shoot camera, giving the viewer the illusion that the actors were in Egypt.

It took eight hours of makeup preparation to transform Boris Karloff into the mummy. At 11:00 A.M., all of his facial skin was covered with wet cotton strips. When the strips dried, they were covered with beauty mud. When that hardened, wrinkles were carved to produce the aged look. Finally, Karloff's body was wrapped with acid-dyed linen. When he stepped on the stage at 7:00 P.M., for shooting, the entire crew gasped. By 2:00 A.M., the resurrection scene was in the can, ready for posterity.

Arthur Tovey was a minor actor in the film, and his experience was almost as unique as Karloff's, but in a different way. Wearing black body makeup, he played one of the Nubian slaves who buried

Imhotep. After the burial, the pharaoh's guards hurled spears at the Nubians, killing them to keep the secret of the resting place. To keep production costs down and the number of extras at a minimum, the two halves of the scene were shot on successive days, with the same extras playing both the Nubians and the pharaoh's guards. One day the guards were filmed throwing spears at the Nubians; the next day the Nubians were filmed dying with spears in them. Tovey played both a guard and a Nubian, thus killing himself!

The Mummy was a great financial success. It was loosely based on the discovery of Tutankhamen's tomb; it featured a mummy, and there was even romance. Later decades would see all kinds of Egyptian-based films.

TEN

The Mummy Goes to the Movies

From the beginning of the movie industry, filmmakers bonded with ancient Egypt. In 1899, *Robbing Cleopatra's Tomb* told a story about a magician who hacks a mummy to pieces to create a female golem (a Frankenstein-like creature). It was the first Egyptian-themed movie, but it was not alone for long. In 1909, a film with the awkward title of *The Mummy of the King Ramses* was showing in theaters. It must have been a success because by 1911 there were three separate films titled *The Mummy*—one French, one British, and one American. All three have been lost, but it is a good bet they bore little resemblance to modern mummy films. In those days, mummies were romantic figures, lovers coming back to life to reconnect with their reincarnated beloveds. It wasn't until Boris Karloff's classic role in *The Mummy* in 1932 that the modern concept of mummies took hold in the cinema.

THE MUMMIES RESURRECT

Universal Studios churned out four sequels to *The Mummy*, but none was as interesting or successful as the original. In *The Mummy's Hand* (1940), the mummy lacks the psychological depth of Boris Karloff's

Imhotep, so fast-paced action replaces the brooding moodiness of the mummy, played by Tom Tyler (who had starred in Westerns and also played Captain Marvel). *The Mummy's Hand* came late in Tyler's career. He was suffering from arthritis, so the mummy's twisted limbs mirrored Tyler's condition.

This film first introduced tanna leaves, a fictional plant, to audiences. The high priest uses three of them to keep the mummy's heart beating and "nine to give him life." The distinction between a heart beating and life is beyond me. The film contains several archaeological howlers, including the use of dynamite to uncover the tomb. In the film, Professor Petrie stares at the seal of the tomb entrance, proclaims that he has waited a lifetime for this moment, then smashes both the seal and door with a pickaxe, destroying them. But the best is yet to come. When Petrie is examining the mummy, he explains that the expression on the mummy's face indicates that he was buried alive. A moment later he comments that its skin is soft and lifelike: "The most amazing example of embalming I've ever seen." This indeed was an unusual mummy, to have been both buried alive *and* embalmed. At the time the film was produced, the great archaeologist Sir Flinders Petrie was still living, and one can only wonder what he must have thought of it.

The Mummy's Hand was followed by *The Mummy's Tomb* (1942), *The Mummy's Ghost* (1944), and *The Mummy's Curse* (1944). All were dreadful. The mummy was now modeled on the mummy of Ramses III in the Egyptian Museum. By the time *The Mummy's Tomb* was filmed, Tyler was completely crippled by arthritis, so Lon Chaney Jr. was cast to play the mummy, although much of the time a stuntman was beneath the wrappings (Fig. 10.1).

In all these sequels, the mummy is little more than a robot. The true protagonists are the High Priests of Karnak (or sometimes Arkam) who thwart modern attempts to violate ancient tombs. The dual nature of Karloff's original role—the revived ancient mummy and his

Fig. 10.1   In The Mummy *(1932), applying Karloff's makeup was so difficult that the mummy only appears in one scene, but that is what everyone remembers.*

alter ego the modern Ardath Bey—had been split into two distinct characters, the priests and the mummy. Just as the Frankenstein films played the monster off against the doctor, mummy films now had a mummy and a high priest. Perhaps the most interesting element of these films is the idea of a secret cult enduring through the millennia, protecting the secrets of the ancient Egyptian religion. In *The Mummy's Hand,* the ancient high priest, played by Eduardo Ciannelli, passes his mantle to a younger George Zucco. In the sequel, *The Mummy's Tomb,* which takes place 30 years later, the wizened Zucco nominates a much younger Turhan Bey to succeed him. In the next sequel, *The Mummy's Ghost,* a rejuvenated Zucco calls on John Carradine. At the end of this film, Carradine and Kharis the mummy wind up fighting over the girl (who is the reincarnation of Kharis's forbidden love, Princess Ananka). The mummy wins, and he and his old flame sink happily into a swamp in Massachusetts. (Yes, it all takes place in America.)

The Mummy's Curse was the last of the series and contains flashes of imagination. Actors Peter Coe and Martin Kosleck are now the guardians of the ancient Egyptian cult. The swamp (mysteriously now located in Louisiana) is drained, Kharis recovered, and the Princess Ananka revived. This time their end comes when an abandoned monastery collapses on them. Universal Studios finally decided that enough was enough, so its next offering with a mummy was a comedy, *Abbott and Costello Meet the Mummy* (1955). Klaris (no typo) the mummy was played by stuntman Eddie Parker, but, in contrast to the earlier films, now he is a non-threatening character the audience can laugh at.

THE MUMMY WITH AN ENGLISH ACCENT

Hammer Films in England produced its own mummy series: *The Mummy* (1959), *The Curse of the Mummy's Tomb* (1964), *The Mummy's Shroud* (1967), and finally *Blood from the Mummy's Tomb* (1971). *The Mummy* starred Peter Cushing as archaeologist John Banning; horror

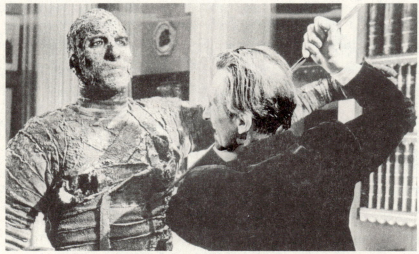

Fig. 10.2   Hammer Studios in England produced its own mummy series starring Christopher Lee as the mummy.

film regular Christopher Lee played Kharis the mummy (Fig. 10.2). Lee turned in a believable performance, but in the process of crashing through doors (which were inadvertently left locked), he dislocated his shoulder.

The 1959 version of *The Mummy* tells the same old story of the princess who died, the lover who attempts to resurrect her, and his subsequent death as punishment for his transgression. Predictable deaths follow at the hands of the mummy once his tomb is discovered. As in the 1932 version, the artifacts found in Tutankhamen's tomb served as models for the props and are faithfully reproduced. The burial of Ananka features an animal-headed funerary couch, Anubis statue, model boat, and alabaster jars patterned after those of the boy king. When the Scroll of Life is removed from its box, Tutankhamen's cartouche is clearly visible. The description of mummification is inaccurate. Viewers are told that the high priest entered the tomb after the coffin, "and behind him, the casket containing the heart of the princess." In Egyptian mummification, the heart was left inside the body. Throughout the film the chief god is Karnak, another Egyptological howler. Karnak is the modern name for a village in Egypt. There was never a god named Karnak.

The Curse of the Mummy's Tomb is one of Hammer Studio's best offerings and presents a new plot. It reuses many elements found in previous mummy films—an Egyptian who falls in love with a modern beauty, a medallion that brings the dead back to life, a curse on those who defile a tomb—but it is done in a thoughtful way.

There are plenty of new elements in the film, but the real novelty is the use of twin sons, one good and one evil. This is very much like the ancient Egyptian myth of Osiris and his evil brother, Seth. Just as in the myth, one brother kills the other, but there are plenty of new twists in the film, which makes for suspenseful viewing. Unfortunately, the same can't be said of its sequel.

The Mummy's Shroud (1967) is best remembered for its poster featuring a gigantic mummy with the heroine in his fist. This image had nothing to do with the movie and was an attempt to cash in on the iconic 1933 King Kong poster with Fay Wray in Kong's hand.

Hammer Studio's final mummy film, *Blood from the Mummy's Tomb,* is based on Bram Stoker's 1903 novel, *The Jewel of Seven Stars.* The movie features an evil female mummy played by the extremely well-endowed Valerie Leon (Fig. 10.3). It is a bit gory, but it has a solid plot and some very good sets. It was remade in 1980 as *The Awakening* starring Charlton Heston as an Egyptologist. That film was so bad that it disappeared from theaters the same week it opened. Two more recent mummy films, *The Mummy* (1999) and *The Mummy Returns* (2001), were huge financial successes but bear little resemblance to traditional mummy movies. These action-packed extravaganzas rely on special effects to give us high-tech mummies. Unlike earlier mummies, he is not

Fig. 10.3   Blood From the Mummy's Tomb *(1971) was based on Bram Stoker's 1903 novel,* Jewel of the Seven Stars.

easy to identify with. The mummy is the most popular theme in films set in ancient Egypt, but Cleopatra is a close second. Cleopatra films starring famous actresses have been a fixture of the film industry since its inception.

CLEOPATRA GOES TO THE MOVIES

In 1917, Theda Bara played Cleopatra wearing her trademark risqué costumes (Color Plate 22). The plot was loosely based on Shakespeare's *Antony and Cleopatra* and cost $500,000, an incredible sum at the time. It was a great success, but the last known copy of the film was destroyed in a fire. All we have left are a few stills and a poster. Claudette Colbert's 1934 femme fatale portrayal of Egypt's last queen did very well at the box office. Directed by Cecil B. DeMille, *Cleopatra* featured spectacular sets and costumes (Fig. 10.4).

Cleopatra's torch was next passed to Vivien Leigh. The 1945 Technicolor hit, *Caesar and Cleopatra,* was based on George Bernard Shaw's 1901 play of the same name. It portrays Cleopatra as a simple-minded nitwit whose beauty, not intellect, captivates Caesar. Perhaps it is best that the public has forgotten this version of *Cleopatra.*

The ultimate *Cleopatra,* the one that will never be forgotten, is the 1963 film starring Elizabeth Taylor and Richard Burton. There are many reasons the movie is memorable, not least of which was the highly publicized love affair between Burton and Taylor, who both happened to be married to other people at the time. The film also featured the highest cost overrun in film history. It was originally budgeted for under $5 million but eventually cost Twentieth Century Fox $44 million. During filming in London, Taylor became critically ill and was rushed to a hospital, where a tracheotomy saved her life. The exotic plants used for the sets died in the damp London climate during

Fig. 10.4   Claudette Colbert's Cleopatra *(1934), directed by Cecil B. DeMille, came on the heels of* The Mummy *(1932). It was a great success.*

the long wait for Miss Taylor's recovery, forcing the crew to relocate in sunnier Rome, where the sets were rebuilt at considerable cost. Still, no expense was spared in the production. Cleopatra's ship cost more than $250,000. Just one scene, her famous entrance into Rome, came in at $500,000. Even the posters, featuring original artwork by Howard Terpning, were expensive (Fig. 10.5). Due to ongoing production delays, they had to be reprinted several times with new opening dates.

By the time director Joseph L. Mankiewicz delivered the film to Twentieth Century Fox, it was six hours long and cost ten times its original estimate. The studio executives realized that it would be a financial disaster because a six-hour film could be shown only twice a

Fig. 10.5   *Elizabeth Taylor's* Cleopatra *(1963) will always be remembered for Miss Taylor's love affair with Richard Burton. Because of cost overruns, it was also the only movie in history to have the largest gross income for the year and lose money.*

day in each theater. They asked Mankiewicz to cut the film to four hours, but he resisted, suggesting that it be made into two separate films, *Caesar and Cleopatra* and *Antony and Cleopatra*. The studio refused. Mankiewicz cut the film, but he had to film additional scenes so the movie would make sense in its shortened version. Eventually it was released at just over three hours, allowing for three viewings per day in each theater.

The film received mixed reviews, but because of all the publicity over the Taylor-Burton affair, viewers flocked to theaters. *Cleopatra* was the highest-grossing film of the year and still lost money, the only film ever to do that. Fox was saved from bankruptcy only by the resounding success of *The Sound of Music* (1965).

EGYPTIAN EPICS HIT THE SCREEN

Cleopatra was not Fox's first Egyptian-themed epic. In 1949, a runaway bestseller, *The Egyptian,* by Finnish novelist Mika Waltari, was sweeping America. The tale of Sinuhe, who rises to become Pharaoh's physician, seemed perfect for the wide screen, so Fox bought the movie rights. From the beginning, it was intended as a big-budget spectacular with an all-star cast (Color Plate 45). Marlon Brando was selected to play Sinuhe but dropped out because he didn't like the script. Michael Wilding played the heretic pharaoh, Akhenaten, with Jean Simmons and Gene Tierney playing leading ladies, but they were upstaged by a spectacular performance by the unknown Bela Darvi as the Babylonian courtesan, Nefer. The stellar cast also included Victor Mature as General Horemheb with Peter Ustinov and John Carradine in other roles. This film is a favorite with Egyptology buffs because the story takes place during the turbulent Amarna period, when Pharaoh Akhenaten became the first to declare that there is but one god. Egyptologist Elizabeth Riefstahl designed the sets, so they are quite accurate, although the film is not without its anachronisms. One gaffe occurs when Nefer turns her back on Sinuhe, revealing a zipper in the back of her costume! *The Egyptian* (1954) is a serious movie worth watching, but it had competition from another Egyptian-themed film released the same year.

Valley of the Kings (1954) starred Robert Taylor as an archaeologist determined to help a colleague's daughter complete her father's life work—finding a lost tomb that would prove the existence of the biblical Joseph. The plot has quite a bit of romance and an adventurous Indiana Jones feel to it, but there is enough solid archaeology to keep it alive among Egyptology film buffs. The best scene is a fight between Taylor and the villain on top of one of the colossal heads of Ramses the Great at the temple of Abu Simbel. This scene may have been the inspiration for Alfred Hitchcock's famous scene in *North by Northwest* where Cary Grant narrowly escapes death on top of Mount Rushmore.

Another favorite with Egyptology buffs is the epic *Land of the Pharaohs* (1955) starring a 22-year-old Joan Collins. Warner Bros. lavished considerable resources on the film, using the new CinemaScope process. They hired William Faulkner as one of the scriptwriters and employed 9,787 extras for just one scene. The plot centers on Pharaoh Khufu, who is building a robber-proof pyramid. To finance it, all foreign lands that pharaoh has conquered must send tribute, but Cyprus is bankrupt, so it sends Joan Collins instead! Pharaoh likes the deal and takes her as his second wife, not knowing that she is as scheming and wicked as he is. She immediately arranges the death of Khufu's first wife, eliminating the competition. Next she decides that the treasures Khufu intends to take with him to the next world should really belong to her, so she engineers his death. In the film's spectacular ending, she enters the pyramid to examine her newly inherited treasure and preside at the sealing of Khufu's sarcophagus. As the high priest demonstrates the pyramid's secret mechanism for keeping tomb robbers out, sand pours down the corridors, blocking stones are released, and the lovely Miss Collins is entombed with her treasures for eternity.

The film's Egyptological trivia make it a cult favorite. When Pharaoh is presented with various plans for his pyramid, the third one he is shown is an accurate diagram of the interior of the Great Pyramid of Giza. Even better for the Egyptology buff, Khufu's burial was filmed at Abu Roash, a remote pyramid site rarely visited by even intrepid travelers.

Of all Egyptian epic films, one stands out above the others, but sadly it is hardly known. The Polish film *Faraon* (1966) was nominated for an Oscar for Best Foreign Film but is rarely shown because of its length (three hours) and use of subtitles. The great Polish Egyptologist Kazimierz Michałowski served as consultant, so the archaeological details are accurate. Near the beginning of the film, the Egyptians have concluded a successful battle, and a soldier walks into frame carrying a basket full of human hands—the Egyptian way of counting the dead.

The plot centers on a transitional point in Egyptian history, the end of the Twentieth Dynasty, when Pharaoh Ramses XI saw his power usurped by the high priests of Amun. Called Ramses XIII in the film, the handsome young protagonist is in a constant power struggle that one senses he will not win. Unlike other Egyptian epics, this one is dark and brooding throughout; there are rarely bright colors or strong sunlight.

Egyptian films have had their share of remakes. Both *Cleopatra* and *The Mummy* have had several reincarnations, but only one Egyptian epic has been remade by the same director. Cecil B. DeMille's *The Ten Commandments* had its first incarnation in 1923 and was then remade in 1956. The original silent version is rarely seen in its two-hour entirety, so hardly anyone knows that the biblical Exodus story is only the first half of the film. The second half is a modern morality play in which one brother, John, follows the Ten Commandments, but his brother, Danny, becomes a corrupt contractor whose shoddily constructed cathedral collapses on his mother, killing her. Her dying words to Danny are that she failed him by not teaching him to follow the Ten Commandments. The second half is so dated that only the Exodus portion is shown in clips today.

The biblical scenes were filmed at California's Nipomo Dunes in San Luis Obispo County. When the filming was over, 1,500 workers buried the giant sets in the dunes, including 35-foot-high statues of Ramses the Great. In recent years, winds have uncovered large sections of the sets, and they have been periodically excavated as part of Hollywood history. The crossing of the Red Sea was partly done in a studio with a slab of Jell-O. The sea-colored Jell-O was sliced in half and jiggled to simulate water. Later this scene was combined with footage of Moses on the dunes leading the Israelites to safety. Appropriately, the film premiered in 1923 at Grauman's Egyptian Theatre in Hollywood.

The film was a box office success, but the 1956 version of *The Ten Commandments* outstripped it, becoming one of the most successful motion pictures ever made. Its all-star cast included Charlton Heston as Moses and Yul Brynner as Ramses II, along with Debra Paget, Sir Cecil Hardwicke, Vincent Price, John Carradine, and Edward G. Robinson (Color Plate 44). The script does not follow the biblical story exactly; characters and scenes were added to help the plot. In spite of inaccuracies, it is still a favorite with Christian organizations and is shown in Bible schools throughout the country. The movie is best remembered for the parting of the Red Sea. DeMille went well beyond Jell-O, and the film won its only Academy Award for Special Effects.

Although most Egyptian-themed films are serious, *Kid Millions* (1934) is a little-known zany movie that has scenes unlike any other. The plot loosely revolves around Eddie Cantor, who inherits an Egyptian treasure from his archaeologist father, but he must go to Egypt to claim it. Various thugs and greedy types try to trick lovable Eddie out of his inheritance, and wackiness ensues.

Eventually Eddie finds himself in an Egyptian tomb with lots of coffins standing up around the walls. In one of the film's funnier moments, the mummies sing a soulful chorus of "Let My People Go."

Eddie stumbles onto the treasure as well as a conveniently located bi-plane that has just enough gas to fly back to New York, and now the movie gets really bizarre.

After seeing Eddie's biplane sputter across the New York skyline, we learn via a spinning newspaper that he opens a gigantic ice-cream factory—and quite a factory it is! The grand finale is one long musical number, complete with dancing girls dressed as factory workers in sparkling jumpsuits and roller skates. The factory comes complete with a four-story-high singing plastic cow, which the gals elegantly milk while roller-skating. To add to the surrealism, this is the only scene in the entire movie filmed in Technicolor. And such colors—Easter egg green, Pepto-Bismol pink; you name it, they used it. In one shot, the gals carry giant chocolate bars up the staircase to a giant mixer. If you look carefully at the dancers, you can spot Lucille Ball, very early in her career. They don't make films like that anymore.

ELEVEN

The Future of Egyptomania

I often think about the shape Egyptomania will take in the future. What events and discoveries will create new waves of interest? What kinds of objects will be out there for me to collect? Will they be stored on a disk? I am convinced that Egyptomania will always be with us in some form, but many aspects of its 3,000-year-old history are gone forever, and that may not be a bad thing.

From the very beginnings of Egyptomania, heads of state were directly involved in bringing Egyptian antiquities to Europe. Roman emperors Augustus and Caligula brought obelisks to Rome as symbols of their power. Napoleon Bonaparte's army discovered the Rosetta Stone, which was in turn claimed by the British. Later in the nineteenth century, France, England, and America all brokered deals that brought obelisks to their shores. This was the elite tier of Egyptomania, which is gone forever. Today Egypt bemoans the loss of its patrimony and has instituted strict laws forbidding the export of any antiquities. In the past, museums and universities excavating in Egypt were rewarded with a division of the finds, which permitted them to return home with artifacts. This practice has also ended. Today, what is found in Egypt stays in Egypt. Excavators dig for knowledge, not to obtain objects. No more obelisks or Rosetta Stones will be leaving Egypt.

Although foreign excavators will no longer bring objects home, loan exhibitions will still fan the flames of Egyptomania. For example, the discovery of Tutankhamen's tomb is an old story, but one the public never tires of hearing. More than 75 years have passed since its discovery, but the public is still fascinated by objects from Tut's tomb. Never have so many people gone so repeatedly to exhibitions on a single topic, and the history of this love affair gives us a clue about Egyptomania's future.

RETURN OF TUTANKHAMEN

In 1961, an exhibition called *Tutankhamen Treasures* opened at the Smithsonian Museum in Washington, DC. This was an era before the blockbuster exhibit, so the display was modest, consisting of only 34 small objects from the tomb.[1] Still, it was a great success, traveling to 18 cities in America and 6 in Canada. In Japan, 3 million people saw the boy king's treasures. In Paris, more than a million lined up for their chance.

In the early 1970s, the British Museum negotiated an agreement with Egypt to display larger objects from Tutankhamen's tomb, including Tut's famous gold mask. The British Museum was an auspicious start for the exhibition. Between March and September 1972, more than a million and a half people came to see Tutankhamen's treasures.[2]

After London, the exhibition went to Russia, Egypt's close political ally at the time. Excited crowds thronged to see the treasures in Moscow, Leningrad, and Kiev. J. Carter Brown, new director of the National Gallery in Washington, DC, decided the time might be right for

America to have its own blockbuster Tut exhibition. Politically, Egypt was moving away from Russia and toward America. Brown seized the moment and flew to Cairo to discuss an exhibition with Dr. Gamal Mokhtar, Egypt's head of antiquities. Mokhtar agreed in principle, but many details had to be worked out: which pieces would be sent, how many cities the exhibit would visit, how it would all be funded. Brown couldn't swing it alone; he knew he would need the help of other American curators. He ended up partnering with Thomas Hoving, the flamboyant new director of the Metropolitan Museum of Art in New York. Hoving, a consummate showman, oversaw not only the creation and marketing of gift shop replicas but also negotiated the final selection of Tut's objects.

In *Making the Mummies Dance,* Hoving gives a very entertaining account of negotiating for the exhibition.[3] It is a tale of bribes, intrigue, and belly dancers, but it would prove to be well worth the trouble. Hoving wanted the exhibition to include one of the beautiful goddess statues surrounding Tutankhamen's shrine, but he was told by Egyptian Museum staff that it would be impossible because the four goddesses and the wood base they rested on were carved out of a single piece of wood. Hoving, trained as an art historian, always did his homework. He knew this was nonsense. When Tutankhamen's tomb was first discovered in 1922, the Metropolitan Museum's photographer, Harry Burton, photographed all the objects as they were found in the tomb. In his photo the four goddesses face the shrine. As Hoving looked at the shrine in the Egyptian Museum, he saw that the statues were reversed, facing away from the shrine. When the shrine had been installed in the Egyptian Museum, the four removable statues were incorrectly replaced looking outward. Hoving, knowing the statues were removable, put on a pair of white gloves, grasped the statue of the goddess Selket, and pulled it out from its base, much to the horror of the museum staff. Selket, one of the stars of the exhibition, was coming to America, along with 55 spectacular objects, gold jewelry, statues, and the iconic gold mask of Tutankhamen. Between 1976 and 1979, more than 8 million Americans in seven cities saw the exhibition. Just like in the 1920s, when the tomb was discovered and Tutmania struck the world, the new blockbuster exhibits once again renewed the frenzy for all things Egyptian.

Plenty of low-brow Tut-related items were produced, from King Tut Party Mix that came in a pyramid-shaped box to King Tut cologne with a stopper looking vaguely like the gold mask (Color Plate 46). Perhaps the greatest King Tut spin-off was created when comedian Steve Martin appeared on the April 22, 1978, *Saturday Night Live* television show and sang "King Tut." The song was directly inspired by the *Treasures of Tutankhamen* exhibition, and, in his introduction to the song, Martin mentions the exhibition. The skit is hilarious, worth searching for on YouTube. People who remember the skit probably recall the unforgettable lines "Born in Arizona, moved to Babylonia, King Tut." But few remember that the lyrics are about a museum exhibition.

> Now when he was a young man,
> He never thought he'd see,
> People stand in line to see the boy king . . .
> (King Tut) Now if I'd known
> They'd line up to see him,
> I'd taken all my money
> And bought me a museum (King Tut)

Fifty years after the discovery of the tomb, the most popular comedy show on television was doing a skit about a museum exhibition! That's how popular Tutankhamen was and still remains.

TUTANKHAMEN'S MURDER?

In 2004, a new Tutankhamen exhibition, *Tutankhamen: The Golden Hereafter,* began touring the world. (It later morphed into *Tutankhamen and the Golden Age of the Pharaohs.*) At the time, I was making my own contribution to Tutmania. As an Egyptologist, I knew the story of the discovery of the tomb and the treasures it held, but I was never particularly interested in the boy king. That changed one evening when I found myself watching an old BBC documentary about him. I was about to turn it off when something caught my eye. Dr. R. G. Harrison, head of the Anatomy Department at the University of Liverpool, was pointing to a dark spot on an x-ray of Tutankhamen's skull. He said it was: "within normal limits, but in fact it could have been caused by a hemorrhage under the membranes overlaying the brain in this region. And this could have been caused by a blow to the back of the head and this in turn could have been responsible for death."

Harrison was very cautious. Consider his phrasing: "could have been," "could have been caused," "could have been responsible for." All very hesitant, and he had good reason to be; the x-ray was far from conclusive, but I was hooked. I knew something Harrison didn't.

Soon after Tutankhamen's death, his young wife, Ankhesenamen, wrote perhaps the strangest letter ever written in ancient Egypt to the king of the Hittites, a traditional enemy of Egypt. She explained that her husband had died, and she had no sons. Would the Hittite king send one of his sons so she could marry him and make him king of Egypt? She ends the letter with this phrase: "Never shall I pick out a servant of mine and make him my husband . . . I am afraid." Why is the queen of Egypt afraid? What is this talk about marrying a servant?

Ankhesenamen's letter was so odd that the Hittite king didn't believe it and sent an ambassador to Egypt to seek the truth. When the ambassador returned from his mission, he reported, yes, the king of Egypt died, the queen had no sons, and she did indeed want to marry a Hittite. The king dispatched his son Zanzana to Egypt, but the prince was murdered on the border of Egypt before he could marry the young widow. And what happened to Ankhesenamen? She ended up marrying the vizier (or prime minister) of Egypt, an old man named Ay, who was a commoner—and, in a sense, Ankhesenamen's servant. After the marriage, Ankhesenamen disappears from history; not even a tomb has been found. This is the stuff of which murder mysteries are made, and that's not the whole story.

The x-ray, combined with the letter and circumstances, led me to speculate that Tutankhamen had been murdered by Ay, the prime minister, who wanted to be king. Ay then had the Hittite prince killed, and he perhaps even murdered Ankhesenamen shortly after their marriage. I became so involved in this theory that I wrote a book, *The Murder of Tutankhamen,* and made a documentary film for The Learning Channel. The book was quite successful, and the film was nominated for an Emmy as Best Documentary. The *New York Times* did a story on the subject, complete with the x-ray, and soon my theory was in newspapers and magazines around the world. Something poignant in the story about the murdered boy king and his frantic teenage widow touched a nerve, and everyone wanted to know more.

TUTANKHAMEN ON LOAN

When the contracts for the latest series of Tutankhamen exhibitions were worked out, Dr. Zahi Hawass, director of the Supreme Council of Antiquities, proved to be a very capable negotiator. Previously, Egypt had gotten a share of the profits only after the museums had deducted their expenses. Hawass wanted Egypt to receive its money, up front, in the form of multimillion-dollar fees from each museum that would host the exhibition. It would be up to the museums to make back the fees however they could. It was a big risk for the museums. No one had ever tried such a venture before. Tutankhamen's star power was well established, but was it enough to raise millions of dollars at each venue?

There were two ways the museums could recoup their loan fees: gift shop sales and special admission fees for the exhibition. Many of the museums had never charged a special admission. Would museum goers pay, and how much? Some museums charged as much as $30 for a ticket at peak times, and still people lined up. For the most part, the gift shops did well. Once again, Tutankhamen proved he could pack the house.

Soon after the exhibition came to America, Roland Emmerich, director of the films *Stargate* and *Independence Day*, optioned the movie rights to my book, so the story of Tutankhamen and Ankhesenamen may be coming to a theater near you. The success of the Tutankhamen exhibitions bodes well for the future of Egyptomania. If an 80-year-old discovery can stir such strong interest in people, think about what a completely new, spectacular discovery might do!

SECRETS OF THE SAND

There are undoubtedly sensational archaeological finds still to be made in Egypt. Tutankhamen's tomb is the only one in the Valley of the Kings ever found intact, but the tomb of his widow, Ankhesenamen, has not been found. Then there's the tomb of Alexander the Great. We know from ancient sources that he was buried at the crossroads of the two main streets of Alexandria, but the city has changed so much in its 2,000-year history that we no longer know where the crossroads were. According to Suetonius, the Roman historian, Julius Caesar and Cleopatra visited Alexander's tomb, so it probably still exists. There is even the possibility that Cleopatra's tomb will be discovered some day. If it is, it will be even bigger news than Tutankhamen's. When Tutankhamen's tomb was discovered in 1922, he was an unknown pharaoh. We know much, much more about Cleopatra. She has had 2,000 years of publicity already. Shakespeare wrote a play about her, movies have told her fabulous story. Who wouldn't go to see her treasures?

WHAT'S NEXT?

Not all fabulous discoveries in the future will be of kings and queens. Plenty of ancient Egyptian noblemen—viziers and generals, architects and royalty—had tombs filled with treasures. Currently excavators are looking for the tomb of Imhotep, the architect of the Step Pyramid of Saqqâra, the first pyramid ever built. It is generally agreed that Imhotep was buried somewhere near that pyramid, and recent soundings by a Polish excavation team suggest that they may be closing in on his tomb. There are many wonderful things still to be found to maintain interest in ancient Egypt, but I think the interest goes far deeper than just the treasures and new discoveries.

On some level, we identify with ancient Egyptians in ways we don't with other ancient civilizations. Every new-ager who is reincarnated seems to have been an Egyptian, not a Viking or an Inca. Why do ten-year-olds want to visit museums' Egyptian galleries but not the Mesoamerican galleries? I have often wondered why the Mayans don't intrigue us the way the Egyptians do. They too built pyramids, they wrote in hieroglyphs, painted murals. Why are we interested in Ramses the Great and Cleopatra, but not the great Maya leader Yax K'uk Mo'? We are closer in time to Yax K'uk Mo' than to Tutankhamen. Why do we build an Egyptian-themed hotel casino in Las Vegas named the Luxor, complete with pyramid and sphinx? Why do we clamor for all things Egyptian but not Mayan?

One reason is that ancient Egyptian pharaohs didn't build pyramids to hold human sacrifices, ripping out the still-beating hearts of their enemies. Mayan rulers pulled slivers of obsidian flakes through their own tongues, which most of us can't identify with. On the other hand, Egyptians had a day of judgment and an afterworld similar to our heaven. We can identify with that. The *Egyptian Book of the Dead* was a passport to heaven. There is also a bit of envy involved. Egyptian mummies appear to have cheated death. Will any of us look that good in 3,000 years? Ancient Egyptians are close enough to us culturally that we can identify with them but far enough away in time that we can fantasize about them. We visit the pyramids and are amazed. We still don't know how they erected their obelisks, and we are left with a sense of mystery and wonder.

This question of why Egypt fascinates is ultimately a psychological one, so it is of particular interest that Sigmund Freud was an enthusiastic participant in Egyptomania. Over the famous couch in his office Freud hung a print of the Egyptian temple of Abu Simbel. On his desk were a dozen statues of Egyptian gods. Along the walls were glass cabinets chock full of antiquities (Fig. 11.1). What was it that drew Freud to ancient Egypt? Fortunately, the great man wrote about his fascination with the land of the pharaohs.

For Freud, the founder of psychoanalysis, archaeology was a metaphor for his profession. Just as the archaeologist, in search of truth, removes layer after layer of a buried civilization, the psychoanalyst uncovers various layers of the psyche in search of earlier truths and memories. This professional connection to ancient Egypt is understandable, but Freud's attraction was also more personal. Freud was Jewish and had studied the Bible. Like Herodotus, the Greek tourist who was proud to trace Greek civilization back to Egypt, Freud happily traced his religion back to the Eighteenth Dynasty and the pharaoh Akhenaten. Akhenaten declared that there was only one god, the Aten, and banished the worship of any other gods. Freud theorized that Moses was an Egyptian priest during the time of Akhenaten and thus Judaism came out of Egypt. When he published his theory in *Moses and Monotheism*,[4] Freud presented little factual evidence; it was nearly pure speculation.

Freud's fascination with ancient Egypt bodes well for the future of Egyptomania. Freud saw the desire to uncover ancient Egypt as

Fig. 11.1   Even Sigmund Freud was fascinated by Egypt. His desk was cluttered with statues of Egyptian gods.

parallel to the psychoanalytical process. Humans have a basic need to discover, to explore, whether searching for the self or for artifacts long buried beneath the sands of Egypt. We may not realize it on a conscious level, but the pull of the hidden is intrinsic to all of us. Like children who want to hear the same story over and over, we will continue to be thrilled by the tale of the discovery of a boy-king who lived 33 centuries ago. Future generations will undoubtedly line up to view exhibitions, buy souvenirs, and sleep on pillowcases decorated with Egyptian lotus flowers. The future of Egyptomania seems assured.

NOTES

CHAPTER 1: BIRTH OF A COLLECTION

1. Thomas Pettigrew, *Egyptian Mummies* (London: Longmans, 1834).
2. There are several versions of this letter written by several people. For a discussion, see Nicholas Reeves and John Taylor, *Howard Carter Before Tutankhamen* (New York: Abrams, 1993), 20–22.

CHAPTER 2: ROME AND THE BIRTH OF EGYPTOMANIA

1. Herodotus, *Histories* (Cambridge, MA: Harvard University Press, 1940), 387.
2. Plato, *Dialogues of Plato, Phaedrus* (Chicago: Encyclopedia Britannica, 1952), 138–139.
3. Euphrosyne Doxiadis, *The Mysterious Fayoum Portraits* (New York: Abrams, 1995), 12.
4. W. Wynn Westcott, *The Isiac Tablet or Bembine Table of Isis* (Los Angeles: Philosophical Research Society, 1976).

CHAPTER 3: NAPOLEON ON THE NILE

1. Vivant Denon, *Travels in Upper and Lower Egypt,* 2 vols. (New York: Heard and Forman, 1803).
2. Richard Pococke, *A Description of the East and Some Other Countries* (London: W. Bower, 1743–1745).
3. Frederik Lewis Norden, *Travels in Egypt and Nubia* (London: Lockyer Davis and Charles Reymers, 1757).
4. Charles Truman, *The Sèvres Egyptian Service 1810–12* (London: Victoria & Albert Museum, 1982).

CHAPTER 4: HOW AN OBELISK AND A CANAL CONQUERED FRANCE

1. M. A. Lebas, *L'Obélisque de Luxor Histoire de sa Translation à Paris* (Paris: Carillian-Goeury, 1839), 1.
2. Ibid., 22.

CHAPTER 5: THE AMAZING VOYAGE OF CLEOPATRA'S NEEDLE

1. W. R. Cooper, *A Short History of the Egyptian Obelisks* (London: Bagster, 1877), 130.
2. Ibid., 140.
3. Ibid., 141.
4. Waynman Dixon, manuscript written on board the *Olga*. In London Metropolitan Archives, Reference Q/CN/3.

CHAPTER 6: EGYPT FOR SALE

1. Anonymous, *The Victorian Pattern Glass & China Book* (New York: Arch Cape Press, 1990), 124.

CHAPTER 7: NEW YORK GETS ITS OBELISK

1. Elbert Farman, *Egypt and Its Betrayal* (New York: Grafton, 1908), 162.
2. Jasper Ridley, *The Freemasons* (New York: Arcade, 1999).
3. Henry H. Gorringe, *Egyptian Obelisks* (Self-published in New York, 1882), 28.
4. Ibid., 33.
5. *New York Times,* October 10, 1880.
6. Albert Bigelow Paine, *Thomas Nast: His Period and His Pictures* (Princeton, NJ: Pyne Press, 1904), 69.

CHAPTER 8: THE MUMMIES SING SONGS OF THE NILE

1. Vincent Rose, *Mummy Mine* (San Francisco: Sherman, Clay, & Co., 1918).
2. Otto Motzan, *My Egyptian Mummy* (New York: Jos. W. Stern, 1913).
3. Maurice Grunsky, *At the Mummy's Ball* (San Francisco: Nat Goldstein, 1921).
4. Jack Coogan, *Cleopatra Had a Jazz Band* (New York: Leo Feist, 1917).
5. Earl and Harry Carroll, '*Neath the Shadow of the Pyramids* (New York: Shapiro, Bernstein & Co., 1914).
6. Grant Clark, *My Sahara Rose* (New York: Irving Berlin, Inc., 1920).
7. Johnny S. Black, *Ilo: A Voice From Mummyland* (New York: Broadway Music Co., 1921).

CHAPTER 9: TUTANKHAMEN, SUPERSTAR

1. Theodore M. Davis, *The Tombs of Harmhabi, and Touatankhamanou* (London: Constable, 1912), 3.
2. For a thrilling and detailed account of the tomb's discovery and excavation, see Howard Carter and A. C. Mace, *The Tomb of Tut-Ankh-Amen,* 3 vols. (London: Cassell and Co., 1923–33).
3. Harry Von Tilzer, *Old King Tut* (New York: Harry Von Tilzer, 1923).
4. Lucien Denni, *Old King Tut Was a Wise Old Nut* (Kansas City: J.W. Jenkins Sons, 1923).
5. Alex Gerber, *3000 Years Ago* (New York: Irving Berlin, 1923).
6. Carlo and Sanders. *Tut-ankh-Amen In the Valley of the Kings* (New York: Jerome H. Remick, 1923).
7. Richard Goyne, *The Kiss of Pharaoh* (New York: Stokes, 1923).
8. Theophile Gautier, *Romance of A Mummy* (Philadelphia: Lippincott, 1892), 1.

9. Ibid., 50.
10. Ibid., 245.
11. Philip J. Riley, ed. *The Mummy* (Absecon, NJ: MagicImage Filmbooks, 1989).

CHAPTER 11: THE FUTURE OF EGYPTOMANIA

1. Rudolf Anthes, *Tutankhamen's Treasures* (Washington, DC: Smithsonian, 1961).
2. I. E. S. Edwards, *The Treasures of Tutankhamen* (New York: Viking Press, 1972).
3. Thomas Hoving, *Making the Mummies Dance: Inside the Metropolitan Museum of Art* (New York: Simon & Schuster, 1993), 401–414.
4. Sigmund Freud, *Moses and Monotheism* (New York: Alfred A. Knopf, 1939).

BIBLIOGRAPHY

CHAPTER 1: BIRTH OF A COLLECTION

Beautheac, Nadine, and Francois-Xavier Bouchart. *L'Europe Exotique*. Paris: Chene, 1985.

Bergman, Edward. *Woodlawn Remembers*. Utica: North Country Books, 1988.

Biblioteca Alexandrina. *The World of Shadi Abdel Salam*. Alexandria: Alexandria Library, 2002.

Bolshoi Ballet. *Pharaoh's Daughter*. New York: Metropolitan Opera House, 2005.

Brier, Bob. *Egyptomania*. Brookville: Hillwood Art Museum, 1994.

———. *Napoleon in Egypt*. Brookville: Hillwood Art Museum, 1990.

Busch, Hans. *Verdi's Aida*. Minneapolis: University of Minnesota Press, 1978.

Carrott, Richard. *The Egyptian Revival 1808–1858*. Berkeley: University of California Press, 1978.

Conner, Patrick. *The Inspiration of Egypt*. Brighton: Manchester City Art Museum, 1983.

Cooper, Wendy. *Classic Taste in America*. Baltimore: Baltimore Art Museum, 1993.

Curl, James. *The Art & Architecture of Freemasonry*. New York: Overlook, 1991.

———. *Egyptomania*. Manchester: Manchester University Press, 1994.

———. *The Egyptian Revival*. London: Allen & Unwin, 1982.

Davison, Joe. *The Art of the Cigar Label*. Secaucus, NJ: Wellfleet, 1989.

Douglas, Ed. *Egypt: The Source and Legacy*. Bronxville: Sara Lawrence College, 1990.

Eisner, Lisa. *Shriners*. Wyoming: Greybull, n.d.

Eldem, Edhem. *Un Orient De Consommation*. Istanbul: Musée de la Banque Ottomane, 2010.

Fels, Thomas. *Fire & Ice: Fredrick Church at Olana*. Ithaca: Dahesh Museum, 2002.

Ficacci, Luigi. *Piranesi*. London: Tashen, n.d.

Fox Theatre. *The Fabulous Fox*. Atlanta: Fox Theatre, 1990.

Gant, Rus. *The Gant Oriental Library and Art Collection*. Self-published, 2004.

Hamilton, Alastair. *Europe and the Arab World*. London: Arcadian Group, 1994.

Hardin, Jennifer. *The Lure of Egypt*. St. Petersburg: Museum of Fine Arts, 1996.

Hobhouse, Hermione. *The Crystal Palace*. London: Continuum, 2002.

Houghton, J. R., and Mr. Priestley. *Delftware and Victorian Ointment Pots*. England: Priestly, 2005.

Humbert, Jean-Marcel. *Egyptomania*. Ottowa: Éditions de la Réunion des Musées Nationaux, 1994.

Ladurie, Emmanuel. *Mémoires D'Égypte: Hommage de l'Europe a Champollion*. Strasbourg: Bibliothèque Nationale, n.d.

Lassell, Michael. *Elton John's and Tim Rice's* Aida. New York: Disney, 2000.

Luxor Hotel. *Map & Directory.* Las Vegas: Luxor Hotel, 2009.

Navratilova, Hana. *Egyptian Revival in Bohemia 1850–1920.* Prague: Set Out, 2003.

Papastratos. *A History of the Greek Cigarette.* Athens: Papastratos, 1997.

Penn State University. *Lavie.* Yearbook of Senior Class. Philadelphia: University of Pennsylvania, 1932.

Pettigrew, Thomas. *Egyptian Mummies.* London: Longman et al., 1834.

Reeves, Nicholas, and John Taylor. *Howard Carter Before Tutankhamen.* New York: Abrams, 1993.

Ringold, Gene, and DeWitt Bodeen. *The Films of Cecil B. DeMille.* New York: Citadel Press, 1969.

Rudok, Judy. *Cartier 1900–1939.* New York: Abrams, 1997.

Scamuzzi, Ernesto. *La Mensa Isiaca.* Roma: Museo di Torino, 1939.

Sutherland, Clara. *The Statue of Liberty.* New York: Barnes & Noble, 2003.

Verdi, G. *Aida.* New York: Edwin Kalmus, n.d.

Verdi, G. *Aida.* New York: Metropolitan Opera, 2005.

Watkin, David, and Philip Hewat-Jabour. *Thomas Hope: Regency Designer.* New Haven, CT: Yale University Press, 2008.

CHAPTER 2: ROME AND THE BIRTH OF EGYPTOMANIA

Boorsch, Suzanne. *The Building of the Vatican.* New York: Metropolitan Museum of Art, 1982.

Dibner, Bern. *Moving the Obelisks.* Cambridge, MA: MIT Press, 1970.

———. *Moving the Obelisks.* Norwalk: Burndy, 1952.

Hassan, Fekri. "Imperialist Appropriations of Egyptian Obelisks." In *Views of Ancient Egypt Since Napoleon Bonaparte,* ed. David Jeffreys. London: UCL Press, 2003.

Herodotus. *Histories.* Cambridge, MA: Harvard University Press, 1940.

Iverson, Erik. *Obelisks in Exile.* 2 vols. Copenhagen: Gad, 1968.

Lazio Regional Tourist Board. *Obelisks of Rome.* Rome: Artemide Editions, 1995.

Parker, John Henry. *Archaeology of Rome: Obelisks.* London: Murray, 1876.

Plato. *Dialogues of Plato, Phaedrus.* Chicago: Encyclopedia Britannica, 1952.

Westcott, W. Wynn. *The Isiac Tablet or The Bembine Table of Isis.* Los Angeles: Philosophical Research Society, 1976.

CHAPTER 3: NAPOLEON ON THE NILE

Abbott, John S. C. *Confidential Correspondence of the Emperor Napoleon and the Empress Josephine.* New York: Mason, 1856.

Abbott, John. *The History of Napoleon Bonaparte.* 4 vols. New York: Harper, 1883.

Ader, Jean-Joseph. *Expédition d'Égypte, et de Syrie.* Paris: Ambroise Dupont, 1826.

———. *Histoire Militaire de Français – de Napoléon.* Paris: Ambroise Dupont, 1826.

Alexander, R. S. *Bonapartism & Revolutionary Tradition in France.* Cambridge: Cambridge University Press, 1991.

Al Jabarti, Abd al Rahman. *Chronicle of the French Occupation.* Princeton: Wiener, 2004.

———. *Journal d'un Notable du Caire Durant L'Expédition Française.* Paris: Michel, 1979.

Anderson, Robert, and Ibrahim Fawzy. *Egypt in 1800, Scenes from Napoleon's Description de l'Égypte.* London: Barrie and Jenkins, 1988.

Anonymous. *Courier de L'Égypte. No. 68.* Cairo: Imprimerie National, 1799.

Anonymous. *Description De L'Égypte.* London: Taschen, 2002.

Anonymous. *La Campagne d'Egypt 1798–1801.* Paris: Hôtel National des Invalides, 1998.

Anonymous. *La Cloche Funèbre de la Politique Européenne.* Cairo: n.p., 1799. Anonymous. *L'État-Major de Kléber en Égypte.* La Vouivre: Fondation Napoléon, 1998.

Anonymous. *Memoirs Relative to Egypt.* London: R. Phillips, 1800.

Anonymous. *Mémoires Sur l'Égypte.* 4 vols. Paris: Didot l'Aine, 1800.

Anonymous. *Napoleon's Book of Fate.* A pamphlet given free by Dr. Chase's Medicines. No publisher, no date.

Anonymous. *Napoleon in Egypt.* Burlington: University of Vermont, 1988.

Anonymous. *Narrative of a Private Soldier.* Philadelphia: United Foreign Missionary Society, 1822.

Anonymous. *Observations sur L'Expédition de General Bonaparte Dan Le Levant.* Paris: Bureau de la Libraire, 1799.

Anonymous. *Napoleon's Oraculum or Book of Fate.* New York: Murray, n.d.

Anonymous. *Relations de l'Expédition de Syrie, de la Bataille d'Aboukir, et de la Reprise.* Paris: Chez Gratiot et Comp., n.d.

Anonymous. *The Egyptian Dream Book.* New York: Bick & Fitzgerald, n.d.

Anonymous. *Traduction Turke des Pièces Recatives a La Procédure et au Jugement de Suleyman El-Haleby, Assassin du General en Chef Kléber.* Cairo: Marcel, 1801.

Arnould, M. *Report sur les Dépenses L'Armée d'Orient en L'an 8.* Paris: Imprimerie Nationale, 1800.

A Savant. *Bonaparte au Caire.* Paris: Prault, An. VII 1799.

Ashton, John. *English Caricature and Satire on Napoleon I.* London: Chatto & Windus, 1888.

Aubry, Octave. *St. Helena.* London: Lippincott, 1936.

Aufrere, Sydney. *Description de L'Égypte.* Tours: Bibliothèque de l'Image, 1993.

Austin, F. Britten. *Forty Centuries Look Down.* New York: Stokes, 1937.

Baird, David. *Life of Sir David Baird.* 2 vols. London: Richard Bentley, 1832.

Barrow, John. *Life and Correspondence of Admiral Sir William Sidney Smith.* Vol. 1. London: Richard Bentley, 1848.

Barthorpe, Michael. *Napoleon's Egyptian Campaigns 1798–1801.* London: Osprey Publishing, 1978.

Barthélemy and Méry. *Napoléon en Égypte.* Paris: Bourdin, 1842.

———. *Napoléon en Égypte.* Paris: Dupont, 1828.

Beaucur, Fernand. *La Campagne d'Égypte 1798–1801.* Levallois: Société de Sauvegarde du Château Imperial de Pont-de-Briques, 1983.

Bednarski, Andrew. *Holding Egypt.* London: Golden House Publications, 2005.

Benoit, Jérémie. *Malmaison et l'Égypte.* Paris: Musée National des Châteaux de Malmaison et Bous-Preau, 1998.

Bernende, Allain, and Gerard-Jean Chaduc. *La Campagne d' Égypte 1798–1801.* Paris: Musée de l' Arme, 1998.

Bernoyer, François. *Avec Bonaparte en Égypte et en Syrie, 1798–1801.* Abbeville: Les Presses Françaises, 1976.

Bert, Alexis. *Description de Désert de Siout a la Mer Rouge.* Cairo: Institute Française d'Archéologie Orientale, 1912.

Bertaud, Jean-Paul. *The Army of the French Revolution.* Princeton: Princeton University Press, 1988.

Berthier, General. *The French Expedition into Syria 1799.* Felling: Worley, 1990.

———. *Relation des Campagnes du General Bonaparte en Égypte et en Syrie.* Paris: Didot L'Armée, 1801.

Bertrand, General. *Campagnes d'Égypte et de Syrie.* 2 vols. with 3rd Atlas vol. Paris: Unis, 1847.

Bierman, Irene, ed. *Napoleon in Egypt.* Reading: Garnet, 2003.

Blanco, Richard L. *Wellington's Surgeon General: Sir James McGrigor.* Durham, NC: Duke University Press, 1974.

Bonnefons, Sergent, and Corporal Cailleux-Brallier. *Souvenirs et Cahiers sur la Campagne d'Égypte.* Paris: Teissedre, 1997.

Boulay de la Meurthe, Count. *Le Directoire et l'Expédition d' Égypte.* Paris: Hachette, 1883.

Boustany, Salah el-din. *Bonaparte's Egypt in Picture and Word 1798–1801.* Cairo: Arab Bookshop, 1986.

———. *The Press During the French Expedition in Egypt, 1798–1801.* Cairo: The American University in Cairo, 1954.

Bradley, Bruce, and William B. Ashworth, Jr. *Napoleon and the Scientific Expedition to Egypt.* Kansas City: Linda Hall Library Trusts, 2006.

Brier, Robert, ed. *The Glory of Ancient Egypt.* New York: Kraus Reprint, 1988.

———. "The Battle of Chobrakit." *The Journal of International Napoleonic Society.* Montreal: International Napoleonic Society, 1998.

———. *Napoleon in Egypt.* Greenvale: Hillwood Art Museum, LIU, 1990.

Browne, Haji A. *Bonaparte in Egypt and the Egyptians of To-Day.* London: T. Fischer Unwin, 1907.

Brunon, Raoul. *Le Musée de L'Empéri.* Salon de Provence: Musée de L'Empéri, 1988.

Brunun, R., and J. Brunun. *Les Mamelukes d'Égypte.* Marseilles: Archives et Collections Raoul et Jean Brunun, n.d.

Bunbury, Lieut.-Gen. Sir Henry. *Narratives of Some Passages in the Great War With France.* London: Richard Bentley, 1854.

Burgoyne, John M. *A Short History of the Naval and Military Operations in Egypt from 1789 to 1802.* Ontario: Poniard, 1996.

Burleigh, Nina. *Mirage.* New York: HarperCollins, 2007.

Bussey, George. *History of Napoleon.* 2 vols. London: Thomas, 1840.

Byrde, Melanie. *The Napoleonic Institute of Egypt.* Ann Arbor, MI: UMI Dissertation Services, 1992.

Calmon, Maitre Philippe. *L'Égypte, Bonaparte, et Champollion.* Figiac: Association Pour le Bicentenaire Champollion, 1990.

Cawthorn, George. *Observations on the Expedition of General Buonaparte to the East.* London: Cawthorn, British Library, 1798.

Charles-Roux, F. *Bonaparte: Governor of Egypt.* London: Methuen & Co., 1936.

Chevallier, Bernard. *L'Abécédaire des Châteaux de Malmaison.* Paris: Flammarion, n.d.

Chuquet, Arthur, *L'École de Mars.* Paris: Plon, 1899.

Clarke, Edward Daniel. *The Tomb of Alexander.* Cambridge: Cambridge University Press, 1805.

Clayeridie, Constantine. *Le Départ de Bonaparte d'Égypte après la Bataille d'Aboukir.* Manuscript of an unpublished play in two acts presented to Empress Josephine. 1801.

Cole, Juan. *Napoleon's Egypt.* New York: Palgrave Macmillan, 2007.

Crowdy, Terry. *French Warship Crews 1789–1805.* London: Osprey Publishing, 2005.

———. *French Soldiers in Egypt: 1798–1801.* London: Osprey Publishing, 2003.

D'Ancemont, R. *The Historical and Unrevealed Memoirs of Napoleon Bonaparte.* London: Self-published, 1820.

Dangell, M. S. *The Cabinet . . . Containing Foreknowledge of Future Events Found in the Cabinet of Bonaparte.* London: n.p., 1833.

De Meulenaire, Philippe. *Bibliographe Raisonnée des Témoignages de l'Expédition d'Égypte 1798–1801.* Paris: Chamonal, 1993.

Denon, Vivant. *Travels in Upper and Lower Egypt*. 2 vols. New York: Heard and Forman, 1803.

Derugy, Jacoues. *Bonaparte en Terre Sainte*. Paris: Fayard, 1993.

Desgenettes, Dr. *Souvenirs d'un Médecin de l'Expédition d'Égypte*. Paris: Levy, 1893.

Devaux, Bernard, ed. *La Campagne d'Égypte 1798–1801 Mythes et Réalités*. Paris: Forman, 1999.

Dewachter, Michel. *Collections Égyptiennes de l'Institut de France*. Paris: Sanolconti, 1987.

Dierkens, Alain. *Henri-Joseph Redoute el d'Expédition de Bonaparte en Égypte*. Bruxelles: Credit Communal, 1993.

Dietrich, William. *Napoleon's Pyramids*. New York: HarperCollins, 2007.

Di Pietro, Dominique. *Voyage Historique en Égypte Pendant les Campagnes des Généraux Bonaparte, Kléber, et Menou*. Paris: Huillier, 1818.

Doguereau, General. *Journal de l'Expédition d'Égypt*. Paris: Perrin, 1904.

Doguereau, Jean-Pierre. *Journal of Napoleon's Expedition*. Westport: Praeger, 2002.

Doyle. *A Non-Military Journal of Observations Made in Egypt*. London: Cadeu, 1803.

Elgood, P. G. *Bonaparte's Adventure in Egypt*. London: Oxford University Press, 1936.

El Turke, Nikoula. *Historie de l'Expédition des Français en Égypte*. Paris: Imprimerie Royale, 1819.

Eton, W. *Survey of the Turkish Empire*. London: T. Cadell, 1801.

Evans, Henry R. "Napoleon in Egypt." *The Master Mason, New Jersey Edition*. New Jersey: Grand Lodge of New Jersey, 1925.

Faivre d'Arcier, Amanry. *Les Agents de Napoléon in Égypte, 1801–1815*. Levallois: Société de Sauvegarde du Châteaux Imperial du Ponte-de-Briques, 1990.

Feydel, Gabriel. *Quatre-Vingt-Onze. Questions Adressées a l'Institut d'Égypte*. Paris: Garney, An. VII 1800.

Fortescue, The Hon. J. W. *A History of the British Army*. Vol. IV. London: Macmillan and Co., 1915.

Francois, Captaine. *Journal par le "Dromadaire d'Égypte."* 2 vols. Paris: Carrington 1903–1904.

Frayling, Christopher. *Napoleon Wrote Fiction*. Salisbury: Compton Press, 1972.

Fregosi, Paul. *Dreams of Empire*. New York: Birch Lane, 1990.

French Army. *Fuite de Bonaparte de l'Égypte*. Paris: Lerouge, 1814.

———. *Correspondance Officielle de l'Armée d'Égypte*. Paris: Pironnet, An IX, 1800.

———. *Copies of the Original Letters from the Army of General Bonaparte in Egypt*. London: J. Wright, 1798.

Funchen, Liliane, and Fred. *Napoléon: le Sultan de Feu*. Paris: de la Porte, 1994. Graphic novel.

Galland, A. *Tableau de l'Égypte Pendant le Séjour de l'Armée Française*. 2 vols. Paris: Galland, An XI 1804.

Galli, H. *L'Armée Française en Égypte 1798–1801*. Paris: Charpentier, 1883.

Garreau, R. *Besson-Bey*. Paris: Société d'Éditions Géographiques, 1949.

Gillispie, Charles Coulston, and Michael Dewachter. *Monuments of Egypt*. 2 vols. Princeton: Princeton Architectural Press, 1988.

———. *Monuments of Egypt*. Old Saybrook, CT: Konecky & Konecky, 1987.

Glover, Michael. *The Napoleonic Wars: an Illustrated History 1792–1815*. New York: Hippocrene Books, 1979.

Glower, Michael. *A Very Slippery Fellow: The Life of Sir Robert Wilson*. London: Oxford University Press, 1978.

Goby, Jean-Edouard. *Premier Institue D'Égypte*. Paris: Darantiere, 1987.

Godfrey, Richard. *English Caricature 1620 to the Present.* Bury St. Edmunds: St. Edmunds Press, 1984.

Godlewska, Anne. *The Napoleonic Survey of Egypt.* Toronto: University of Toronto Press, 1988.

Goodwin, Peter. *Nelson's Victory.* Annapolis, MD: Naval Institute Press, 2000.

Green, Jeremy. "A Year Against the Odds." *Military Heritage.* Vol. 4, No. 6. McLean, VA: Military Heritage, 2003.

Grobert, J. *Description des Pyramides de Ghize de la Ville du Kaire et de ses Environs.* Paris: Logeret-Petiet/Remont, 1801.

Guitry, Commandant. *L'Armée de Bonaparte en Égypte.* Paris: Flammarion, 1898.

Guyader, Herve le. *Geoffroy Saint-Hilaire: A Visionary Naturalist.* Chicago: University of Chicago Press, 2004.

Hamelin, Antonine-Romain. *Douze ans de Ma Vie.* n.p., n.d.

Hayward, Joel. *For God and Glory: Lord Nelson and His Way of War.* Annapolis, MD: Naval Institute Press, 2003.

Herbin de Halle, P.-E. *Conquêtes des Français en Égypte.* Paris: Pouglens, An VII 1799.

Herold, J. Christopher. *Bonaparte in Egypt.* London: Hamish Hamilton, 1963.

Hery, Francois-Xavier, and Thierry Endel. *L'Univers de l'Égypte, Révèle Par Bonaparte.* Aix en Provence: Chaudoreille, 1992.

Hill, Draper, ed. *The Satirical Etchings of James Gillray.* Toronto: Dover Publications 1976.

Holland, Ann Marie. *Napoleon's Expedition to Egypt.* Montreal: McGill University Press, 1998.

Horward, Donald. *Consortium on Revolutionary Europe 1750–1850.* Tallahassee: Florida State University, 1998.

———. *Napoleon and Iberia.* Tallahassee: Florida State University, 1980. Autographed.

Jones, Proctor. *Napoleon: An Intimate Account of the Years of Supremacy 1800–1814.* San Francisco: Proctor Jones Publishing Company, 1992.

Kasabarian-Bricout, Beatrice. *L'Odyssée Mamelouke.* Paris: Harmattan, 1988.

Kelsey Museum of Archaeology. *Napoleon's Legacy: the European Exploration of Egypt.* Kelsey, MI: Kelsey Museum of Archaeology, 1984.

Kirchenhoffer, H. *The Book of Fate Formerly in the Possession of Napoleon.* Scranton: Personal Arts, 1929.

———. *The Book of Fate Formerly in the Possession of Napoleon.* London: Arnold, 1834.

———. *The Book of Fate Formerly in the Possession of Napoleon.* London: Arnold, 1826.

———. *The Book of Fate.* London: J. McGowan, 1822.

———. *The Book of Fate Formerly in the Possession of Napoleon.* New York: Anglo-American Association, n.d.

Krettly, Captaine. *Souvenirs Historiques.* Vol. 2. Paris: Berlandier, 1839.

Lacouture, Jean, and Somonne. *Egypt in Transition.* London: Methuen, 1958.

Lacroix, Desire. *Bonaparte en Égypte* 1798–1799. Paris: Garnier, 1897.

Laissus, Yves. *Il Y A 200 Ans, Les Savants en Égypte.* Paris: Museum National D'Histoire, 1998.

———. *L' Égypte, une Aventure Savante 1798–1800.* Paris: Fayard, 1993.

———, ed. *Les Savants en Égypte.* Paris: Nathan, 1998.

La Jonquiere, Clement. *L'Expédition d'Égypte.* 5 vols. Paris: Charles-Lavauzelle, 1910.

Lapurte, Joseph. *Mon Voyage en Égypte et en Syrie.* Paris: Presses Universitaires de France, 2007.

La Revue Napoléon. Nos. 1–10. February 2000–May 2002. 10 vols.

Larrey, Baron Dominique Jean. *Memoirs of Baron Larrey.* Chippenham, Wiltshire: Great Britain, 1997.

Laurens, Henry. *Campagnes d'Égypte et de Syrie.* Paris: Imprimerie Nationale, 1998.

————. *L'Expédition d'Égypte 1798–1801.* Paris: Armand Colin, 1989.

————. *Kléber en Égypte 1798–1800.* 2 vols. Paris: Institute Français D'Archéologie Orientale, 1988.

Laus de Boissy, Louis. *Bonaparte au Caire.* Paris: Prault, An VII 1799.

Lavalliette, Count. *Memoirs.* Philadelphia: Ash, 1832.

Lavery, Brian. *Nelson on the Nile.* London: Chatham Publishing, 1998.

Legrain, Georges. *Les Savants de Bonaparte en Égypte.* Cairo: Gillet, 1913.

Lenoir, Albert. *Le Tombeau de Napoléon Premier aux Invalides.* Paris: Libraire Classique, n.d.

Le Quesne, Charles. *Queseir.* Cairo: American University Press in Cairo, 2007.

Lloyd, Christopher. *The Nile Campaign, Nelson and Napoleon in Egypt.* London: David and Charles Holdings Ltd., 1973.

Malus, Etienne Louis. *L'Agenda de Malus: Souvenirs de l'Expédition d'Égypte.* Paris: Champion, 1892.

Mangrel, Maxim. *Capitane Gérard.* 5 vols. Paris: Charles-Lavauzelle, 1910.

Marcellino, Fred. *I Crocodile.* New York: HarperCollins, 1999.

Marchand, Louis-Joseph. *Memoirs.* Sacramento: Proctor Jones, 1998.

Martea-Becker, F. *General Desaix.* Paris: Didier, 1852.

Martin, P. *Histoire de l'Expédition Française en Égypte.* 2 vols. Paris: Eberhart, 1815.

Menenal, Count. *Memoirs of Napoleon Bonaparte.* 3 vols. New York: Collier 1910.

Menuau, Commandant. *Journal d'un Dragon d'Égypte.* Paris: Dubois, 1899.

Metz, Jean, and Georges Legrain. *Au Pays de Napoléon, l'Égypte.* Grenoble: Rey, 1913.

Meysen, Jean Joseph. *Mémoire et Souvenirs.* A 202-page manuscript by one of Napoleon's soldiers in the Egyptian Campaign.

Milleliri, Jean-Marie. *Médecins et Soldats Pendant L'Expédition D'Égypte 1798–1799.* Nice: Giouanangeli, 1993.

Millet, Chasseu Pierre. *Souvenirs de la Campagne d'Égypte.* Paris: Emile-Paul, 1903.

Millet, Stanslas. *Le Chasseur Pierro Millet.* Paris: Emile-Paul, 1903.

Miot, Jacques. *Mémoires Pour Server A L'Histoire des Expéditions en Égypte et en Syrie.* Paris: Demonville, 1804.

Miot, M. J. *Memoires of My Service in the French Expedition to Egypt and Syria.* Tyne and Wear: Worley Publications, 1997.

Moiret, Captain Joseph-Marie. *Memoirs of Napoleon's Egyptian Expedition 1798–1801.* London: Greenhill Books, 2001.

Moiret, Joseph-Marie. *Mémoires sur l'Expédition d'Égypte.* Paris: Belfond, 1987.

Morand, General Charles. *Lettres sur L'Expédition D'Égypte* La Vouivre: Fondation Napoléon, 1998.

Munier, H. *Tables de la Description de l'Égypte.* Cairo: Société Royale de Géographie d'Égypte, 1943.

Murat, Laure. *L'Expédition d'Égypte.* Paris: Gallimard, 1998.

————. *A la Découverte de l'Égypte.* Paris: Paris Muses, 1998.

Napoleon Journal. Nos. 13–15. 3 vols. Berkley, CA: Napoleon LLC (Fall 1998–Winter 1999).

Neret, Gilles. *Description of Egypt.* London: Taschen, 2002.

Newton, Alfred. *Audouin's Explication Sommaire des Planches.* London: The Willoughby Society, 1883.

Norden, Frederik Lewis. *Travels in Egypt and Nubia.* London: Lockyer Davis and Charles Reymer, 1757.

Norry, Charles. *Relation de l'Expédition d'Égypte.* Paris: Ch. Pougens et Magimel, An VII 1798.

Norry, Charles. *Relation de l'Expédition d'Égypte.* Paris: Pougens, 1799.

Nowinski, Judith. *Baron Dominique Vivant Denon.* Rutherford, NJ: Fairleigh Dickinson University Press, 1970.

Orlandi, Enzo, ed. *The Life and Times of Napoleon.* Philadelphia: The Curtis Publishing Company, 1966.

Parker, Bonnie. *Napoleon's Book of Fate.* Wellingborough: Aquarian Press, 1988.

Parker, Harold. *The Cult of Antiquity and the French Revolution.* Chicago: University of Chicago Press, 1937.

Pawley, Ronald. *Napoleon's Mamelukes.* Osceola: Ospray, 2006.

Pelleport, General. *Souvenirs Militaires et Intimes.* 2 vols. Paris: Didier, 1857.

Phillip, Thomas. *Acre: Rise and Fall of a Palestinian City.* New York: Columbia University Press, 2001.

Pococke, Richard. *A Description of the East and Some Other Countries.* London: W. Bower, 1743–1745.

Polowetzky, Michael. *A Bond Never Broken.* Rutherford, NJ: Farleigh Dickinson Press, 1993.

Postgate, Raymond. *Story of a Year: 1798.* New York: Harcourt, Brace & World, 1969.

Rawson, Geoffrey. *Nelson's Letters.* London: Dent, 1960.

Raymond, Andre. *Égyptiens et Français au Caire 1798–1801.* Paris: Institut Français d'Archéologie Orientale, 1998.

Remini, Robert V. *Joseph Smith.* New York: Penguin Group, 2002.

Revue du Souvenir Napoléonien. May–June 1998 issue devoted to Bicentennial of Bonaparte in Egypt.

Reybaud, Marcel. *Histoire Scientifique et Militaire de l' Expédition Française en Égypte.* Paris: Denain, 1830–6. Ten volumes of text and two atlas volumes of plates.

Reynier, General. *De l'Égypte Après La Bataille d'Héliopolis.* London: Cox, 1802.

Reynier, Jean Louis. *The State of Egypt after the Battle of Heliopolis.* London: G. Robinson, 1802.

———. *Campaign Between the French Army of the East and the British and Turkish Forces in Egypt.* London: Ridgway, 1802.

Richardson, Robert. G. *Larrey Surgeon to Napoleon's Imperial Guard.* London: John Murray, 1974.

Richardt, Lieutenant-Colonel. *Nouveaux mémoire sur L'Armée Française en Égypte en Syrie.* Paris: Correard, 1848.

Ridley, Ronald T. *Napoleon's Proconsul in Egypt, The Life and Times of Bernardino Drovetti.* London: Rubicon Press, n.d.

Ripaud, Citizen. *Report of the Commission of Arts to the First Consul Bonaparte, of the Antiquities of Upper Egypt.* London: J. Debett, 1800.

Roider, Karl, and John Horgan. *The Consortium on Revolutionary Europe 1750–1850.* Tallahassee: Florida State University, 1992.

Roy, J. J. *Les Français en Égypte.* Tours: Mame, 1868.

Russell, Terence M. *The Discovery of Egypt.* UK: Sutton Publishing Ltd., 2005.

Saisons d'Alsace. 20, no. 4 (1953). Issue devoted to the 200 anniversary of the death of General Kléber.

Sangle-Ferrière, François-Etienne. *Souvenirs de l'Expédition d'Égypte.* Paris: Teissedre, 1998.

Sarrazin, General. *Confession de General Bonaparte.* London: Vogel, 1811.

Savigny, Jules-Cesar. *Histoire Naturelle et Mythologique de l'Ibis.* Paris: Allais, 1805.

Schur, Nathan. *Napoleon in the Holy Land.* London: Greenhill Books, 1999.

Schwartz, Constance, and Franklin Hill Perrill. *Napoleon and His Age.* Roslyn, NY: Nassau County Museum of Art, 2000.

Serino, Franco. *Description de l'Égypte.* Cairo: University of Cairo Press, 2003.

———. *Description de l'Égypte.* Vercelli: White Star, 2003.

Silvera, Alain. *Napoleon in Egypt in Laurels.* New York: The American Society of the French Legion of Honor, 1983.

Small, Lisa. *Napoleon on the Nile.* New York: Dahesh Museum, 2006.

Sole, Robert. *Bonaparte a la Conquête de l'Égypte.* Paris: Seuil, 2006.

———. *Les Savants de Bonaparte.* Paris: Seuil, 1998.

Sonnini, C. S. *Travels in Upper and Lower Egypt.* London: Debrett, 1800.

St.-Hilaire, Etienne Geoffroy. *Lettres Écrites D'Égypte.* Paris: Hachette, 1901.

Stoddard, John, L. *Napoleon from Corsica to St. Helena.* Chicago: The Werner Company, n.d.

Strathen, Paul. *Napoleon in Egypt.* New York: Bantam Dell, 2008.

Taschin. *Description of Egypt: 30 Postcards.* Koln: Taschen, 1995.

———. *Description of Egypt: 6 Posters.* Koln: Taschen, 1995.

Thiers, Louis. *Expédition de Bonaparte En Égypte.* New York: Holt, 1894.

Thurman, Capitaine. *Bonaparte en Égypte.* Paris: E.-Paul, 1902.

Tortel, Christian, and Patricia Carlier. *Bonaparte de Toulon au Caire.* France: Armine-Ediculture, 1996.

Tranie, Jean, and J. C. Carmigniani. *Bonaparte la Campagne d'Égypte.* Paris: Pygmailion, 1988.

Trecourt, Jean-Baptiste. *Memories Sur Égypte.* Cairo: Royal Geographical Society of Egypt, 1942.

Truman, Charles. *The Sèvres Egyptian Service 1810–12.* London: Victoria and Albert Museum, 1982.

University of Pennsylvania. *The Museum Journal.* Philadelphia: University of Pennsylvania Press, 1913.

Vaxeclaire, J. C. *Mémoires d'un Vétéran de L'Ancienne Armée 1791–1800.* Paris: Delagrave, 1899.

Veron-Denise, Daniele. *Des Livres Pour l'Exil. La Bibliothèque de Napoléon I a l'Ile d'Elbe.* Fontainebleau: Musée National du Château de Fontainebleau, 1998.

Walsh, Thomas. *Journal of the Late Campaign in Egypt.* London: Candell, Jun & Davies, 1803.

———. *Journal of the Late Campaign in Egypt.* London: Elibron Classics, 2005.

Warner, Oliver. *Nelson's Battles.* London: Pen and Sword, 1965.

———. *The Battle of the Nile.* London: Batsford, 1960.

Watson, S. J. *By Command of the Emperor, A Life of Marshal Berthier.* Chippenham, Wiltshire: Antony Wiltshire, 1957.

Weider, Ben. *The Poisoning of Napoleon: The Final Proof.* Montreal: Ben Weider, 1995.

Wheatly, Dennis. *The Sultan's Daughter.* London: The Book Club, 1963.

Wilson, Sir Robert Thomas. *History of the British Expedition to Egypt.* London: C. Roworth, 1803.

Zamoyski, Adam. *Rites of Peace: The Fall of Napoleon and the Congress of Vienna.* New York: Harper, 2007.

CHAPTER 4: HOW AN OBELISK AND A CANAL CONQUERED FRANCE

Anonymous. "The Obelisk of Luxor." *The Penny Magazine* 120 (February 15, 1834): 61–63; and 121 (February 22, 1834): 66–67.

Barker, A. J. *Suez.* London: Farber and Farber, 1864.

Beaty, Charles. *De Lesseps of Suez.* New York: Harpers, 1956.

Department of State. *The Suez Canal Problem.* Washington, DC: U.S. Government Printing Office, 1956.

Karabell, Zachary. *Parting the Desert.* New York: Alfred A. Knopf, 2003.

Kinross, Lord. *Between Two Seas.* New York: Morrow, 1969.

Lebas, M. A. *L'Obélisque de Louxor Histoire de sa Translation à Paris.* Paris: Carillian-Goeury, 1839.

Nourse, J. E. *The Maritime Canal of Suez.* Washington, DC: Government Printing Office, 1884.

Thomas, Hugh. *Suez.* New York: Harper & Row, 1867.

CHAPTER 5: THE AMAZING VOYAGE OF CLEOPATRA'S NEEDLE

Alexander, James. *Cleopatra's Needle.* London: Chatto & Windus, 1879. Anonymous. *The Complete History of Cleopatra and All about Her Needle.* London: Sutton, 1879.

Budge, E. A. Wallis. *Cleopatra's Needles and Other Egyptian Obelisks.* London: Religious Tract Society, 1926.

Cooper, W. R. *A Short History of the Egyptian Obelisk.* London: Bagster, 1877.

Dixon, Waynman. Manuscript written on board the *Olga.* London Metropolitan Archives, Reference Q/CN/3.

Engelbach, Rex. *The Problem of the Obelisks.* London: Fisher Unwin, 1923.

Habachi, Labib. *The Obelisks of Egypt.* New York: Scribner's, 1977.

Hayward, R. *Cleopatra's Needles.* Buxton: Moorland, 1978.

King, Rev. James. *Cleopatra's Needle.* London: Religious Tract Society, 1886.

Noakes, Aubry. *Cleopatra's Needles.* London: Witherby, 1962.

Wilson, Erasmus. *Cleopatra's Needle.* London: Brain, 1878.

CHAPTER 6: EGYPT FOR SALE

Anonymous. *The Victorian Pattern Glass & China Book.* New York: Arch Cape Press, 1990.

Crosby, Deborah. *Victorian Pencils.* Atlglen, PA: Schiffer Publishing, 1998.

Davison, Joe. *The Art of the Cigar Label.* Seaucus: Wellfleet Press, 1989.

Nichols, Dale Reeves. *Egyptian Revival Jewelry & Design.* Atglen, PA: Schiffer Publishing, 2006.

Sherman, Milton M. *All About Tobacco.* New York: Sherman National Corp., 1970.

CHAPTER 7: NEW YORK GETS ITS OBELISK

Anonymous. *Translation of Ancient Egyptian Hieroglyphics . . . On the Sides of the Ancient Egyptian Masonic Obelisk.* New York: Reading & Co. Masonic Publishers, 1881.

Cooper, Basil. "Cleopatra's Needle and Other Monoliths." *Frank Leslie's Popular Monthly* 5 (May 1878): 593–601.

Darling, Gen. Charles. *The Obelisk at Central Park New York.* Privately printed, 1898.

D'Alton, Martina. *The New York Obelisk.* New York: Metropolitan Museum of Art, 1993.

Farman, Elbert. *Along the Nile.* New York: Grafton, 1908.

———. *Cleopatra's Needle.* New York: Grafton, 1908.

———. *Egypt and Its Betrayal.* New York: Grafton, 1908.

Gorringe, Henry H. *Egyptian Obelisks.* New York: Self-published, 1882.

Julien, Alexis. *Notes of Research on the New York Obelisk.* New York: American Geographical Society, 1893.

Moldenke, Harold. *The New York Obelisk.* New York: Randolph, 1891.

———. *The New York Obelisk.* Lancaster: Lancaster Press, 1935.

New York Times, October 10, 1880.

Paine, Albert Bigelow. *Thomas Nast: His Period and His Pictures.* Princeton, NJ: Pyne Press, 1904.

Ridley, Jasper. *The Freemasons.* New York: Arcade, 1999.

Tompkins, Peter. *The Magic of Obelisks.* New York: Harper, 1981.

Weisse, John A. *The Obelisk and Freemasonry.* New York: Bauton, 1880.

World Newspaper. *Programme of the Masonic Ceremonies attending the Laying of the Corner Stone of the Obelisk.* New York: World, 1880.

Young, John Russell. *Around the World with General Grant.* 2 vols. New York: American News Department, 1879.

CHAPTER 8: THE MUMMIES SING SONGS OF THE NILE

Adams, Stanley, and Lecouna, Ernesto. *Dust on the Moon.* New York: Edward Marks, 1934.

Artis, Hal. *Karzan.* Cleveland: Sam Fox, 1919.

Barron, Irma. *'Neath the Shadows: An Egyptian Romance.* New York: Shapiro & Bernstein, 1911.

Berlin, Irving. *Araby.* New York: Waterson, Berlin & Snyder, 1915.

Black, Johnny S. *Ilo: A Voice from Mummyland.* New York: Broadway Music Corp., 1921.

———. *When the Sun Goes Down in Cairo Town.* New York: McCarthy & Fisher, 1920.

Bowers, Rob't Wood. *The Maid and the Mummy: A Musical Farce in Three Acts.* New York: M. Witmark & Sons, 1904.

Broomstock, I. L. *Thebes.* New York: F. B. Haviland, 1906.

Browning, H. *My Queen of the Caravan.* New York: H. I. Browning, 1918.

Caire, Reda. *Mon Egyptienne.* Paris: Paul Beuscher, 1937.

Carlo and Sanders. *Tut-Ankh-Amen In the Valley of the Kings.* New York: Jerome H. Remick, 1923.

Carroll, Earl, and Harry. *'Neath the Shadow of the Pyramids: Ballad.* New York: Shapiro, Bernstein, & Co. 1914.

Casey, James W. *Egyptland.* Chicago: Forster, 1919.

Clark, Grant. *My Sahara Rose.* New York: Irving Berlin, Inc., 1920.

Conrad, John. *Peacock Walk.* St. Louis: Conrad, 1920.

Coogan, Jack. *Cleopatra Had a Jazz Band.* New York: Leo Feist, 1917.

Cooper, John. *My Desert Love: An Oriental Love Song.* New York: M. Witmark & Sons, 1919.

Costello, Bartley. *Egypt.* New York: Triangle Music, 1927.

Crist, Bainbridge. *Egyptian Impressions.* New York: Carl Fischer, 1915.

De Silva, Bud. *My Cairo Maid.* Los Angeles: W. A. Quincke, 1917.

Delhaxhe, Jules. *Sérénade Égyptienne: Morceau Caractéristique pour Piano.* Bruxelles: E. De Saedler and E. Possoz, n.d.

Denni, Lucien. *Old King Tut Was a Wise Old Nut.* Kansas City: J. W. Jenkins Sons, 1923.

Doyle, Walter. *Egyptian Ella.* New York: Skidmore Music Co., 1931.

Dulmage, Will E. *Cairo Land.* Battle Creek: Chas. Roat, 1923.

Earl, Mary. *Mohammed.* New York: Shapiro, Bernstein & Co., 1920.

Fillmore, Henry. *Vashti.* Cincinnati: Fillmore Bros., 1904.

Flynn, Alan. *Egyptian Nights.* New York: Al Piantadosi, 1919.

Freed, Arthur. *Love Songs of the Nile.* New York: Robbins Music Co., 1933.

———. *Cairo.* San Francisco: Sherman, Clay & Co., 1919.

Freeman, Harold R. *Rose of Egypt Land.* Providence: Harold Freeman, 1919.

Friedland, Anatol. *My Sweet Egyptian Rose.* New York: Jos. W. Stern, 1917.

Frost, Harold. *Oasis, a Desert Romance.* Chicago: Frank K. Root, 1918.

Gay, Byron. *Just a Little Drink.* San Francisco: Villa Moret, 1925.

———. *Fate: It Was Fate When I First Met You.* New York: M. Whitmark & Sons, 1922.

———. *Sand Dunes.* New York: Leo Feist, 1919.

Gerber, Alex. *3000 Years Ago.* New York: Irving Berlin, 1923.

Goetzl, Anselm. *Aphrodite.* New York: M. Witmark & Sons, 1919.

Goldstein, Nat. *At the Mummies Ball.* San Francisco: Nat Goldstein, 1921.

Goldston, Margaret. *I Want My Mummy.* Van Nuys, CA: Alfred Publishing, n.d.

Green, Bud. *Mystic Nile.* New York: Al Piantadosi, 1920.

Grofé, Ferdie, and Peter de Rose. *Suez.* New York: Triangle, 1922.

Gunsey, M. J. *Goddess of the Nile.* San Francisco: Adrian-Reece, 1919.

Hagen, Milt, and Roslyn Clephane. *Dromedary.* New York: Edward B. Marks, 1925.

Hartmann, Albert. *Cleopatra's Needle Waltz.* London: J. B. Cramer 1879.

Hearn, Edward. *Song of Araby.* St. Louis: Art Publication Society, 1955.

Henlere, Hershel. *Kismet.* Chicago: Will Rossiter, 1920.

Henry, S. R., and O. Onivas. *Pahjamah.* New York: Jos. W. Stern, 1919.

Herbert, Victor. "Star Light Star Bright." From *Wizard of the Nile.* New York: Edward Schuberth, 1895.

Herscher, Louis. *Bound in Morocco.* New York: Leo Feist, 1920.

Hewitt, J. F. *Mummy Monarch.* New York: John Church, 1907.

Jones, Clarence. *Mid The Pyramids.* Chicago: Will Rossiter, 1918.

Jones, Isham. *Lady of the Nile.* Chicago: Milton Weil, 1925.

Kalmar, Bert, and Harry Ruby. *Rebecca Come Back from Mecca.* New York: Waterson, Berlin & Snyder, 1921.

Kendall, Edwin I. *Arabs Dream.* New York: Seminary Music, 1909.

Kerr, Harry. *My Cairo Love.* Cleveland: Sam Fox, 1919.

Ketelby, Albert W. *Au Pays Mystique D'Égypte.* Bruxelles: Bosworth, 1931.

Kummer, Clare. *Egypt, My Cleopatra.* New York: Josh W. Stern, 1903.

Lamb, Arthur. *Pride of the Caravan.* New York: Joe Morris, 1919.

Lardie, Max B. *Whispering Sunbird.* Detroit: Arthur Brothers, 1923.

Leininger, Lillian. *If I Could Read Your Heart.* New York: American Advance Music Co., 1905.

Lenzberg, Julius. *Moonlight on the Nile.* New York: Jerome Remick, 1919.

Lewin, Leonard. *Desert Dreams.* New York: Waterson, Berlin & Snyder, 1920.

Lewis, Ted. *Bo-La-Bo.* New York: M. Witmark & Sons, 1919.

Lincke, Paul. *Amina, Egyptian Serenade.* London: Hawkes & Son, 1907.

Litchfield, E. S. *Zoma.* New York: Geo. A. Friedman, 1919.

Losey, F. H. *Under Egyptian Skies.* Williamsport: Vandersloot, 1912.

———. *Flower of the Nile.* Williamsport: Vandersloot, 1908.

Markell, D. *Desert Nights.* Los Angeles: Southern California Music Co., 1920.

McPhail, Lindsay, and Walter Michels. *San.* New York: Curtis, 1924.

Moore, Elizabeth. *Arabian Song Cycle.* Cincinnati: John Church, 1923.

Motzan, Otto. *My Egyptian Mummy.* New York: Jos. W. Stern, 1913.

Nicholls, Horatio. *Saharh.* Paris: Francis-Day, 1924.

Odie, Basil. *In Cairo.* London: Bowerman, 1923.

Penn, Arthur. *Alexandria.* New York: M. Witmark & Sons, 1919.

Perillo, Carl, and Howard Rossman. *Cairo Blues: Oriental Fox Trot.* Scranton: Whitmore, 1919.

Phillips, A. Fred. *Egyptian Moonlight: An Oriental Love Song.* Boston: Ted Garton,1919.

Powell, W. G. *Cairo, Intermesso Patrol.* New York: Church, Paxon & Co., 1911.

Roberts, Lee S., and J. Will Callahan. *Cleo.* Chicago: Forster, 1919.

Rogee, Leon. *Americans on the Nile.* New York: Edgar Selden, 1912.

Romberg, Sigmund. *The Desert Song.* Santa Monica: Southern California Music Co., 1926.

Rose, Vincent. *Mummy Mine.* San Francisco: Sherman, Clay, & Co., 1918.

Roy, Rae. *Gyptia Fox Trot.* London: Baker & Bond, 1920.

Shannon, J. R. *Where the Desert Meets the Nile.* Detroit: Grinnell Bros., 1910.

Shean, Al, and Ed Gallagher. *Oh Mister Gallagher and Mister Shean.* New York: Jack Mills, 1922.

Shepheard, Fred H. *On the Nile.* New York: F. B. Haviland, 1904.

Siedle, Carl. *I Am Dying, Egypt.* Cincinnati: A. C. Peters, 1865.

Silverman & Mehr. *Cairo Valse.* London: Silberman & Grock, 1918.

Smith, Harry B., and Francis Wheeler. *The Sheik of Araby.* New York: Berlin & Snyder, 1922.

Smith, Walter. *By the Temple Gate.* Kansas City: Jenkins Sons, 1924.

Spencer, Herbert. *There's Egypt in Your Dreamy Eyes.* New York: Jerome H. Remick, 1917.

Squires, Harry D., and Bob Haring. *Pharaoh Land.* New York: Joe Morris, 1922.

Von Tilzer, Harry. *Old King Tut.* New York: Harry Von Tilzer, 1923.

Waite, C. L. *Sons of The Desert, Sphinx Temple Marching Song.* Hartford: Sphinx Temple, 1930.

Wells, William. *Sahara.* New York: Frederick V. Bowers, 1919.

Whiting, Richard. *In the Valley of the Nile.* New York: Jerome Remick, 1915.

Wiedoef, Ruby, and Olman, Abe. *Karavan.* Chicago: Forster, 1919.

Williams, Gene. *En Caravan.* Paris: Francis Day, 1924.

Williams, Harry H. *Prince of Pyramid Land.* Providence: Williams, 1915.

Yellen, Jack. *By the Silvery Nile.* Chicago: Forster, 1921.

CHAPTER 9: TUTANKHAMEN, SUPERSTAR

Adams, John. *The Millionaire and the Mummies: Theodore Davis's Gilded Age in the Valley of the Kings.* New York: St. Martin's Press, 2013.

Administrators of the Egyptian Museum. *Notice Sommaire sur Objects Provenant de la Tombe de Toutankhamon.* Cairo: Institut Français, 1926.

Bell, Archie. *King Tut-Ankh-Amen.* London: L. C. Page, 1923.

Budge, E. A. Wallis. *Tutankhamen, Amenism, and Egyptian Monotheism.* New York: Bell, n.d.

Capart, Jean. *Tout-Ankh-Amon.* Bruxellles: Vromant, 1923.

Carter, Howard. *The Tomb of Tut-Ankh-Amen. Statement with Documents as to the Events Which Occurred in the Winter of 1923–24.* London: Cassell and Company, 1924.

———, and A. C. Mace. *The Tomb of Tut-Ankh-Amen.* 3 vols. London: Cassell and Co., 1923–1933.

Carter, Michael. *Tutankhamen.* New York: David McKay, 1972.

Corlett, Dudley S. "Art on the Screen; or the Film of Tutankhamen." *Art and Archaeology* XVI, 6 (December 1923): 231–240.

Cottrell, Leonard. *The Secrets of Tutankhamen's Tomb.* Greenwich: New York Graphic Society, 1964.

Curators of the Egyptian Museum. *A Short Description of Objects from the Tomb of Tutankhamun.* Cairo: Institut Français, 1927.

Current History Magazine. *Splendors in the Tomb of the Egyptian King Tutenkhamon.* New York: New York Times Company, 1924.

Dowdall, Ernest S. *The Man Tutankhamen.* London: Ed. J. Burrow, 1923.

Eckenstein, L. *Tutankh-Aten.* London: Jonathan Cape, 1924.

Fazzini, Richard. *Tutankhamun and the African Heritage.* New York: Metropolitan Museum of Art, 1978.

Gautier, Théophile. *Romance of a Mummy.* Philadelphia: Lippincott, 1882.

Goyne, Richard. *The Kiss of Pharaoh.* New York: Stokes, 1923.

James, T. G. H. *Howard Carter*. London: Kegan Paul, 1992.

Nahas, Bishara. *The Life and Times of Tut-Ankh-Amen*. New York: American Library Service, 1923.

Piankoff, Alexandre. *The Shrines of Tut-Ankh-Amon*. Princeton, NJ: Princeton University Press, 1977.

Reeves, Nicholas. *The Complete Tutankhamen*. London: Thames and Hudson, 1990.

Smith, G. Elliot. *Tutankhamen*. London: Routledge, 1923.

Taboulis, G. R. *The Private Life of Tutankhamen*. New York: McBride, 1929.

Tyldsley, Joyce. *Tutankhamen*. New York: Basic Books, 2012.

Weigall, Arthur. *Tutankhamen and Other Essays*. New York: Doran, 1924.

Williams, Maynard Owen. "At the Tomb of Tutankhamen." *National Geographic Magazine* XLIII, 5 (May 1923): 461–508.

Winlock, H. E. *Materials Used at the Embalming of King Tut-Ankh-Amun*. New York: Metropolitan Museum of Art, 1941.

Winstone, H. V. F. *Howard Carter*. London: Constable, 1991.

Wise, William. *The Two Reigns of Tutankhamen*. New York: G. P. Putnam's, 1964.

Wynne, Barry. *Behind The Mask of Tutankhamen*. New York: Taplinger, 1972.

CHAPTER 10: THE MUMMY GOES TO THE MOVIES

Anonymous. *House of Horror: The Complete Hammer Films Story*. London: Creation Books, 1973.

Frank, Alan. *Horror Films*. London: Spring Books, 1977.

Hutchinson, Tim. *Horror & Fantasy in the Movies*. New York: Crescent Books, 1974.

Riley, Philip J., ed. *The Mummy*. Absecon, NJ: MagicImage Filmbooks, 1989.

Ringgold, Gene, and DeWitt Bodeen. New York: Citadel Press, 1969.

CHAPTER 11: THE FUTURE OF EGYPTOMANIA

Anonymous. *The Treasures of Tutankhamun in San Francisco*. San Francisco: California Living Books, 1979.

Anonymous. *The Guide to Tutankhamun and the Golden Age of the Pharaohs*. Fort Lauderdale: Museum of Art, 2005.

Anonymous. *The Treasures of Tutankhamun*. New York: Metropolitan Museum of Art, 1976.

Anthes, Rudolf. *Tutankhamun's Treasures*. Washington DC: Smithsonian, 1961.

Desroches-Noblecourt, Christiane. *Tutankhamun*. New York: New York Graphic Society, 1963.

Edwards, I. E. S. *The Treasures of Tutankhamen*. New York: Viking Press, 1972.

Ford, John. *Tutankhamen's Treasures*. Secaucus, NJ: Chartwell Books, 1978.

Fox, Penelope. *Tutankhamun's Treasure*. London: Oxford University Press, 1951.

Frayling, Christopher. *The Face of Tutankhamun*. London: Farber and Farber, 1992.

Freud, Sigmund. *Collected Papers*. 5 Vols. New York: Basic Books, 1959.

———. *Moses and Monotheism*. New York: Alfred A. Knopf, 1939.

Hawass, Zahi. "DNA Sheds New Light on the Boy King's Life and Death." *National Geographic Magazine* 218, 3 (September 2010): 34–59.

———. *The Golden Age of Tutankhamun*. Cairo: American University of Cairo Press, 2004.

———. *Tutankhamun, The Golden King and the Great Pharaohs*. Washington, DC: National Geographic, n.d.

————, et al. "Ancestry and Pathology in King Tutankhamun's Family." *JAMA* 303, 7 (February 17, 2010): 638–647.

Hoving, Thomas. *Tutankhamun, The Untold Story.* New York: Simon and Schuster, 1978.

Jones, Edward L. *Tutankhamun.* Seattle: Time Printing, 1978.

Kemp, David. "King of New York." *Vanity Fair* (April 2013): 158–172.

Kolos, Daniel, and Hany Assad. *The Name of the Dead, Tutankhamen Translated.* Ontario: Benben Books, 1979.

Metropolitan Museum of Art. *The Treasures of Tutankhamun.* New York: Metropolitan Museum of Art, n.d.

Reeves, C. N., ed. *After Tutankhamen.* London: Kegan Paul, 1992.

Reeves, Nicholas, and John H. Taylor. *Howard Carter Before Tutankhamun.* New York: Abrams, 1993.

Romer, John, and Elizabeth. *The Rape of Tutankhamun.* London: Michael O'Mara, 1993.

Silverman, David P. *Masterpieces of Tutankhamun.* New York: Abbeville Press, 1978.

Weiss, Walter. *Tutankhamun, His Tomb and Treasures.* Semmel Concerts, n.d.

INDEX